# Mom Minus Dad

Dearest Jane!
Thank you so much
for all the support
you and Jim
minded my family
during Dads sickness
and after his death.
I will never forget
your kindness. You
are a kind and
I appreciate your wisdom!
kindness and warm spirit—
I'd swear you had wings
on your back.
much love,
XO Jamieson
Love,
Jamieson
[illegible]

# Mom Minus Dad

---

## THE ESSENTIAL RESOURCE GUIDE
## FOR BUSY ADULTS
## WITH A NEWLY WIDOWED PARENT

---

# Jamieson Haverkampf

Blooming Women Press L.L.C.
Atlanta, Georgia

For updates and additional resources,
visit www.theparentlossbook.com

Blooming Women Press L.L.C.
4355 Cobb Parkway, Suite J608
Atlanta, GA 30339

orders@theparentlossbook.com
http://www.theparentlossbook.com

ISBN: 978-1-934953-19-8
Library of Congress Control Number: 2008920216
**Library of Congress subject heading**: Death-Dying, Bereavement, Grief, Loss, Parents, Widows and Widowers-Widowhood.

Cover and book design by Burtch Hunter Design

1.0

**Legal Disclaimer**

This book is not intended to serve as a substitute for advice from a physician, attorney, accountant, counselor, financial advisor, or other professional on some of the issues addressed in this book. We've done our best to provide useful and accurate resources in this book, but information in this area changes frequently and is subject to differing interpretations. If you want specific professional advice, please seek such from a professional in that field of interest. The books, Web sites, organizations, associations, and nonprofit organizations listed as resources in this book are provided as a convenience and for informational purposes only; they do not constitute endorsement or approval by the author of any of the products, services, or opinions of the respective corporation, organization, or individual. The author bears no responsibility for the accuracy, legality, or content of these resources. If you use the resources listed in this book, it is your responsibility to make sure that the facts and general advice contained in it are applicable to your situation.

*Mom Minus Dad is dedicated to God and His Son, Jesus Christ,*

*for daily guidance, and to my earthly mother and father,*

*for the countless sacrifices they both made on my behalf.*

# WHAT OTHERS ARE SAYING

*Mom Minus Dad* is like having a best friend to guide you through one of the toughest times of your life. Compassionate, concise, and packed with resources and the advice you need just when you need it most. A *must read* for caregivers of ill or aging parents.

> ~ **Sheila Warnock**, founder and president, SharetheCaregiving, Inc. Coauthor, *Share the Care, How to Organize a Group to Care for Someone Who Is Seriously Ill*
> **www.sharethecare.org**

I believe Jamieson Haverkampf's book, *Mom Minus Dad*, provides a real service to anyone facing the death of a loved one. No one in our culture wants to discuss death and its surrounding grief and responsibilities. Jamieson not only provides an encyclopedic guide to resources and information but also shares her own personal struggle with her father's death. By sharing the experiences she, her mother, and sister Ivy endured, she will make the journey for others less difficult.

> ~ **Carolyn Newton Curry PhD**, founder and director, Women Alone Together®
> **www.womenalonetogether.org**

This is the most incredible resource I have ever seen—prepared with such care and concern, as well as always-needed humor and reassurance. Ms. Haverkampf not only shares from her own experience but also has organized exhaustive research, which will make your journey much easier!

> ~ **Lulu Orr**, executive director, Good Grief Center for Bereavement Support
> **www.goodgriefcenter.com**

Jamieson and her family have lived the nightmare that keeps the rest of us awake at night—just thinking about the journey ahead. This is a journey that you *do not* need to take alone. *Mom Minus Dad* acts as the travel guide for adult children and aging parents to follow as they face the inevitable end-of-life issues. On the road map, Jamieson has posted warning signs based upon personal experience to keep you on the right track, and she offers pothole-free roads to follow with her extensive resource listing. This is a must-have resource book for all families.

> ~ **Jeanne K. Smith**, estate organization expert Founder of Exit Stage Right®
> **www.exitstageright.com**

# ACKNOWLEDGMENTS

Many thanks to all my friends and family members for their support while I wrote *Mom Minus Dad*. I could not have completed the book without your love, interest, and time.

Thank you to God for my constant strength and great blessings; to my father, John; my sister, Ivy, and my mom, Caroline, for all their love and support; the Buckhead Church community and Andy Stanley for inspiring, encouraging, giving me strength, and healing my heart; to Dr. Jan Thorpe for her constant support, insights, wisdom, and encouragement; to the Maui Writers Retreat and Conference writers, editors, agents, teachers, and speakers who nurtured, encouraged, and inspired me; to Sharon Dotson and Heather Zarrett for continuing to be the greatest of friends; to the G9 for supporting me at my father's memorial service; to Melinda Schomaker, Abby Schomaker, Peter and Susie Haverkampf, Joan Von Lessen, and Leslie Johnson for coming to Houston; to the early readers of the book: Laura Blossey, Neale Kitchens, Cynthia Black, Janet Haverkampf, Julie McNulty, Meg Young, Patti Styles, Ivy Haverkampf, Caroline Haverkampf, Ardith Ashton, Kathryn Sant, Elaine Sims, Alisa Barry, Peggy Post, Robin Lesses, and Kathleen Gulbransen; to Stacy Milrany for her creativity; to Melissa Libby for her generosity in sharing information and ideas; to my editors, Bobbie Christmas, Janis Whipple, and Carolyn Pincus; to my book designer Burtch Hunter, to all the doctors and nurses at the Massey Cancer Center, Georgetown Hospital, and M. D. Anderson Cancer Center for all you did to try to save my father; to Meg Young, Sonya Whitmire, Samantha Hughes, Traci Bloodworth, and Jennifer Pipin for your friendship and support; to Dan Poynter for opening the doors of publishing opportunity; and to Dr. John Roberts for your early belief in me as a writer.

In addition, I would like to thank the many experts who generously provided their wisdom and expertise for this project, including: Kathy Baltzell MA; Michele Blair; Martha Bolton; Jeffrey Brantley MD; Yvette Colón PhD, MSW, ACSW, BCD; Candice Courtney, Carolyn Newton Curry PhD; Raphael Cushnir; Tom Ellis MA, MFT; Jennifer Dempsey Fox JD, MBA, CFP; Donna M. Genett PhD; Janine Goben; Tom Golden LCSW; Peg Guild; Chris Hartwell MSW; Heather Clauson Haughian; Martha Whitmore Hickman; Cathy Hounsell, Judy Jordan MFT; Alexandra

Kennedy MA; Grace Lebow LCSW-C; Cendra Lynn PhD; Ron Manheimer PhD; Marta Gordon Martinez; Jane Monachelli MA, LPC; David Morrill; Cathy Olivetti JD; Lulu Orr; Gene L. Osofsky JD; Ashley Davis Prend LCSW, ACSW; the Publishers Marketing Association; Donna Robbins; Debbie Rodgers; Maria Savage; Jeanne K. Smith; Anne Bryan Smollin; Lisa Thompson; Dennis Toman JD; and Sheila Warnock. Thank you.

And finally, thank you to all the adult children with widowed parents who give much of their time, love, and support to enhance the lives of others.

# CONTENTS

# APPENDIXES

# Mom Minus Dad

*Mom Minus Dad* was not written to assist you in managing your grief after the loss of a parent, but instead to support you with resources and ideas as you juggle new responsibilities and life changes with a newly widowed parent. Grief looms large as a natural emotion associated with the death and loss that affects people in numerous ways and at unpredictable times. Although I am trained as a Grief ❣ Recovery Specialist, I am not a professional therapist. Because grief is an important emotion to understand as you deal with loss, below are two well-known resources for managing and understanding grief and its symptoms to complement the resources and suggestions in *Mom Minus Dad*.

Elisabeth Kübler-Ross became a pioneer in identifying and labeling the various grieving stages when she wrote her book, **On Death and Dying** (p. 170), published in 1969. She based her information on her evaluation of the grieving stages of terminally ill patients. Those stages quickly became used in the grief-and-loss field, and the media's use of them created mainstream acceptance of Kübler-Ross's finding. Kübler-Ross's five grief stages are denial, anger, bargaining, depression, and acceptance. For more information on Elisabeth Kübler-Ross's work and her many books, see Part III: Resources.

Another respected and well-known grief resource, the **Grief ❣ Recovery Institute** (p. 236) has provided grief assistance for more than twenty years. Through seminars, programs, and literature, the Grief ❣ Recovery Institute builds skills and tools both for grieving individuals and those who counsel others through their grief. The institute's three book offerings include **The Grief ❣ Recovery Handbook: The Action Program for Moving beyond Death, Divorce, and Other Losses** (p. 170); **When Children Grieve** (p. 170); and **Moving On: Dump Your Relationship Baggage and Make Room for the Love of Your Life** (p. 170). These books explore and lay out a grief-recovery action program using a loss-history graph, letter-writing techniques, and community as resource. The coauthors of these books are Grief ❣ Recovery Specialists and have trained and certified others to teach Grief ❣ Recovery workshops throughout the United States.

Elisabeth Kübler-Ross and the Grief ❣ Recovery Institute are only two grief resources of many available in the marketplace. Review other grief books in Part

III: Resources under the First Weeks after Loss section. Find a grief resource or two that works for you when you want to understand or need to go deeper as you work with your personal grief.

## How to Use This Book

*Mom Minus Dad* grew out of my and my sister's personal experience aiding my mother in the months and years following my father's unexpected death. Ivy and I did not have such a comprehensive guide to follow, so this book was written in hopes of offering you a manual as you walk down this difficult path as the adult child of a widowed parent.

You have already noticed the boldfaced type in the above references to the Grief ❣ Recovery Institute. Throughout this book, you will find numerous bold-faced references to help point you to a huge array of resources. Behind each reference is a page number that corresponds to the page where the full information on this reference can be found in Part III: Resources. In addition, a lengthy index can help you pull up resources as you need them, and an annotated table of contents can help you navigate your way through the book in the areas you have need. As with many resource guides, *Mom Minus Dad* is written and designed for you to delve into the areas that you most need at the time, and skim over those that do not apply to your current situation. Part I introduces you to our family's story and struggles following Dad's death. Part II offers ten corresponding dilemmas and numerous solutions to help you in your own situation. At the end of each section in the chapters, you'll also find a list of questions to help you evaluate you and your parent's current needs regarding that topic. Part III is a large list of resources we compiled through our own needs and research.

In addition, throughout the book, I have woven in pieces of our story—mine, my sister Ivy's, and Mom's—as we walked together through the struggles after such a great loss, many of which can last for years. Whether you are minus a mom or minus a dad, my hope is that you will find *Mom Minus Dad* an invaluable resource during your and your widowed parent's time of grief and recovery.

*Warm Wishes,*
Jamieson Haverkampf
Atlanta, Georgia

# ICONS USED IN THIS BOOK

To help you quickly locate the information you need as you seek resources for your particular situation, five different icons identify specific content throughout the book. Here's what each icon means:

## Our Story

When you see two conversation bubbles, this icon indicates a short section on how my family managed, struggled, or succeeded with the chapter topic.

## Benefits

A thumbs-up icon alerts you to the benefits of addressing the chapter topic.

## Special Note

A pointing-finger icon signals a special tip related to the chapter topic.

## Resources

Next to the lightbulb icon, you will find the best resources to assist you and your parent with more information on the chapter topic.

## Questions

A question mark alerts you to a section of questions for you to ask yourself or your parent regarding the chapter topic. These questions help you brainstorm solutions for your particular situation.

**PART I**

# Introduction

# INTRODUCTION

## TWO DAUGHTERS FACE THE CHALLENGES OF THE LOSS OF A PARENT AND A NEWLY WIDOWED PARENT

My phone rang for the tenth time that day with Mom on the other end of the phone two thousand miles away. Six months prior, cancer had taken the life of my sixty-two-year old father, who was my mother's husband and partner for thirty-four years. Mom cried into the phone uncontrollably when I answered. I cried too. I was torn deeply between the two worlds I most cared about—my mother and my own life. When your newly widowed parent needs your assistance, how do you determine where your job as a loving daughter or son ends so you can also take care of your own life? My sister, Ivy, and I both wrestled daily with the answer to that question. One day compassion for our mother led our decisions, the next day our own worries came first.

Dad's death from cancer was unexpected because we were told by doctors that the remission rate for stage-three non-Hodgkin's lymphoma was high—80 percent after five years. When Dad was diagnosed in September 2000, we talked to doctors and friends to determine the best treatment. We considered many treatments, doctors, and facilities for treating his lymphoma, such as Memorial Sloan-Kettering Center, Johns Hopkins Hospital, the Mayo Clinic, and the University of Washington Medical Center. In the end, we selected Virginia Commonwealth

University's Massey Cancer Center in Richmond, Virginia, because it was one of sixty National Cancer Institute–designated centers in the United States and had a highly respected lymphoma doctor who could administer Dad's recommended chemotherapy treatment. Treated at Massey, my father could live at home with all his creature comforts. Of all Dad's choices, the Massey Cancer Center seemed ideal. We expected him to survive; however, after months of chemotherapy, a failed stem-cell transplant at Georgetown University Hospital, and an experimental clinical trial at M. D. Anderson Cancer Center, Dad died in hospice eleven months after his initial diagnosis.

After Dad's death, Mom was lost. Our family of four had defined Mom's world, and she created her identity from the family role she played. She tried to work in the real estate, interior design, and horticulture fields, but my stockbroker father always needed her to travel on short notice for important business events. Therefore Mom adapted and put her husband's career first. Her choice to support her husband and children's dreams built her whole adult life; she fundamentally knew no other.

## NEW SURROGATE SPOUSE ROLES

Forced into an unimaginable world without Dad's support, Mom sought advice from her next-best-trusted confidants, her two daughters. Together Ivy and I temporarily became surrogate spouses to Mom, guiding her through seemingly endless meetings with her estate attorney, investment advisors, and CPAs.

Initially my sister and I planned to stay a week or two in Richmond after Dad's funeral to straighten out estate paperwork and be with Mom. We lived across the country in San Francisco. At the time, we thought two weeks was long enough to sort out everything. Mom needed our eyes, ears, and shoulders to manage the piles of old and new paperwork, create a new bill-paying system, find a grief counselor, and organize the first steps to settle Dad's estate. Because Dad had paid the monthly bills and managed the investments, Mom needed guidance for creating a new budget and understanding her financial situation. My parents' finances were complicated because Dad worked as an investor. In those beginning weeks when Mom faced new widowhood, we wished we had known about many of the financial resources listed in **Paperwork and Finances** (p. 217).

At the same time, my sister and I still owed rent on our San Francisco apartment and we had to figure out a way to restore the shambles of our lives. We talked about moving back to Richmond, but because Ivy and I loved the people and opportunities in San Francisco, we decided to return there. However, our new responsibilities to aid Mom weighed heavily on our minds and hearts. We did not know how to leave Mom and attend to the other parts of our lives. There was too much to do and Mom was lost. My sister and I needed support in order to continue to function as Mom's cheerleaders and advisors. Grief-and-loss resources were expensive and hard to find. Mom needed new money management, paperwork, and accounting systems—fast.

Because Dad's death was unexpected, no one was prepared for the consequences and problems we faced—especially Ivy and me. We struggled with the shock of loss, exhaustion, and the reality of living far away from a widowed parent. Our divided attention created a loss of steady income, which amplified our stress. Boundaries grew murky. Parental-loss grief groups proved hard to find. Our health suffered as we gained weight, drank too much coffee for energy, and ate junk food on the run. Family members and friends didn't know how to help. Mom was isolated, depressed, and had lost her thirty-four-year identity as a married woman. We all faced innumerable challenges, but my sister and I, as adult children of a fifty-six-year-old newly widowed mother, faced ten particularly tough ordeals. (These ten issues, or dilemmas, form the basis for the ten chapters in part II.)

## EXHAUSTION FROM CAREGIVING A SICK PARENT

After Dad died, my sister and I were exhausted from caring for our sick father and distraught mother during the previous eleven months. During Dad's eight months of chemotherapy treatments and later stem-cell transplant, my sister and I flew across the country from San Francisco to Richmond one week a month to boost Mom and Dad's morale. At my parents' home, we spent long hours surfing the Internet for any nugget of information to make the nightmare go away. We eventually left San Francisco for three months to be with Mom and Dad during the last months of Dad's life at M. D. Anderson Cancer Center in Houston, Texas, as a clinical-trial drug was administered. Every day for two and a half months, Mom, Ivy, and I walked from our hotel to the connecting bridge to Dad's hospital room for the 7:30 a.m. blood count evaluations to see if the new drug was working. We jockeyed between spending time with our father, researching on the Internet, or being on the phone seeking clinical-trial drugs or advice. We hired a few night nurses, but we caught all of them asleep on the job. When we walked into my parents' home a day after Dad's death, we practically collapsed.

Mom had been my father's sole caregiver for the prior few years before his death. Three years before the cancer invasion, my mother nursed my father after emergency surgery in which the doctors removed a large portion of Dad's large intestine. Soon after he recovered from that, he needed a hip replacement. For Mom, Dad's ailments never seemed to end. Mom shuffled through the tough last year of Dad's life with cancer as an exhausted caregiver.

After an eleven-month nightmare, planning Dad's funeral and memorial service was the last task we wanted to take on, but Mom, Ivy, and I figured out the many details. We had to decide about costs, memorial service locations, and catering options for both an Atlanta funeral and memorial service and a second service in Richmond. Review chapter 1 and **First Weeks after Loss** (p. 161) for better suggestions on how to handle a funeral, memorial service, and the many tasks surrounding both events.

## TWO THOUSAND MILES APART

The two thousand miles between our home in San Francisco and Mom's in Richmond, Virginia, created another problem. A trip from San Francisco to Richmond was a four-hundred-dollar plane flight and a four-to-six hour cross-country flight one-way. Mom called daily with questions about the location of files, bills, passwords, paperwork, or tech support needs. Because I lived so far away, I couldn't drive over after work to find what Mom needed. Because other family members lived in Chicago, Arizona, and Atlanta, they were not able to offer Mom regular local assistance in Richmond.

If we had known about the **National Association of Professional Organizers** (p. 164), **AARP's local offices** (p. 165), **the National Alliance for Caregiving** (p. 208),

**Geek Squad** (p. 231), or **GoToMyPC** (p. 234), the distance between our homes might have been more manageable.

## LACK OF INCOME

Three months before our father's diagnosis, my sister and I drove from Atlanta to San Francisco together, armed with a craving for adventure but with no place to live and no jobs. In our twenties, we both had pursued various fields after college. My career included work in art direction, graphic design, and illustration, whereas my sister's included Internet sales, research, and fashion. Like our parents, Ivy and I were and are entrepreneurs at heart with restless and curious spirits. After Dad was diagnosed, we worked in San Francisco in temporary or part-time jobs that accommodated our need for a flexible schedule to fly to our parents' home frequently.

Since we were virtually self-employed, the **Family Leave and Medical Act** (p. 174)—a government program that allows qualified employees of companies to leave work on unpaid leave for a maximum of twelve weeks—did not apply to us. We had no guarantee of jobs or income waiting for us after we took time off to assist my dying father, and later, our widowed mother. After Dad died we struggled with where to best spend our time—help Mom manage her investments, pursue graduate degrees, or continue to work in the red-hot California real estate and mortgage businesses in 2001.

## LOSS OF MOM'S FINANCIAL MANAGER AND INVESTMENT ADVISOR

During my parents' decades of marriage, they shared the assorted responsibilities of running a household. My father paid the bills, made the money, and managed the investment decisions because he worked in the world of finance as a stockbroker. Mom embraced her role as a homemaker in charge of social planning and entertaining my father's clients' wives on business trips. She enjoyed and excelled at the role of family social director. Mom orchestrated our household—from ren-

ovations to cooking dinner to finishing projects that my father energetically started, then abandoned when business called.

Because Mom grew up in a traditional gender-role family where the husband
managed the money, she was stunned and full of fear when Dad's death put her
in charge of managing the investments they had built together. She had learned
about stock investments by being married to Dad, but relied heavily on my father
to make larger investment decisions. Mom was used to managing a smaller portion of their household budget, not the entire household's budget and complicated investments.

The first few months after Dad's death, Mom was vulnerable and worried
about handling all the financial responsibilities. We worried about her being
approached by an unethical financial person who wanted to take advantage of
her or by a man offering to marry her and take care of her financial worries. We
knew Mom, in her weakened state, could be a target for romantic swindlers and
financial shams.

Apparently Mom and Dad didn't regularly discuss their finances or household
budget together. Money management was understood to be Dad's job in their marriage. If Dad had delegated more financial and investment responsibility to Mom,
automated their regular bills, or outsourced their accounting to a firm, we would-
n't have had so much to manage. If we had known about **Women's Institute for
Financial Education** (p. 227), **American Association of Retired Persons' Finance
Guide** (p. 221), **Women's Institute for a Secure Retirement** (p. 227), **American
Association of Individual Investors** (p. 226), or the **National Association of
Professional Organizers** (p. 164), all of which offered financial advice, Mom's
financial management transition might have been easier.

## MOM'S ADDITIONAL JOB AS EXECUTOR

Mom's job as executor of Dad's estate forced her into a year of paperwork and legal
overload. The executor's job required Mom to assemble a list of my father's assets,
including all things big and small, such as his car and any U.S. bonds he had purchased. Mom started to worry that she wouldn't have enough money to support
herself. After we spoke with her estate attorney, Ivy and I assisted Mom with the

search for necessary estate documents and tried to help Mom see and understand her real financial situation.

When he was alive, Dad did not discuss the majority of my parents' financial and legal issues with my sister and me either. He also did not leave a note in a safety deposit box or in a file outlining who to call and where specific files were located if something happened to him. We looked for anything that resembled an account. We reviewed old copies of Dad's resumé to see if any companies he worked for in the past might still be holding an unredeemed pension benefit. We sorted through files and made a list of people to call. Dad's paper files went back thirty years. Fortunately for us, Dad's files showed understandable categories. Yet this was only the beginning of Mom's job as executor; the job took Mom and her estate attorney fifteen months to complete.

I wish we had known then about **AARP's grief-and-loss checklists for settling an estate** (p. 165), the **Internal Revenue Service's booklet #559** (p. 222), or **Treasury Direct** (p. 225), or read *Facing a Death in the Family: Caring for Someone Through Illness and Dying, Arranging the Funeral, Dealing with the Will and Estate* (p. 169) when Mom first became executor.

## LIMITED FAMILY SUPPORT

Our limited family support added to our liabilities. Dad had been a strong support to all of us, and we didn't have a strong faith community to lean on. Because we have a smaller-sized family and Ivy and I were unmarried, we didn't have access to any family members or extended family who were CPAs, lawyers, accountants, or money managers to ask for advice. Some family members assisted us with various needs initially, but after some time had passed, their focus understandably turned back to their own lives, and my sister and I were on our own to answer Mom's questions. Two other deaths in the family the same year my father died—my mother's father and my father's mother—contributed to other family members' restricted abilities to offer us stronger assistance. Mom, Ivy, and I wanted to support each other's needs, but constant stress ran rampant through all of us.

## GRIEF SUPPORT HARD TO FIND

My sister and I faced compounding losses: our father, our family as we knew it, our sense of home, income, personal time, career, and future dreams. We needed grief counselors to help us work through our own grief. Because Dad died in hospice, we did eventually find out we all could receive one year of free hospice counseling through the **Medicare Hospice Benefit, section 40.2.3 (p. 203)**; however, at the time, when we searched for grief counselors through hospice programs, we did not receive useful counsel. If you are in a similar situation, I suggest doing research on multiple hospice counselors available in your local area and understanding their counseling methods prior to making an appointment. This will help you avoid negative or awkward experiences. For example, I went to one hospice counselor without understanding her background or counseling methods. The first time I talked with her, she told me to fall on my knees and beg God for mercy. At the time I wasn't an overly religious person, and this comment wasn't helpful in my fragile state. In those first few months after the loss of my father, I craved a nurturing counselor to be present for me, to simply listen and offer useful suggestions, based on his or her knowledge of working with grief and loss, as I sorted through my struggle of multiple losses and new decisions.

Since finances and time were limited due to our many responsibilities, we didn't want to spend extra money or time on other counselors. Friends were empathetic but many couldn't relate to our situation. We coped by trying to support each other, yet without a regular grief support group, we lacked perspective. If we had known about the many other local and online grief-support options, such as **Griefshare** (p. 177), **Vitas Innovative Hospice Care** (p. 177), **Kara** (p. 179) or **GriefNet** (p. 200), we could have found parental-loss grief support early after our father's death to vent our own grief and concerns for our mother.

Because Dad died in a hospice out of town, Mom searched for new grief-and-loss resources back in Richmond. When she couldn't find a hospice or grief counselor initially after Dad's funeral, she searched for widows' groups in Richmond. The only grief support groups she could find had either much older members or members grieving a different kind of loss. She craved a support group with women closer to her age who had lost a spouse. In the meantime, Ivy and I functioned as Mom's motivational cheerleaders when she had a rough day. When we went home a few months after my father's death, we found for Mom, through our research on the Internet, a useful grief counselor who practiced in Richmond. If Mom had known about **AARP's grief-and-loss message boards** (p. 200), **Healing the Spirit** (p. 196), **Senior Navigator** (p. 196), or **GriefShare** (p. 177), she would have had found grief support earlier, reduced her isolation, and lessened our worry about her.

## MY DETERIORATING HEALTH

During the three years after Dad died, my health spiraled out of control. I was juggling too many new responsibilities between Mom's needs and running my real estate business. Workouts became optional instead of part of my regular routine. My sister and I lived on easy-to-grab, low-nutrition food and caffeine to keep us going. I worried about Mom's health and survival too. Three years after my father died, my cholesterol hit three hundred. Eventually I burned out. I wish I had read **The Hour-Long Vacation** (p. 210) or **Grounding Yourself** (p. 209) and consulted the corresponding resources at the time to have known better ways to take care of myself in the years after Dad's death. If I had known about **Dinewise** (p. 163), **Home Bistro** (p. 164) or **Magic Kitchen** (p. 164), my sister, mother, and I might have been able to eat healthier the first few months after the loss of my father, reducing the extra task of going to the grocery store or cooking meals.

## NO RESOURCE GUIDE TO AID BUSY ADULTS WITH A NEWLY WIDOWED PARENT

Ivy and I needed resources and trustworthy people to delegate the mounting responsibilities of encouraging and guiding Mom with her numerous and major financial choices, in addition to our many other needs. Yet we could not locate any practical resource guides anywhere to assist us—the adult children of a newly widowed parent. My sister and I painstakingly found bits and pieces of resources as we went along. We needed information about many new issues, such as finding grief counselors to guide us with a widowed parent's issues and needs and coping with huge family dynamic changes. We looked for outside aid to provide Mom with technology support issues that drained my sister's and my energies. We searched for easy systems for Mom to set up to manage tasks on her own.

A thorough resource book with practical advice, Web sites, and organizations to aid adult children with widowed parents was nowhere to be found. The only grief and loss books available focused on guiding the widow or widower, not assisting adult children to become strong and balanced advisors to their widowed parent. We needed a book offering the majority of the resources for adult children along with additional resources for widows, because the issues are intertwined. We needed advice specific to our own needs along with guidance for acting as a widowed parent's main trusted support system. After three years of fruitless searching for a comprehensive resource book for adult children with a newly widowed parent, the idea for *Mom Minus Dad* was born.

*Mom Minus Dad* is a compilation of the resources and strategies my sister and I found or wish we had found during my father's illness and the years after his death. Part II describes specific situations you could encounter with a widowed parent and the specific resources that may be of assistance. Part III lists descriptions and further information about more than five hundred useful associations, Web sites, books, nonprofit organizations, and other resources mentioned throughout the text of the book. The resources give you a starting point to reach out to others for advice, information, counseling, groups, or whatever you might need.

Even though my story of loss may be distinctly dissimilar from yours, my hope in *Mom Minus Dad* is for you to use the solutions, suggestions, ideas, and resources listed in this book as a place to start to find assistance to keep your life more balanced while aiding your newly widowed parent.

# PART II

# Dilemmas and Solutions after the Loss of a Parent

# FIRST WEEKS AFTER LOSS

The first days and weeks following the death of a loved one are difficult for many reasons. First is the huge shock of loss and onset of the grieving process, which is experienced differently among family members. Then, to add to the emotional onslaught, many important and difficult decisions must be made quickly and definitively by those who are reeling from the impact of the loss of one they dearly loved. The suggestions that follow will help you and your surviving parent navigate the difficult and emotional first weeks following the loss of your mom or dad.

## DO ONLY ESSENTIAL TASKS

I can't imagine how you feel after the loss of your parent. You may be in shock, sad, relieved, or plain exhausted—depending on how the death happened. When a parent's death takes place, no matter if the death was unexpected or not, new roles, responsibilities, choices, and changes fall into the widow or widower's, and other family members' laps. Especially when an unexpected death of a parent occurs, many families aren't prepared to deal with the many consequences.

Your widowed parent may turn to you to figure out immediate solutions to pressing problems, including finding wills, organizing a funeral and memorial service, and writing obituaries and eulogies. Other family members may stick to the sidelines not knowing how to help. Meanwhile, your own life, jam-packed with activities and responsibilities, screams for your attention. Torn between two worlds you care about, you try to juggle both. You think you have no choice. Actually, you do.

## One Solution for the First Weeks after the Loss of a Parent

After the loss of a parent, people want to contribute and can do a good—if not better—job than you can. No one judges your performance at your time of grief. Life's pace bounces hectically around you, but if you need to bow out of the spotlight temporarily, it's okay. Do what you can, but access resources and solicit support from others to assist with the funeral and memorial service planning. Friends, extended family members, clergy or other religious leaders, funeral directors, and even professional organizers can offer assistance. Friends and family members want to donate their time and energy; tell them how.

## Our Story

When my sister, mother, and I walked back into my parents' home after losing Dad to cancer, the exhaustion and stress of those last eleven months piled high on our shoulders. Our grief coursed through our veins. The idea of turning to friends to plan the funeral and memorial service seemed selfish. My mother, my sister, Ivy, and I all went into robotic organizer mode. We knocked out tasks methodically one at a time. When I wrote Dad's obituary, I hit my breaking point.

We all struggled with releasing control to others because everything seemed important to handle personally. The dark circles under our eyes darkened even more while we drank coffee practically nonstop and pushed on day after day. After my sister and I spent months away from our home in San Francisco, neglected work and bills called for our attention. After difficult nights of little to no sleep, we were all a mess. The workload was too much. Finally we sought help from other people, which provided solutions and reduced our tasks.

We took one task at a time and determined which duties were important for us personally to handle and which could be accomplished by others. Good friends made some of the necessary phone calls and coached us in making decisions about funeral and memorial service details. After we released some control and tasks to others we trusted, sleep came easier. We then had time to take care of ourselves by taking breaks or a walk, calling supportive friends, getting a manicure, or simply taking a nap.

We ignored our own needs when we tried to do everything ourselves. Your family may want you to take part in the planning, but you also need to take care of yourself. You may be captive to unexpected public meltdowns of emotion when you take on too much. If you try to avoid the grief that comes along with the death of a mother or father, unresolved grief only delays your natural grieving process.

### Grieving Your Own Way

Everyone grieves uniquely. Your distinctive circumstances create specific issues to sort out. You don't "get over" the death of a parent; you process and release grief at your own pace. You may ask, "How can I be okay with being selfish after the loss of a parent or spouse?" I'm not saying to be selfish, but don't forget about your own health and needs.

### Resources for Grief

To find book, audio, and video products about grief and loss, go to the Web sites of **In-Sight Books** (p. 171), **Roberts Press** (p. 171), **Compassion Books** (p. 171), the **Grief ❣ Recovery Institute** (p. 177), or **Elizabeth Kübler-Ross** (p. 170 also p. 172). Other insightful and helpful books about grief include *This Thing Called Grief* (p. 169), *I Wasn't Ready to Say Good-bye* (p. 171), and the daily reader *Healing after Loss* (p. 170). If you find yourself thinking about your parent's death and his or her well-being after death, you might want to check out *Life after Death* (p. 172), *What They Saw . . . at the Hour of Death* (p. 172), or *Life after Life* (p. 172).

### Resources for Time Off Work

You may not be able to afford to quit or jeopardize your job. If possible, though, try to reduce your job from full-time to part-time or at least take off as many days as possible without causing problems. If receiving time off work is an issue for you, contact your employer or your local **U.S. Department of Labor's Wage and Hour District Office** (p. 174) to see if you qualify for twelve weeks of legal leave from work through the **Family and Medical Leave Act (FMLA)** (p. 174). Read the section Time Off from Work in chapter 3 for more information.

### Resources for Eating Healthy after Loss

Food may be the last thing on anyone's mind, but when hunger strikes, available food brings comfort. Friends will ask how to support you. An easy answer is to ask them to make or order food to be delivered to your home. Friends who want to provide support with food needs can either cook meals for you or arrange a week or two of fresh meal delivery for your family from companies such as **Gourmet Grocery Online** (p. 163), **Dinewise** (p. 163), **Home Bistro** (p. 164), or **Magic Kitchen** (p. 164). Food gift baskets from catalogues such as **Harry and David** (p. 164) also provide healthy eating options for grieving families.

Another option is to have friends arrange for personal chefs like **Big City Chefs** (p. 163) to come to your home to make food for your family. Organic food is another healthy food choice for friends or family members during times of grief. Arrange to have it delivered to the home from companies such as **Diamond Organics** (p. 163). Friends can also order takeout from local restaurants and have food delivered from a service such as **Takeout Taxi** (p. 164). Even small gifts of food from other people bring you and your family comfort and reduce stress.

If you live far away from your parent, friends can order groceries to be delivered to your parent's home. Online grocers who make home deliveries include **Peapod** (p. 173), **Netgrocer** (p. 173), and **Safeway** (p. 173). Let someone else exert energy picking out groceries and delivering them. You and your parent need to conserve all your energy and reduce the daily decisions you need to make.

## Resources for Additional Funeral or Memorial Service Help

If you need additional funeral or memorial service assistance outside family members, friends, clergy or funeral directors, try contacting the **National Association of Professional Organizers** (p. 164) to find a professional organizer. Your local **Chamber of Commerce** (p. 164) may provide referrals of event planners to aid in organizing a memorial service. For more information on planning a funeral or memorial service, read the next section, Create an Energy Team. Check out Part III: Resources, under "First Weeks after Loss" for more grief, funeral, and memorial service resources.

## Questions to Ask about Only Doing Essential Tasks

* Why does my parent or I have to do everything?
* What do I miss when I let a few things go?
* What few comforting things can I do for myself if I have extra time? Speak with a grief counselor? Get a nurturing massage? Take a long walk?
* What can I postpone until later?
* What can I not do or what simply doesn't have to be done at all?

Go ahead and flex your muscles from time to time, but try to let friends and family take over when you need a break. Down the road, you will get a chance to flex your muscles for them. Life promises that fact.

> *What do we live for, if not to make life*
> *less difficult for each other?*
>
> GEORGE ELLIOT

## CREATE AN ENERGY TEAM

When you snow ski down a "black diamond" run for the first time, navigating the hill's unexpected moguls and hazardous ice patches can be quite a challenge. A sudden blizzard can make it worse. Back at the top of the mountain, your skiing buddies offered encouragement and spiked your confidence. They promised to pay for a large hot cocoa and lunch if you arrived inside the lodge in ten minutes. Halfway down the run, your friends' waves revive your motivation to keep going.

Sometimes we all need someone else to fill us with hope and encouragement when we are pushed to our limit. If you forge alone through the first weeks after the loss of a parent without an assembled support team, you might push yourself beyond what you can handle. When you're alone, the work and grief loom large. With support, burdens shrink.

### How to Remedy Low Energy
One solution is for you to create an "energy team" from the beginning. An energy team is a group of friends or family members taking on separate funeral or memorial service duties, which allows immediate family members to conserve

energy for essential tasks. An energy team provides motivating vigor, liveliness, and oomph for you when you are depleted.

Over the next few months, your depleted energy because of loss and grief might only be able to help you manage a few critical jobs for your widowed parent. Your body needs to conserve energy for the transition that lies in the days ahead. During the first weeks after loss, with an energy team in place, you conserve energy that will pay off in the days, months, and even years ahead.

## Our Story

After the eleven-month nightmare of my father's failing health, the last tasks we wanted to tackle were creating plans for a funeral and multiple memorial services, but choices and decisions were required. Thankfully other family members, whom were in the Houston hospice when Dad died, took care of managing the delicate procedures with the funeral home and cremation facilities.

At my parents' home, we numbly made calls and sorted three months of mail, energized solely by coffee or diet colas. We tried to sleep, but almost nightly we took prescribed or over-the-counter sleeping pills to aid our restless nights. We had lots to do to plan the funeral and services and we had no energy.

## How to Build an Energy Team

Unfortunately for us, we took on most of our tasks ourselves. If I had everything to do all over again, I would gather seven friends or family members with various talents and ask them to be our energy team. Our energy team could've supplied the energy we lacked for tasks.

Build your energy team and watch yourself call on them again and again. A team consists of energy team managers, funeral managers, memorial service planners, writer/Web site designers, house-sitter coordinators, home and estate organizers, and a small transportation team. You may not need all seven positions; we could have used them all. In choosing to have more than one person working on each job, the workload is less burdensome. With two people per team, people can discuss choices together and cover for each other when one person has an emergency or is out of town.

**Energy Team Managers:** The first members of the team, the energy team managers, are close friends of the family who work as a contact between the family and the rest of the team. If possible, they live in the community where the funeral and memorial service will be held. The main three jobs for the energy team managers is to assist the other managers on the team; track gifts, food, and other assistance provided during the first few weeks after loss so the family members can send thank-you notes later; and gather a meeting with the energy team members and the family.

The energy team members can initially gather the rest of the team members with the family to meet and discuss the family's needs and specific requests and introduce themselves to each other. This meeting can also function as a brainstorming session to make a list of others to fill empty positions. By setting up this meeting, the family can state their wishes once to everyone involved, freeing up their energy to tend to their grief and other needs.

**Funeral Managers:** Ask your most decisive friends with prior experience with funerals to manage details with the funeral home. These funeral managers can present to the family reduced selections and options regarding urns or caskets; take care of cremation, organ donation, or embalming requests of the family; and handle burial plot questions and calls from the funeral home. The funeral managers coordinate plans with a minister, rabbi, or other spiritual advisor for the family. The handling and positioning of **flowers** (p. 162), donation materials, sign-in books, and framed photographs are other tasks for the funeral managers. If family members want to play a larger role in the funeral decision-making process, their direct involvement with your funeral managers and funeral director may assist in the family members' grieving process.

The many decisions a funeral requires are overwhelming. Many online resources make your many choices easier. If you or your funeral managers have questions about funeral protocol, read **Emily Post's etiquette book**'s (p. 172) chapter on grieving and condolence. The **Funeral Planning 101** Web site (p. 167) offers all kinds of information on planning funerals, including contrary religious traditions, writing a eulogy, funeral costs, and memorials. The **National Funeral Directors Association** Web site (p. 168) connects you to grief-related organizations, discusses end-of-life issues, and provides a list of charitable organizations. Read about the **Federal Trade Commission's Funeral Rule Law** (p. 166) as well as its two informative brochures about your rights as a consumer when you purchase funeral goods and services. If your deceased parent was a veteran, you can ask your funeral manager to call the **U.S. Department of Veterans Affairs** (p. 168) for information on funeral, burial plot, and other death benefits available to your family. Refer to the books *Caring for the Dead* (p. 169) or *Facing a Death in the Family* (p. 169) for more detailed funeral information. Also, see appendix D for information about payment options for funeral homes. If you are on a tight budget, go to the **Funeral Help** Web site (p. 167). Funeral Help offers advice and a book on saving money in planning funerals.

For information on bereavement airfares, go to the **About** Web site (p. 161) and type in "Family Emergencies and Bereavement Fares." Also try the **Smarter Travel** Web site (p. 162) and review its article on bereavement fares.

**Memorial Service Planners:** Your most competent juggler and detail-oriented friends should be your memorial service planners. Friends who regularly plan parties, weddings, or special events may be a good selection. Your memorial service planners coordinate the memorial service and location(s), create the invitation list, screen phone calls from the service location, and coordinate food and beverages. Your memorial service planners can also handle the flowers, donation materials, sign-in book, and framed photographs if these are not supervised by the funeral manager. Memorial services typically take place at a church, restaurant, favorite place of the deceased, your home, the beach, or wherever seems appropriate for your family's needs.

For alternative memorial services, see the **Eternal Reef** Web site (p. 166) or **AARP**'s (p. 165) "Ways to Remember" article on its Web site. If you need charitable organization ideas, go to the **Guidestar** Web site (p. 167).

**Writers and Web Site Designers:** Your next team members to identify are obituary writers and Web site designers, if you want to create a memorial Web site. The best people for the job are close friends with good writing or computer skills who knew your deceased parent.

Your writers work with the family to write an obituary. An obituary creates a biographical account of a person's life in a summarized form. The obituary might include a person's life's work, education, awards, achievements, and surviving family members. You will also want to list where people can make donations in the deceased's name, where to send flowers, and any Web site created in honor of the deceased. Take a look at **Legacy** (p. 168) for ideas on obituaries from more than 175 newspapers. After the family approves the obituary, the writer distributes the obituary to the appropriate newspaper(s).

### Special Note

See appendix A for three sample obituaries: someone who has lived a good, ordinary life; a successful businessman—an attorney; and a woman who was an academic.

Additionally the writers can create a handout for the memorial service with the obituary, donation information, and the address to which friends, neighbors, and out-of-town attendees can send flowers to the family after the memorial service and funeral. One suggestion we used on our handout was to add family members' mailing addresses, e-mail addresses, and phone numbers to allow attendees to write condolence notes or contact the family after the funeral to offer support. For privacy reasons, you may not wish to include personal information. For us, out-of-touch friends who attended the services were easily able to contact us later to offer support and reestablish friendships.

If the family desires a memorial Web site, the designers can post a simple one-page site with all the funeral and memorial service information. This can be a fast way to reduce the number of phone calls you'll receive from people asking about details. You may want to consider setting up a blog for the family or the Web site designer to keep friends and family informed with regular updates on funeral or memorial service plans. Friends can post comments to the blog offering support to the family. If you are interested in learning more about building a memorial Web site, go to **Memory-Of** (p. 168).

**House-Sitter Coordinators:** Assign two friends to be your house-sitter coordinators, who arrange for two people to stay at the family's home during the funeral or memorial service. Many homes are broken into during funerals by thieves who read the newspaper obituaries to find out which homes will be empty and when. Two house-sitters can ensure activity in the home if they rotate lights and place cars in the driveway.

**Home and Estate Organizers:** As your paperwork builds, the home and estate organizers begin assisting the family by putting both bills and estate papers in order during the first two weeks after loss. Because of the confidentiality of certain estate papers, you may want to select one person, the home organizer, to handle the less-sensitive home paperwork—including utilities, magazine subscriptions, and junk mail—and the other person to manage the more sensitive estate paperwork. The home organizer could be a friend, extended family member, professional organizer, or assistant. The estate organizer needs to be resourceful, organized, and someone you trust with your confidential papers.

During the initial weeks after the death, you or your estate organizer will be required to get a few papers together, such as ten to fifteen certified copies of the death certificate, marriage and birth certificates, life insurance policies, and will and/or trust(s). Missing life insurance policies can be found using suggestions from the **American Council of Life Insurance Policy**'s Web site (p. 174) or **Medical Information Bureau Policy Locator Service** (p. 225). Death certificates are acquired from your funeral director, your local city hall, or **Vitalchek** (p. 174). Your estate organizer can assist your parent in contacting the **Social Security Administration** (p. 174) to stop benefits of the deceased parent, if any, and inquire about your parent's eligibility for widow or widower's benefits. The estate organizer can also help you contact health and life insurance companies, your deceased parent's employer, credit card companies, as well as transferring automobile titles.

In addition, you may have been out of town for a period of time before planning the funeral and have other bills and mail to sort through. If you are completely trusting of your Home Organizer with going into personal effects and bills, they can sift through those papers and present the family with the most urgent ones first and take care of them as required. The Estate Organizer should review online or order the **American Association of Retired Persons** (AARP) book *Final Details* from the **AARP** Web site (p. 165) for a list of paperwork to assemble. See also the General Paperwork to Gather worksheet in appendix C.

**Transportation Team:** Many grievers don't think clearly during the shock of initial grief and are susceptible to car accidents. Your transportation team assists with driving family members to funeral homes, attorney meetings, friends' homes, grocery stores, or any other location they need to go. Consider assigning one or two people to manage and coordinate other volunteer drivers. The size of your transportation team depends on the number of family members who need assistance. Drivers for the family members during the initial weeks after death can reduce the risk of injury to grieving family members. Friends are the best source of volunteer drivers. If friends are not available, check with reputable local staffing companies for temporary workers or post an ad on **Craigslist** (p. 228) and ask for drivers' references before hiring anyone you don't know.

You may have other specific needs or jobs that are not listed above. Add or delete positions that best suit your family and aid in alleviating stress and tasks.

 ### Benefits of an Energy Team

You create more time to grieve and get the support you need from friends, family members, and counselors after you assign those seven roles. You and your family benefit from answering fewer phone calls often filled with emotionally difficult questions from strangers. You also benefit from not having to talk with everyone and go through numerous explanations, repeatedly answering the same questions about what happened and how everyone is doing. With an energy team, you and your family can spend more time calling friends and family members and making important time-sensitive decisions. An energy team can substantially reduce your stress.

All seven team member assignments may not be necessary for you and your family. You may not want a Web site designed, for instance. If seven people aren't available, team members can expand their duties. If you can relieve at least some tasks from the family, you can greatly reduce the stress family members' experience.

You may already have friends working on similar tasks, and you can adapt them to build your own energy team. If you want to take on all those roles yourself, reduce your own life's workload to make things easier.

Wherever you stand with the funeral and memorial service plans, start to assemble your team and delegate tasks. As each friend takes over duties, your energy refills its empty well, and you can focus on your most pressing needs and conserve energy. For more energy team resources, browse Part III: Resources (p. 155), under "First Weeks after Loss." If you are struggling with depleted energy from caring for a terminally ill surviving parent, read *Share the Care: How to Organize a Group to Care for Someone Who Is Seriously Ill* (p. 162).

## Questions to Ask about Funeral and Memorial Service Duties

- Who can my parent or I ask for support?
- Do I really have the energy for all those tasks?
- What can my widowed parent, siblings, or other family members supervise or manage?
- Do I want to run the loss marathon alone? Why?
- What local friends want to provide time and energy to assist with funeral and memorial service duties? What are their talents?
- Which seven friends can build a strong energy team for me?

You might be on a black-diamond run—the most difficult ski slope—for the first time in your life. Alone, the current list of to-do tasks may loom as difficult moguls and ice patches. If you attempt to tackle each obstacle and ice patch alone, you may suffer burnout or exhaustion, and feel overwhelmed. If friends or family members are available to assist, accept their offers. After conquering a black-diamond run in a blizzard, nothing beats sharing steaming hot cups of cocoa together with friends inside a warm lodge.

> *The truest help we can render an afflicted man is not to take his burden from him, but to call out his best energy, that he may be able to bear the burden.*
>
> **PHILLIP BROOKS**

# CHAPTER TWO

# BUILD YOUR SUPPORT TEAM

Grieving the loss of someone you loved, especially a spouse or parent, is a long, emotional path with many ups and downs. You and your parent will not quickly run through the steps of grief and then move on. You will need not only each other but many others to help you through the days, weeks, and years to come. How you develop that support system is not as crucial as the fact that you intentionally do build a support team around you to help you in many ways. You and your surviving parent will need that support, and you can find a variety of options to build that foundation.

## SUPPORT GROUPS: WHAT ARE YOUR OPTIONS?

Support is critical while grieving and assisting a widow or widower. Support can be received from friends, spouses, family members, or community groups. However, sometimes an unbiased perspective from grief-and-loss, widow, or parental-loss support groups can be valuable.

As you hear other people's stories and struggles in groups, the magnitude of your own loss may be lessened. Support-group members give you valuable feedback that allows you to see your own growth and progress. While you listen to how others handled various situations, you may gather new ideas and tools to deal with your own grief or situation. Grief is not a mental illness or sickness, but part of everyone's life.

## Four Ideas about Support Groups

When seeking the right grief-and-loss support group, keep four key ideas in mind:

1. If you spend time and test diverse groups, you will find a good support group.
2. Because grief counseling traditionally caters to the senior market, the majority of spousal and parental-loss support groups have older members. If you or your widowed parent prefers support groups with members closer to your ages, seek groups with members in a similar age range. The ages and personalities in a group may be a hodgepodge, though the wisdom of the group may be exactly what you need to hear.
3. Online grief-and-loss groups may provide another tool for managing grief along with an in-person group. Busy schedules, managing young children, or work may make in-person support groups difficult to attend.
4. Groups with a professional moderator or facilitator may monitor the group to make sure the conversation sticks to the group's guidelines as well as maintaining a safe nurturing place to share your feelings.

## Our Story

In Houston at M. D. Anderson Cancer Center, where Dad was receiving care, my mother, my sister, Ivy, and I were burdened with everything we had to do for my father, therefore we didn't allocate time to find strong support groups. Initially the three of us went to one or two cancer support groups at M. D. Anderson while Dad was undergoing evaluation and clinical trials. We were torn between spending time with my father and seeking support for ourselves, which felt selfish. A close friend suggested I look at the Yahoo groups online under Dad's disease, non-Hodgkin's lymphoma, to find support and information after Dad was asleep at night. I joined an online group and found an incredible amount of support and knowledge from both patients and caregivers of family members with non-Hodgkin's lymphoma. Their daily posts of support and inspirational stories kept me going.

Looking back, our decision not to prioritize community support took its toll. Back in Richmond, Mom looked into widow grief groups at churches and other community centers, but became only more depressed because every woman in the group was twenty years older than she. Unfortunately the grief groups Mom attended either did not have a professional group leader experienced in grief and loss or had a poorly experienced leader. Therefore, none of the group leaders guided Mom toward a more age-appropriate grief group.

As our lives have stabilized and the years have passed, we each have looked into more faith-based support groups and individual therapy. I enjoy my faith-based support group because women in the group provide consistent support, feedback, inspiration, and perspective. When I hear other people's struggles and problems, my heart fills with compassion for their lives and gratitude for the gifts in my own life, while my own problems lessen in severity.

## How to Find a Support Group

To find a support group, call your friends and ask them if they know of any active local grief-and-loss support groups. Spend time checking out your local community center, gym, church, or even online grief chat rooms, bulletin boards, listservs, or e-mail support groups if you are comfortable with the idea of seeking support online. Read "Online Support Groups" in this chapter for more information. Another option is to check with the **Grief ❣ Recovery Institute** (p. 177) to see if any local grief-recovery personal workshops are offered where you live.

The **American Heart Association** (p. 202), the **American Cancer Society** (p. 202), churches, temples, and other spiritual centers can be a great place to find immediate support. **Vitas Innovative Hospice Care** (p. 177), **Griefshare** (p. 177), or **2-1-1** (p. 176) can provide connections to support groups. If your parent needs support from other widows or widowers, check to see if your local AARP office supports a **Widowed Persons Service** (p. 177) where your parent lives. Community center and health-club bulletin boards usually have postings for support groups. Hospitals or rehabilitation centers that deal with addictions usually have grief and support groups to support the issue of loss, which is a big part of their patients' recovery process. For a list of **support groups for all fifty states and various other countries**, look in Part III: Resources under **"Support by Location"** (p. 178).

Group work isn't easy. When you share in a group, you test your courage, your open-mindedness, and the guts to be vulnerable. Groups may seem awkward to you at first, but attend a handful of groups before you decide if support groups in general are for you. If you keep attending, support groups will ease the unpredictable phases of grief.

## If You're Uncomfortable with Support Groups

Maybe support groups are not for you or your widowed parent. You may search for the right group and get frustrated. Or maybe the vibe of the group doesn't work for you or the age differences make it difficult to find common ground. Whatever your reasons, support groups simply may not be the right fit for you. If you try a particular group and the group doesn't work for you, that's okay. Try another group, consider individual counseling sessions, or find assistance through other books or CDs. When you continue to seek tools to work through your grief, benefits abound. Read the next section "Individual Therapy: Is Therapy for Me?" if you are interested in learning more about individual counseling instead of group therapy.

## Children and Support Groups

Grief organizations providing support for children are well-established and widely available. Try contacting **Rainbows** (p. 206), the **National Institute for Trauma and Loss in Children** (p. 205), or **A Little HOPE** (p. 205). The Grief ❣ Recovery Institute created a book specifically for assisting grieving children called ***When Children Grieve*** (p. 170).

## Questions to Ask about Support Groups

- Is my parent or I interested in finding a support group?
- If I cannot talk to a group of people about my grief-and-loss issues, whom can I confide in to work through those issues?
- Is individual therapy a more comfortable solution for me?
- If I am not ready for support groups yet, what other personal ways can I deal with my grief regularly, such as journaling, taking time to meditate, or otherwise spending time reflecting on my grief and expressing my feelings of loss, hurt, anger or whatever else surfaces?

As you cast a wide net, your search may leave you empty-handed or turn up a good group or two. No matter what kind of grief support you try—group or individual—keep searching until you find the right fit. Grief support may seem as if you are wasting your time, but you're not. You will be rewarded with hope, courage, and gradual healing if you reach out to others.

Support groups provide you with stability in the middle of chaos and changes in a life after loss. You may have to spend some time researching the right group, but the benefits of an additional support system outweigh the loss of time. Pick a group and give group support a try.

> *Find out how much God has given you and from it take what you need; the remainder is needed by others.*
>
> SAINT AUGUSTINE

## INDIVIDUAL THERAPY: IS IT FOR ME?

When you sit inside a doctor's examining room for the first time, the room can be cold and uncomfortable. You don't know if you should disrobe for a complete stranger or greet him or her sitting fully clothed. Let's face it—the situation is awkward for everyone in a similar position. A first therapy appointment can be comparable.

In a new therapy session, you are meeting a complete stranger who wants you to reveal intimate problems or emotions. The therapist may provide some framework and suggest tools to try, depending on what you share. In a session, emotional conversations may leave you feeling exposed. For therapy to work, you will need ongoing courage to be vulnerable to another person. The process can be humiliating and embarrassing, but it can also provide invaluable help in the grieving process.

### Two Ideas about One-On-One Therapy

Individual therapy, like group therapy, can provide you with support in terms of tools, feedback, and perspective after your loss. Before undertaking individual therapy, take into account these two ideas:

1. Like finding a support group, finding the right therapist may take some time.

If affordable, try three distinctive therapists and evaluate their insights into your problem and your ease when talking to them. Trust your gut instinct. If individual therapists don't work for you, move on to other options.

2. If you find yourself uncomfortable in a one-on-one situation with the spotlight on you, look into group therapy. It's usually less expensive, and you receive a variety of perspectives and feedback from many people instead of one therapist. Group therapy usually is most beneficial when a trained leader guides the group.

## Our Story

After Dad died, Mom, my sister, Ivy, and I were not much support for each other. Each of us dealt with our own grief in our own way; we all had many new life choices and responsibilities to manage. The three of us were overwhelmed individually and together.

Luckily Ivy and I discovered that if a parent passes away in hospice, the family can receive one year of free hospice counseling. Under the **Medicare Hospice Benefit, section 40.2.3** (p. 203), bereavement counseling to family members must be made available after a patient's death in a hospice. To learn more about the Medicare Hospice Benefit policy, review the guidelines on the **Medicare** Web site (p. 203).

Mom actively sought support; however, at age fifty-six, compatible grief support was hard to find. Mom tried hospice counselors, social workers, psychotherapists, and local church programs and finally found a hospice counselor in her hometown about three to four months after Dad's death. Once Mom had professional support, my sister and I received relief from the constant daily emotional support Mom required. As our responsibility lessened, we diverted our energy back to rejuvenating our own lives.

Eventually we all found counselors who were a good fit for our individual personalities and needs. Therapy appointments created some structure for all of us, structure that hadn't been there for the first months after my father's death. The most successful counseling strategy for all of us was a blend of faith-based group therapy and individual counseling.

## Benefits of Individual Therapy

After getting into individual counseling with a compatible therapist, I found many benefits. My therapist provided me with tools to implement, options for my circumstances, and unbiased feedback from someone outside my family and friends. She provided a fresh perspective of my situation and a confidential, stable place to go to talk through new problems and concerns.

## If Individual Therapy or Group Therapy Doesn't Work

Combining individual and group therapy may not work for you. That's fine. Try other successful ways of dealing with your grief, such as journaling, taking vacation time from work, or talking with other friends who have lost parents or loved ones. Whatever you decide to do, don't avoid dealing with your grief. It is important to work through grief, in whatever way or time that is successful for you.

## Yes, Therapy Is Awkward, But . . .

Yes, the first visit to a therapist's office can be excruciatingly uncomfortable and awkward. You may only want to reveal a little at a time. That's okay. Without any kind of grief therapy, you miss out on a large amount of available support. When you withdraw from support, you lose an outside perspective, new ideas for dealing with new loss issues, and beneficial structures for dealing with your grief.

## Resources and Options

As soon as you are able, start investigating your options. Call friends who have experienced working through loss in therapy and ask for referrals. Many types of therapists treat grief-and-loss issues—psychotherapists, social workers, and psychologists. Ask each therapist you contact if they have experience in counseling patients dealing with grief.

For other referrals, try a local hospice, such as **Vitas Innovative Hospice Care** (p. 177), as well as talking to individual grief-and-loss counselors. Try *Psychology Today*'s Web site (p. 204), the **National Board of Certified Counselors** (p. 204) Web site, or the **Family and Marriage Counseling Online Directory** (p. 205) for searchable databases of counselors by state, marriage and family counselors, or psychotherapists in your neighborhood. If those resources aren't the right fit, find social workers through the **National Association of Social Workers** Web site (p. 204) or look for church programs. The **Society of Military Widows** (p. 204) and **2-1-1** (p. 176) also have grief-and-loss resources. You can talk to licensed counselors by phone through

**Phone Counseling** (p. 204).

Keep knocking on doors, and eventually a good one will open. If individual therapy isn't right for you, find out more about group therapy in the previous section. For additional resources, take a look at Part III: Resources under the "Support Groups, Grief-and-Loss Centers, and Individual Therapy" sections.

 ## Questions to Ask about Individual Therapy

- Is my parent or I ready to talk with a therapist about unsettling issues?
- Is a group setting more comfortable for me?
- Who in my network of friends and family can I go to for advice or support if I am not comfortable talking with a therapist?

A good therapist's office should put you at ease and create a safe place to expose your feelings. Fortunately you have many choices. Select an educated and experienced counselor to assist you in managing and working through all the emotions loss can create. Typically when you lose your fear of vulnerability, other people can offer support that quickly improves your life. Put fear aside and watch the universe place someone on your path to bring you new hope.

---

*The best way out of a problem is through it.*

**ANONYMOUS**

---

# ONLINE SUPPORT GROUPS

When you open your e-mail inbox, it could be filled with supportive and heart-filled messages from Australia, Greece, or even Hong Kong. Online support groups provide another tool for dealing with grief along with the traditional support options of group or individual therapy.

## Five Ideas about Online Support Groups

Online support works best in five situations:

1. You want to remain anonymous.
2. It is difficult to attend or find local in-person support groups close to work or home.
3. You require support immediately and can't wait until a scheduled meeting. Online groups are available twenty-four hours a day, seven days a week.
4. You want another tool for dealing with grief or loss of a parent in addition to group or individual therapy.
5. The online support group is either monitored daily for adherence to the group guidelines for communication or the group e-mails are censored or moderated by a professional counselor before they are sent to the group. Censorship is especially important in children's online support groups.

## Our Story

When I was at M. D. Anderson Cancer Center in the last months of my father's life, a Yahoo online support group for non-Hodgkin's lymphoma fit my needs perfectly. Away from home and surrounded by unfamiliar people and services, I had no easy immediate support options. I was getting only minimal assistance in Houston where I was temporarily located, and my schedule was erratic. During our two-and-a-half month stay in Houston, I needed daily support. The members of the Yahoo online group supported me with inspiration and information on the disease, specialists, and hospitals. Additionally, I was able to connect late at night after Dad was asleep and still be with him during the day.

When I left Houston, I had difficulty finding grief support from support groups or individual therapists where my parents lived in Richmond and in San Francisco where I lived. Because I was focused on accomplishing funeral and memorial service tasks with Mom, I often forgot to take care of my own needs. I wish I had spent the time to find an online grief support group after Dad's death. Even though I had many friends offering support, when I talked with people who had lost a loved one, their understanding and reassurance brought me great comfort.

## Benefits of Online Support Groups

Traditional support groups are usually held in person at a designated place and time. Many people who could benefit from a traditional group still prefer to participate in an online forum. I believe the greatest benefit comes from combining online support groups with in-person support.

Online groups offer many advantages, such as serving people who are unable to participate in a face-to-face group and providing low-cost grief therapy moderated by a professional counselor or peer leader. Web-based groups can include video, sound, or computer graphics along with text, and participants can review information multiple times. Online group members can participate from a private, comfortable environment, and the relative anonymity of an online support group may help facilitate meaningful dialogue. A person can receive help and support simply by reading about the experiences and comforting words others have posted.

## Drawbacks of Online Support

An online group wasn't perfect, but the Yahoo group was the best I could find for my circumstances. As the years have passed, I have gotten involved with local faith-based support groups. I found they have provided more encouragement as I connected with group members in person. Besides, they provide additional local resources and the physicality I miss online. Online support is not perfect. People can misrepresent themselves in chat groups. Read "How to Stay Safe Online" in this section for more information.

## If Online Support Is a Bad Fit

If you try an online group and don't find the comments useful, the forum may be the wrong one for you or maybe online support is not the right support avenue. Individual therapy or an in-person support group may be a better fit. When you find grief therapy that suits you, the process should ease you forward through your grief.

## Special Note: Different Online Group Formats

Online groups can be conducted either in "virtual time" or "real time." When you write to members in a "virtual time" support group, the other members may not be in front of their computers as you write. Examples of "virtual time" support groups are message boards or e-mail listserv groups. Alternatively in a "real time" support group everyone is in front of their computers at a designated time. Chat rooms are examples of "real time" support groups.

Cendra Lynn, founder of **GriefNet** (p. 200), says that e-mail virtual support groups, such as the fifty groups she monitors on GriefNet, create a greater intimacy because each member receives each message posted, creating a greater sense of community. This creates more of a personal letter environment that facilitates intimacy without the typical nonverbal distractions people face when involved with an in-person group. Online groups are divided into three categories:

**Chat Group (or Chat Room):** A chat group is a real-time exchange in which everyone is at their computers at the same time, "chatting" with each other—much like a telephone conference call. At a predetermined time, the members of the group sign into the group using a special chat program so they can communicate with each other. **GROWW** (p. 199) has chat rooms available for adults facing parent or grandparent loss.

**Bulletin Board (or Message Board):** A bulletin board is a Web program or location in which participants can read and write messages at any time that can be read by any other participant. The messages remain for the duration of the group, posted sequentially and usually organized by topic. The **AARP's grief-and-loss message boards** (p. 200) and **Beyond Indigo** (p. 200) are examples of bulletin boards.

**Mailing Lists (or Listserv):** A mailing list is a private e-mail subscription in which each subscriber receives a separate copy, via e-mail, of each message that is posted. Through these messages, members can maintain ongoing communication with other list members who share a particular situation or common concern. **Yahoo Groups** (p. 200) and **GriefNet** (p. 200) are examples of listservs.

## Resources and Options

A good place to start for a grief support message board is **Beyond Indigo** (p. 200). Click on its message-board tab and either search past the listed topic postings or register to become a member and post to the discussions. For loss-of-parent groups, try **GriefNet** (p. 200) or **Healthboards** (p. 201). For widows or widowers try **Grief Support Services** (p. 201), **GriefNet** (p. 200), or **AARP's grief-and-loss message boards** (p. 200). For a list of other online groups, go to Part III: Resources.

## Questions to Ask about Online Support Choices

- Does my parent or I want to use the Internet as a grief-support tool?
- Do I have time to review additional e-mail every day?
- How will I go about finding the right online groups for me?
- Is my current schedule inconsistent? Will online support work better for my current lifestyle?

## Special Note: How to Stay Safe Online

Here are some general safety guidelines to understand before getting involved with an online support group. For additional online security information go to **Stay Safe Online** (p. 201) or **OnGuardOnline** (p. 201).

1. If you are feeling suicidal, then you need in-person help either through your emergency room or national hotline numbers (U.S. National Suicide Hotlines: 1-800-SUICIDE or 1-800-273-TALK).

2. Because the Internet can create a place for fraudulent identities and inaccurate information, use caution and withhold sensitive personal information in online conversations. Do not post information about your surviving children if they are under the age of eighteen, such as name, place of residence, school, and activities. Make up a name if you wish to refer to them by name instead of daughter, son, etc. Many people look on message boards to find information about children to abuse them. Once you get to know someone, swap information through e-mail. Play it safe.

3. If you are still having depressive symptoms after six months of grieving, you definitely need in-person support as well as online.

4. Online support is never a replacement for professional help.

5. Remember that posting online is public information. This means people can search by your name or the information you put in the post and it will appear in a search engine.

Sharing with others can provide new ideas, directions, or guidance on how to work through our unique situations. Sometimes it's best to sit at home in your pajamas and surf online. Whether you go online, find a local group, or seek individual counseling, find support that works. Reaching out is the critical action. Try an online group or two and see how the interaction fits your life and needs. If the e-mails get to be too much, try other support methods when the time seems right. Support exists in abundance no matter where you search.

> *Nobody makes a greater mistake than he*
> *who did nothing because he could only do a little.*
>
> **EDMUND BURKE**

CHAPTER THREE

# TAKING CARE OF YOURSELF

You have experienced one of the most difficult transitions in life—the loss of a parent. Yet you cannot simply go away and grieve, because your surviving parent now needs you in ways he or she never has before. If you do not take care of yourself during these next days, weeks, and months, you will not be able to provide the support to your newly widowed parent that you genuinely desire to give. You must consider how to protect and preserve yourself and still be available to help your mom or dad.

## TIME OFF FROM WORK

Life insurance policies can be expensive, but the price usually pays off if the policy or policies provide financial security for the family or heirs after a death. While assisting your widowed parent, you may want to invest in your own version of an insurance policy—a "priority policy." Intense self-care after loss is critical because grief affects you physically and can threaten your own health as well as your newly widowed parent's health. When you prioritize and reduce or shift work and extracurricular activities in your schedule, you buy the best insurance money can acquire—sanity and better health. Additionally, with a "priority policy," you may suffer a short-term financial setback but you'll prevent a long-term financial or health crisis.

### Four Time-Off-Work Options

A priority policy, my own concept, is a fictitious policy for creating sanity and taking care of yourself. You create a priority policy when you combine time management and prioritize new and current tasks. When creating your priority policy, four options are available:

1. See if unpaid leave under the **U.S. Department of Labor's Family and Medical Leave Act** (p. 174) is an option for you. The Family and Medical Leave Act, a government program, allows qualified employees to leave work on unpaid leave for a maximum of twelve weeks. If you don't qualify or can't afford to leave work, reduce your hours, if manageable and allowed by an employer. Employers sometimes are able to offer you flexible schedules, reduced hours, telecommuting, or four-day workweeks for a reduction in pay. It doesn't hurt to ask. Take a look at **Telecommuting Jobs** (p. 216) or **QuintCareers** (p. 216) online for more information on flexible job options.

2. If your employer is unwilling to reduce your hours or days at work, freelance. With the Internet, e-mail and cell phones, work options have changed. If you work in the creative, intelligence technology, programming, writing, accounting, administration, research, or consulting industries, many freelancing opportunities are posted online. Be aware, however, that freelancing may lead to a reduced income or take time to create steady income. If freelancing is of interest to you, take a look at **Elance** (p. 215) or **Guru** (p. 215) online.

3. Part-time assistance for you through a virtual or personal assistant may be an option. New companies such as **AssistU** (p. 215) offer virtual assistants at affordable rates.

4. If none of the options above seem plausible, temporarily reduce all or most of your extracurricular activities. After experiencing parental loss, it's important to maintain some activities to provide you with a diversion; however, new responsibilities combined with a previously packed schedule may become too much to handle. Read the book *Six Months Off: How to Plan, Negotiate, and Take the Break You Need without Burning Bridges or Going Broke* (p. 215) for more ideas.

 ## Our Story

My sister, Ivy, and I had been working in part-time jobs since our father was diagnosed. When we returned after Dad's funeral, we had established strong friendships in California and wanted to stay there rather than move back to Richmond to live closer to Mom.

Because of our decision and the weak job market in San Francisco at the time, we started our own businesses in mortgages and real estate to pay our bills. During the next four years, Ivy and I struggled financially and emotionally trying to build new lives, run our businesses, and take care of issues with Mom. We had put too much work pressure on ourselves and underestimated the effects of my father's death. Eventually the stress of managing everything from opposite coasts overcame us. We burned out and made the decision to move back to Mom's new home in Atlanta.

Looking back, I have mixed emotions about my decision to stay in California and not move immediately; however, because we started new businesses while stressed and grieving, they were destined to fail. It was too much. I misjudged the time required to aid Mom with new needs and major decisions she wasn't prepared to make alone.

If I had all the responsibilities to do all over again, my business and volunteering priorities would have been reduced from the beginning. Instead of starting a new business, I would have temporarily worked for someone else. When Mom's issues and new responsibilities stabilized, I would have taken more career and financial risks.

## Benefits of a Priority Policy

If you invest in a priority policy for yourself, you avoid becoming overwhelmed. Instead of running on survival mode and showing poor performance at work or with children because of your new responsibilities, with a priority policy, you maintain good relationships, preserve your reputation in the business community, and maintain your self-esteem. When you create a more workable schedule, you also reduce the possibility of harboring resentments toward your widowed parent or other family members. If you have a flexible schedule or can afford assistance, you are in the best position to address all the issues that may emerge after a death. Because of your priority policy, you are able to be more sensitive, balanced, and healthy.

If the additional tasks of assisting your widowed parent will not affect your current schedule, that's fine. However, if your tasks become too much to handle, create a priority policy.

As you make extra time to tend to your widowed parent's issues, you may miss your own life. Remember, the change is only temporary. You're actually protecting your life. If you temporarily stop or reduce your workload, you manage your stress levels, keep yourself healthy, and reduce the time spent sorting everything out. Remind yourself that reducing your own schedule is only temporary until your widowed parent is able to manage the majority of tasks on his or her own.

## Resources and Options

Be realistic and look at your individual situation. For the time being, stop or reduce your community service or volunteering efforts. Look into the **Family and Medical Leave Work Act** (p. 174) or call your boss to discuss options. Search online and look in Part III: Resources, for freelance job–posting Web sites and other resources to aid in making work decisions.

## Questions to Ask about Priorities

- Can I afford to take some time off work?
- Can I manage my current schedule along with new tasks to assist my widowed parent?
- Does the physical distance between my widowed parent and me make things more difficult?
- Can siblings or relatives who live closer to our parent handle things without me?
- Can I do my job from a remote location?
- Can I reduce my work week?
- Can I take on freelance projects to pay my bills while I assist my widowed parent?
- Will my ability to pay my bills remain intact if I make a job change or cut back on work hours?
- What is the best for my family's situation?

Investing in a priority policy for yourself takes time and usually some sacrifice but will pay huge dividends later. Paychecks and health benefits are great to have, but if your sanity, positive attitude, and reputation are lost because of excessive responsibilities, your job might not be the insurance policy you need. Strategizing and prioritizing ahead of time brings a sense of balance to an otherwise potentially chaotic and difficult situation.

> *The way to be safe is never to be secure.*
>
> **BENJAMIN FRANKLIN**

## HEALTHY BOUNDARIES

Switzerland is notorious for being politically neutral. In the middle of Europe and close to feuding countries, Switzerland stands its ground. It's small but powerful because of its strong stance. The country guards its borders, as they are tested all the time. While inside the country, its citizens ski, enjoy the picturesque countryside, and protect their country's peaceful ways. As you work through your own grief-and-loss issues, you must build your own secure sanctuary—a mythical Switzerland.

### Three Strategies for Building Healthy Boundaries

To build your own secure sanctuary or protected place, you need to assess three areas:

1. Consider how much short-term and long-term assistance your widowed parent will require. Be realistic.
2. Define for yourself what is essential in your life to maintain balance with regard to your time, energy, and money.
3. Figure out what tasks to give to others and who will be selected to accomplish those tasks.

### Our Story

After I lost Dad, my secure sanctuary was destroyed. As I focused on taking care of too many of Mom's needs and ignoring too many of my own, I experienced weight gain, souring friendships, health troubles, and income loss. Periodically I tried to address these growing concerns but was drawn back into the whirlwind of Mom's crises. My own life's boundaries became blurred when I was determining how much to put my life's activities on hold to support my grieving mother. The tug-of-war between my needs and my mother's went on inside me for years until I learned to maintain stronger personal boundaries. Learning to say no was empowering and allowed me to say yes to important needs in my own life.

Four years after my father's death, I looked at my life, which previously had sparkled with fun, friends, and creativity. Instead I had a life I did not want. I knew I had to set boundaries if I wanted to get my life back on track.

First, I determined what needed to be reestablished for me to maintain my previous levels of energy, time, and money. For me, regular exercise and better time management became essential to preserve my own sanctuary. I established two boundaries—exercise and my own work and personal schedule. I found making time for self-care provided more energy to support my mother when she needed comfort.

As I continued to sort through unsatisfactory areas of my life, I reestablished activities and new boundaries. I joined a support group and took time for fun-filled breaks. My sister and I guided Mom in hiring new advisors and local handymen. Mom called us less with daily emergencies as she grew accustomed to the newly built systems—such as online bill pay—we created to help with all her new responsibilities. I learned to say no to preserve my own life. Eventually I restored my own secure sanctuary guarding my life.

## Build a Protected Place

Without saying no when appropriate, you lose yourself. After the loss of a spouse, a widowed parent's new needs are important, but the adult children's needs are equally important, especially since adult children typically look after the widowed parent the most. As you assist your parent, establish early boundaries, perhaps as your parent did while raising you. Parent-child roles may get reversed, but the essential job of encouraging and assisting each other has not changed. You both grow. Of course you will have occasional emergencies. The borders of your secure sanctuary aren't meant to be permanently rigid walls but bridges that allow entrance when urgent needs arise.

## If Boundaries are Not Maintained

If you don't take the time to reassess your personal boundaries, you react to whatever circumstances are thrown your way. Without any grounding in your own routine or rituals, you operate lopsided. If boundaries are not established, the widowed parent's new needs could consistently override an adult child's own energy, time, and financial needs. Clear communication and respect for each other's lives should be a high priority for both the widowed parent and adult children.

Without honest communication and understood boundaries, you and others may ignore the time you need for daily rituals that give you energy, grounding, and soul feeding. You may lie awake at night wondering what happened to time during the day. Unpaid bills may lie untouched in your mailbox while late payment charges accumulate. When you have no boundaries, many of your needs become blurred and sometimes forgotten.

### Resources and Options

If you already have strongly maintained boundaries, stick to them. If not, read the book *Boundaries: When to Say Yes, When to Say No to Take Control of Your Life* (p. 207). If you have an elderly parent, review **Eldercare Resources** (p. 297) for additional assistance in managing the needs of elderly parents, and read *Coping with Your Difficult Older Parent: A Guide for Stressed-Out Children* (p. 297) for more ideas and boundary-setting strategies with parents.

### Questions to Ask about Boundaries

* Do my parent and I respect each other's boundaries?
* What is essential for my own life to run on survival mode for a little while?
* What activities could I reduce and not miss?
* How will I carve out small amounts of personal time to unwind?
* What areas will I be flexible with, and which boundaries need to be permanently closed to others?

Your mythical Switzerland is always vulnerable to boundary attacks. As its only commander in chief, your job is to protect and monitor your boundaries while balancing the needs of a widowed parent. Remember, saying no to others means saying yes to yourself.

*The best place to find a helping hand*
*is at the end of your own arm.*

**SWEDISH PROVERB**

# SHOULD WE CREATE A CAREGIVER CONTRACT?

Housewives get a bad rap. Many housewives, especially those who take care of children, also perform income-worthy tasks. Many duties they perform—paying bills, cleaning the home, running errands, doing laundry, washing windows, and grocery shopping—are full- or part-time legitimate jobs and businesses.

Nowadays, full-time bookkeepers, housecleaners, errand runners, window washers, and personal assistants do these same tasks for other people; it is their job. The employees or freelancers who perform those payable jobs charge from fifteen to a hundred dollars an hour, depending on their location and expertise.

When you or another family member leave full-time work, or work part-time to support a widowed parent, you may perform payable jobs for your parent, such as tech support, housecleaning, errand running, coaching, organizing, moving, and bill paying. If it's affordable for your parent, getting paid for your time will balance your income loss and reduce resentments between you and your parent—possibly other siblings or family members. You may want to consult an attorney if you choose to draft a caregiver contract.

## What Is a Caregiver Contract?

A caregiver or personal care contract—if between family members—is a written legal agreement between a caregiver and a parent. The contract outlines salary, terms of payment, schedule, duties, performance reviews, pay increases, restrictions, dismissal, and termination options. A caregiver contract creates a legitimate way for a parent to pay adult child caregivers financial compensation for their assistance, which provides income for the caregiver and, in some cases, may reduce so-called "death taxes" on the parent's estate.

## Not an Option for Everyone

A caregiver contract may not work for you or your parent. Many people can't afford to pay for assistance. In such a case, you or other family members will spend time executing tasks, possibly reducing your own income or personal time. Maybe other things of value can be bartered for your time, such as a lunch or dinner at Mom or Dad's home or free babysitting if you have children.

### Four Caregiver Contract Considerations

When determining if a caregiver contract is right for your situation, keep four considerations in mind:

1. If you or another family member were not facilitating tasks for your widowed parent, he or she might have to pay someone else to do them.

2. If you leave your job or take time off work to assist your widowed parent, you will face the consequences of your choice. Those consequences may be loss of income, loss of health benefits, or loss of job security, all of which have financial repercussions.

3. As you receive an income from your time spent taking care of your widowed parent, you reduce resentment toward your widowed parent or other family members for not contributing assistance.

4. When your widowed parent pays you or other family members, payments may reduce the estate, which may result in reduced "death taxes" upon the parent's demise, (i.e. estate taxes, probate fees, and in some states, inheritance taxes). Also, if these payments are made from the parent's savings, the payments may legitimately reduce the parent's countable resources and—in some cases—thereby render the parent eligible for Medicaid, which a widowed parent may need. Many families contact elder-law attorneys to create a written caregiver contract, summarizing the tasks and fees agreed to by the parent, and his or her adult children.

### Our Story

When my mother was widowed, my sister and I each spent close to thirty hours a week assisting Mom with financial, technological, and paperwork issues, and we lost income opportunities. We assisted Mom through long-distance phone calls and cross-country trips to Virginia. The financial implications for my sister and me were tremendous. We paid for travel and long-distance phone bills and sacrificed time away from income-producing jobs. Mom assisted with some expenses when she could. We maintained that crazy pace for three years.

Because my sister and I were self-employed, we had limited income-producing options. We were torn between Mom's new needs and tending to our own lives, two worlds that were both important. Our parent and child roles reversed.

My sister and I struggled with choices that Mom made over the years we were growing up, sacrificing for us. As Mom chose when we were growing up, Ivy and I decided what was okay to sacrifice in our lives and when Mom's issues needed critical immediate attention.

I developed health problems and became depressed. My sadness grew for my compounding losses. I lost my Dad, my sense of home, my income, and my personal relaxation time with friends and dates. My career and life plans were put on hold. Mom had changed from a fun-loving energetic mother to a lost friend who needed constant advice and comfort. Our whole situation broke my heart.

### You May Need to Rethink Your Situation after the Loss of a Parent

About nine months after my father died, Mom sold the Virginia home that had been our family home for the previous twelve years and rented in various cities for three years. At the end of three years, Mom decided to move to Atlanta permanently. Soon after Mom bought her Atlanta home, Ivy and I left San Francisco and the three-year-old businesses we built there to move temporarily to Mom's Atlanta home.

We moved to build a less financially stressful life for ourselves and to aid Mom with important tasks and decisions. As we untangled Mom's financial and accounting issues, we all decided my sister and I should get paid for our time. In our situation, having Mom compensate us for our time was the right thing to do.

### The Benefits of a Caregiver Contract

After Mom talked with professional money managers, organizers, and bookkeepers and learned how much they charged for the tasks my sister and I were doing for her, she valued our efforts all the more. Because we received payment for work completed to aid our mother, we reduced resentments and created some income for ourselves as we pursued new careers. Our agreement created the beginning of some financial stability for my Ivy and me. The biggest benefit was that all three of our relationships became less strained.

### Unexpected Times Call for Creative Solutions

Money is a sensitive topic. If you talk with your parents about money exchanging hands or creating a caregiver contract, discussions can be awkward. If you have the extra time to do a few tasks for your parent, that's great. Simply make sure that you are not being so generous with your time and resources that you forget about taking care of yourself. Brainstorm creative and maybe unconventional bartering solutions that benefit both you and your parent.

## Resources and Options

Contact the **National Academy of Elder Law Attorneys** (p. 208), the **National Alliance for Caregiving** (p. 208), or the **National Family Caregivers Association** (p. 208) for more information about creating a caregiver contract.

## Questions to Ask about a Caregiver Contract

* Is my parent willing to pay a family member(s) for caregiving assistance?
* Could my family create a caregiver contract that benefits everyone involved?
* How much time each week will caregiving tasks require?
* Will I have to quit my job to do caregiving tasks for my parent?
* Does my parent want my assistance?
* What do other professionals charge to take care of tasks?
* Do I currently do too much and resent my widowed parent or other family members for not pitching in more?
* What are the consequences for me in taking on additional responsibilities?

Most likely you are doing tasks for your widowed parent that a legitimate business or service provides for someone else. If you have had to reduce your own income to provide specific support, talk to your parent about getting paid or compensated in another way for your time. Talk with an elder-law attorney to see if you can craft a legal caregiver contract outlining your caregiving duties and compensation. When you make the situation clear, emotion plays a less important role. The agreement becomes a business arrangement between parties.

If you ignore your own financial needs, you will face the consequences. Value yourself, your talents, and your time. Give as much as you can, but if you are resentful, irritated, or bitter, it's time to make some changes. When you both value and respect each other's talents and time, everyone wins.

> *Circumstances are the rulers of the weak;*
> *they are but the instruments of the wise.*
>
> **SAMUEL LOVER**

## THE HOUR-LONG VACATION

When you go to a movie, you snuggle into the theater's padded bucket chair; pop your drink into its holder; and crunch on salty, butter-drenched handfuls of pop-corn. Happily settled in your seat, you're ready to be entertained and escape from your problems. Going to the movies is a healthy one-to-two-hour vacation for the brain. As your brain swirls around your parent's numerous new problems, you may need to take short one-to-two-hour vacations regularly to provide relief.

### Four Hour-Long Vacation Ideas

When creating your one-hour vacations, take into account these four ideas:

1.  Get out of your normal environment. If you normally walk, take a yoga class. If you live in a city, drive to the country for a hike. Spend an hour in a botanical garden. Whatever your situation, do something you don't normally do in your everyday life.

2.  Invigorate yourself through your senses—smell, touch, sight, sound, or touch. Make an appointment for a spa treatment. Go see a movie. Listen to relaxing music. Order flowers for your office. Write in a brand-new journal. Take an exotic cooking class or stretching class. Take a hike or volunteer. (Volunteer only if tasks are easy for you and they replenish your soul.) Do whatever rejuvenates.

3.  Laugh. See a stand-up comic live or listen to a comedy performance on audio. Go see a silly movie. Try to laugh. Laugh often. Laughter eases stress.

4.  When you go on your hour vacation, don't think. Give your brain a break from problem solving. Let your brain enjoy time off and whatever sight, smell, touch, taste, or sound you bring to its attention.

## Our Story

After we spent a month at M. D. Anderson Cancer Center in Houston with Dad, our brains were fried. Every day was filled with new and complicated decisions, adrenaline rushes, and exhaustion. Our brains swirled twenty-four hours a day trying to figure out a way to save Dad's life while dealing with our own needs. We were in dire need of a break from hospitals, blood-test results, and bad hospital and on-the-go convenience food.

One day my sister suggested seeing a movie. During the movie, for the first time in the month we had spent at M. D. Anderson, I felt my brain relax a little. Sure, I thought about my father from time to time, but the story kept me entertained enough to experience some relief and escape.

As we have collaborated with Mom on her new and big decisions over the years since Dad died, a walk or bike ride provided me with the best one-hour vacations. Daily walks or bike rides in nature revitalized all my deadened senses. While walking or riding my bike, I focused on everything going on around me, not the problems in my head I had been intensely trying to solve. Many times a solution came to me during my one-hour vacation.

Before I tried the one-hour vacation, I used to focus on solving my mother's problems all the time. Soon I realized focusing on Mom's problems and not my own wasn't working for me. I needed a new strategy to relax and take a break. Repeatedly rehashing problems in my mind or with others did not create solutions. It only made me worry more.

## Benefits of One-Hour Vacations

I shifted gears and tried the one-hour vacation idea. Because I took a break, got out of my normal environment, and stimulated my senses, workable solutions to Mom's problems surfaced. Constant focus and worry about your current situation won't make solutions come. Realize your parent's new problems can't be solved in one afternoon. Inject time for quiet and fun, and you create better balance for yourself and reduce stress. New environments, smells, sounds, and sights can quiet the logical mind and turn on the more creative and intuitive brain. When you turn off logic to solve the problem, the solution may come sooner.

## Resources and Options

Some people's schedules allow one hour off a day, while other people's schedules may only have five free minutes. Any kind of break from five minutes to a few hours can create a change in perspective and a break from the intensive decision making. The one-hour vacation doesn't have to be complicated: take a cooking class such as **Viking** (p. 210) or find one on **Shaw Guides** (p. 210), eat healthy food from your local **farmers' market** (p. 211), watch a movie (try **Netflix** [p. 212]), or listen to a comedian (try **Comedy Day** [p. 212]). **Botanical gardens** (p. 211) can be very relaxing. If you like outdoor or weekend breaks, look at the Web sites **Gorp** (p. 213) or **Worldwide Bed and Breakfast** (p. 210) for ideas. To find a spa, go to the **SpaFinder** Web site (p. 213). Do what invigorates you. For more hour-long vacation ideas, look in Part III: Resources.

## Questions to Ask about One-Hour Vacations

- What could I do to dramatically change my environment in one to two hours?
- What places are located nearby that I have always wanted to visit but never had the time?
- Which one of my senses is really in a need of a fix?
- What do my body, mind, and spirit need to refresh? An Italian meal? A mineral bath? An art gallery? A botanical garden? A concert?
- Has my brain been working too hard on solving one big problem?
- Am I willing to try several one-hour vacation strategies?
- After I stopped and took a break, did the time off clear my mind or did new ideas come to me?

Don't overplan your one-hour vacation. Make the escape fun and not a task on your to-do list. Enjoy your time off; you deserve it. If your brain is working overtime, take at least an hour off every day to chill out.

> *Nowhere can man find a quieter*
> *or more untroubled retreat then in his own soul.*
>
> **MARCUS AURELIUS**

## GROUND YOURSELF

Many athletes, dancers, and chefs prepare themselves for their jobs and daily lives through grounding practices, habits, or rituals. Without their daily practice or routine, they don't nurture themselves, and their performance suffers. By learning to practice mindfulness—a friendly and nonjudging attention to inner and outer experience—we can "ground" or "center" ourselves in the present moment whenever we wish—even in the most challenging situations.

### How Do You Ground Yourself?

People often use terms like *grounding, focus,* or *centering* to refer to an experience of coming back into the present moment with conscious attention. Mindfulness, or coming back to the present moment, is easier than you may think, but it does require knowing that grounding is important, and having some skills for directing and stabilizing your attention in the present moment.

According to Dr. Jeff Brantley, founder and director of the Mindfulness-Based Stress Reduction Program at Duke University's Center for Integrative Medicine, mindfulness is a natural human capacity for awareness that arises when you pay attention on purpose without trying to change or judge what you notice. Dr. Brantley suggests that you can develop your capacity for mindfulness by starting to notice your inner life, the sensations of breathing and walking, and letting a kind and compassionate attitude inform your attention to that and all other experience. Dr. Brantley says when your mind wanders or your attention moves elsewhere, you have not made a mistake or done anything wrong. Have patience with yourself and gently bring attention back to your focus in the present moment, noticing your breathing, body sensations, or sounds for example.[1]

### Three Grounding Ideas

When taking on new caregiving responsibilities in your new role, a daily grounding practice may protect your own life, needs, and boundaries. Grounding assists you in not losing yourself. As you explore new grounding routines, keep three important ideas in mind:

1. It is paramount to put yourself first daily. When you are pulled in many

directions, you must first meet your own needs.

2. A grounding routine can include listening to music, a walk in the woods, making a phone call, journaling, or your established spiritual practice. Choose a good fit for your personality and interests.

3. Your sleep and relaxing time are equally as important to establishing a regular grounding practice. As you rest and relax, your body is able to repair itself. Setting your personal sleeping times or daily resting breaks can be healthy new practices.

 ## Our Story

After a few years of coaching Mom, I had become much too focused on her needs and not mine. Ignored and forgotten, my own life had shriveled into a lifeless mess. Instead of focusing on my own life, I concentrated on tasks that made Mom's situation easier. Before my life got any worse, I knew I needed to find *me* again and get grounded.

As a writer and voracious reader, I chose to take an hour each morning and read from inspirational books and write in a journal. I still use journaling and reading inspirational books for my daily ritual. If I miss my hour, I am off balance and get easily stressed out, lacking a healthy perspective. As I have grown in my own mindfulness, I have explored prayer, meditation, and yoga as well as other new practices to learn to stay centered in present-moment awareness.

My restless sleep was also an issue. I couldn't quiet my mind from worry. A nutritionist prescribed a natural sleep remedy for me that led to more peaceful sleep. Instead of tossing and turning for five hours a night, over time I started sleeping for seven to eight hours a night in a calm, deep sleep. Over time I needed the natural sleeping remedy only sporadically and changed to using meditative CDs to relax my mind before sleep. One good meditative CD to try is ***Your Present: A Half Hour of Peace*** (p. 213). For more ideas on how to improve your sleep, read the book ***How to Get a Good Night's Sleep: More than 100 Ways You Can Improve Your Sleep*** (p. 215).

When I did not have a daily grounding routine to keep the focus on myself, I got lost in Mom's task list. When I took care of myself first and established a personal practice, I rebuilt a healthy new life. During my most challenging days, an hour of focused nurturing brought soul-warming rewards. My resentment toward others was reduced. As I protected my sleep, my invigorated body burst with new energy. I found huge benefits in taking the time to ground myself every day.

## Nurturing Benefits of Grounding Yourself

Dr. Jeff Brantley suggests three reasons why the experience of being grounded or present is felt as nurturing:

> First, our lives happen only in the present moment, so to return there, bringing our attention back from past ruminations, or future worries and plans, can be liberating. In addition, by establishing attention steadily in the present moment, we free ourselves from being hijacked by habits of reactivity in mind and body that tend to feed feelings of inner distress and upset, and to lead to neglect of important activities such as self-care and stress management. Finally, establishing ourselves consciously, and repeatedly here, in the present moment, has the benefit of putting us back in touch with our wholeness as human beings. When we can feel our bodies again, notice our breathing, or hear sounds around us, we gain immediate respite from the proliferating thought chains and inner narratives that can drive and narrow our lives.[2]

When you center yourself with a comfortable daily routine or practice, you create strong footing from which you can build activities of the day. Grounding roots and reconnects you with your innermost soul. When you take the time to cultivate a daily calming practice, you balance yourself and your mind for the work you are about to do. Grounding yourself provides stability, confidence, and a comfortable daily place to find comfort.

If you already do something every day that grounds you, stick with your practice. If you're hesitant or don't think you have time, reconsider. Try a short five-minute practice and watch the changes in your stress, reactions, and state of mind.

## Resources and Options

What's the risk? Try putting yourself first and create a new practice or routine. Set a sleeping schedule and slip into bed at the hour you establish as bedtime. As you try new ideas, see what grounds you in your day. If you are searching for inspirational daily readers, try *Simple Abundance* (p. 208) or *Journey to the Heart* (p. 208). For information on using journaling to work through grief, check out **How to Journal through Grief** (p. 211) or the **Center for Journal Therapy** (p. 211).

Dr. Jeff Brantley has written three books with Wendy Millstine on mindfulness-based stress reduction, including *Five Good Minutes in the Morning: 100 Morning Practices to Help You Stay Calm and Focused All Day Long* (p. 209), *Five Good Minutes in the Evening: 100 Mindful Practices to Help You Unwind from the Day and Make the Most of Your Night* (p. 209), and *Five Good Minutes at Work: 100 Mindful Practices to Help You Relieve Stress and Bring Your Best to Work* (p. 209). Each of these books offer a wide variety of mindfulness-based practices that can be a foundation or support for personal rituals and ceremonies that can help with living a richer and more balanced life. For additional ideas on daily routines and practices, check out *True Balance* (p. 209) or Part III: Resources.

 ## Questions to Ask about a Grounding Routine or Practice
- What routines or practice(s) could ground me daily, weekly, or monthly?
- Am I putting myself first daily?
- If not, why not?
- Does getting more sleep or sticking to a regular schedule give me more energy during the day?
- What benefit does grounding create in my life?
- Am I more grounded and less stressed when talking with my parent?

Be smart and start a grounding routine or practice. Put yourself first on your to-do list. If you're sleepy, take a nap; your body may need the rest. Quiet your mind and body before your day begins. Athletes do it. Dancers do it. You may need to do it too.

---

*Nothing can bring you peace but yourself.*

**RALPH WALDO EMERSON**

# PAPERWORK

One of the more mundane and frustrating
your parent's death is the location, organiz
finances, and the estate. Juggling attorne)
accountants is hard enough in your daily life, ....g your
widowed parent deal with it all while grieving s .... The following suggestions can help you avoid costly or emotional mistakes in dealing with paperwork
and finances at this time.

## ORGANIZERS, ASSISTANTS, AND BOOKKEEPERS

Imagine a CPA's desk on April 14, papers piled high with random manila folders
peeking out of askew paper stacks. Orange, pink, and neon green Post-it notes stick
out everywhere, attempting to organize the chaos. As you familiarize yourself with
your own paperwork situation, choose what's more important to you–your time or
your money.

### Three Questions to Ask

Before you hire extra assistance, you may want to know the answers to three
important questions:

1. Is your widowed parent willing to release control of personal paperwork?
2. How involved does your parent want to be?
3. Do you have time for your parent's weekly or even daily paperwork questions
   while you also manage your own affairs?

g Dad's last treatment efforts and his funeral and memorial serv-
_ and I were in no condition to tackle the mounds of paperwork at
home with her. Because Dad managed the household bills and records,
m was unfamiliar with his paperwork management systems. Together we had
to create new systems for Mom while unraveling foreign-looking life insurance
policies as well as numerous hospital billing requests for information.

To be honest, we still struggle to find information at tax time regarding my
father's previous investments. Mom tried a few professional organizers but hasn't
found the right fit yet. We recently hired a part-time bookkeeper to organize
Mom's accounting, files, and tax information. I wish we had hired a bookkeeper
from the beginning.

After a few years of trying to manage everything ourselves, I realized the paperwork issue was about control, trust, and time versus money. Yet without Mom's
online bank passwords, a local assistant or organizer could have relieved my sister
and me of most paperwork problems during the first year after our father's death.

A part-time personal assistant could have provided Mom daily companionship
while sorting through paperwork. Without an assistant, no one acted as a buffer to
handle emotionally difficult questions with phone calls from the hospitals and
Mom's attorney. With Mom's daily support in place, our focus could have shifted
back to rebuilding our own lives.

## You Don't Have to Pay Everyone

If you've determined that you need additional helping hands but don't have the
resources to pay others, ask your parents' or your friends. Rally a small group of
three to five people to spend an hour or two on alternate days handling tasks. Give
them a specific task for several weeks or cycles. Sharing the work avoids too much
pressure on one person. Volunteers at local churches or your **local AARP chapter**
(p. 165) can also be good resources to look for low-cost assistance. If you have privacy concerns, ask friends or volunteers to handle less sensitive documents such as
household bills or phone calls to hospitals or insurance companies.

Set boundaries if you do the work yourself. Maybe two hours a week is all the
extra time you can feasibly spend while maintaining balance in your own life. Talk
openly with your spouse or significant other about the extra time you need to

spend with your parent assisting them with paperwork.

## If Extra Paperwork or Systems Don't Create a Problem

Some lucky people have parents who share their paperwork systems and their overall financial picture with each other, even if they divide household roles. If your parents shared financial information or household records regularly with each other, you won't have to be as involved or hire assistance, because your parent will know what to do. However, even if your parents were quite competent in these matters before the death occurred, a grieving parent might need additional support. You may want to suggest a parent temporarily hire an organizer, part-time assistant, or bookkeeper.

## Resources and Options

Remember that CPA's desk on April 14? You could be sitting behind that desk—by default—if you aren't careful. As paperwork grows after the funeral, you may need a game plan to manage the work. First, take into account the actual extra time you have to dedicate to those matters, and then talk to your parent about specific assistance needs. If financially viable, hire advisors and delegate as much paperwork to others as possible. Planning ahead may prevent inundation later. Don't wait. Get started right away.

If you need a bookkeeper, contact the **American Institute for Professional Bookkeepers** (p. 217). To find an organizer, contact the **National Association for Professional Organizers** (p. 164). Personal assistants can be found through **Craigslist** (p. 228), **AssistU** (p. 215), **Domestic Placement Network** (p. 228) or the **International Association of Administrative Professionals** (p. 229). The **Lindquist Group** (p. 229) places top-notch domestic support staff in cities such as New York, Greenwich, Atlanta, London, or Palm Beach. Check out Part III: Resources for other assistance suggestions.

## Questions to Discuss with Your Parent about Hiring Assistance

* Does my parent want paperwork assistance?
* How does my parent want assistance handled?
* What in my life am I willing to relinquish to have time to assist my parent?
* Could I delegate some tasks and handle the rest with my parent?

- At what point will I draw the line and say no to more responsibility?
- How many hours a week or month or year can I realistically handle managing those new duties along with my own schedule?
- How could I sacrifice some control and thus be less overwhelmed?

If you or your parent thought you could handle all the paperwork and accounting but you're having second thoughts, you're not alone. Competent part-time employees and freelancers are ready to work. Whether you choose a team of friends, a professional, or yourself, extra hands make lighter work. Usually CPAs have a team working for them and you may want a team too. It's the only way CPAs see the tops of their desks on April 16.

*The smartest thing I ever said was, "Help Me!"*

**ANONYMOUS**

## MERGE, PURGE, AND AUTOMATE

The offices of famous organizers such as Martha Stewart or **Peter Walsh** (p. 218), a professional organizer from the Learning Channel's *Clean Sweep* TV show, may be perfectly painted and in near perfect order. Categorized, color-coordinated, and labeled files may be standard office protocol. Franklin Covey planners or BlackBerrys may keep all of Martha's or Peter's activities flawlessly coordinated. Fresh flowers may bloom daily on their desks. Unneeded papers may be shredded by personal assistants. They may have created true office bliss.

Is your parent's office similar? How about your parent's files? If your parent's office or files are not as organized, do you expect to see an office more like one that Einstein or Andy Warhol used? If your parent requests your assistance in reorganizing files, the job will no doubt be easier if your parent had either Martha's or Peter's organizing vision. I hope your parents created offices like

Martha or Peter. If not, don't fear.

No matter whether your parents are married, divorced, remarried, or single, they have some kind of filing or accounting system. They may make piles, folders, or stuffed shoeboxes. Their system may not make any sense to you; however, the system worked for them.

As you dig into your parents' paperwork and bills, two dissimilar systems, no system, or one system without a user's manual may exist. Blending those two worlds sooner rather than later will divert questions and frustration ahead. You can merge those two worlds using a solid strategy.

If you were born into a family that keeps neat, orderly files and online accounts similar to a professional organizer, you are incredibly blessed. Your parent may already know about his or her spouse's filing, bill paying, and money management system. If not, read on.

## Four Paperwork Choices

Before tackling the paperwork piles, you have four choices:

1. Ignore the paperwork and hope someone else offers assistance.
2. Leave the paperwork to your widowed parent to figure out; but your parent will probably call you frequently to ask questions.
3. Take the time to coach your parent immediately by suggesting the most efficient way to arrange a new system and shred the old one.
4. Hire a professional bookkeeper, organizer, or accountant with high ethics and privacy standards to create a new filing, bill-paying, or general paperwork system for your parent.

## Our Story

Dad's death changed everything for Mom. Dad paid all the bills and kept all the important files organized. After he died, Mom's thirty-four-year marriage role changed overnight. For the first time, Mom had to pay all the bills, maintain tax-receipt files, and organize new filing systems to manage all the financial and legal household paperwork. The piles of paper grew into problems for all of us. Mom needed new working systems fast.

First we paid the current bills. Next my sister and I pulled out all the statements from Dad's files and entered new payees into our parents' joint online bank account. You can write paper checks if you are uncomfortable with online banking; however, we preferred online banking because of the option to automate payments.

## Special Note

Online banking is more comfortable for some people than others. Because money is a sensitive topic for widows and widowers, automatic drafts from bank accounts and the release of control of managing their bills themselves creates vulnerability. Some people embrace technology, while others are hesitant. Explore your parent's wishes about paper statements, online bill paying, and automatic drafts before implementing.

While we typed in Mom's payee information in her bank accounts online, we reduced her paperwork by stopping delivery of her paper statements. We installed **Quicken** (p. 219), a money-management program, to download her transactions until we could find a bookkeeper. We installed the money-management program, even though implementing a computer program was an additional step, because the electronic program made Mom's budgeting and tax preparation easier.

After some stressful discussions with Mom's accountant, we took more action. With color-coded folders, a good shredder, and a list from the accountant on what files to keep, we dug in. We labeled new files with categories my mother could understand and use. We went through her accumulated paper piles and filed only the important ones. Finally, we tackled Dad's files. We purged unnecessary papers and incorporated the rest into Mom's new system. The establishment of Mom's new filing system was a good start.

## Benefits of Creating a New System

Mom's new system, without Dad's handwriting on all the files reminding Mom of her loss, reduced her emotional stress. After we finished, she had an easily accessible system that was tailored to her new needs. Mom traveled more confidently, knowing she could pay her bills online. At first she felt uncomfortable not receiving paper statements, but eventually she saw the advantages. We now are all less stressed about bills and finding papers because we took the time to create new systems.

Accountants, lawyers, and the Internal Revenue Service request various estate papers years after your parent's passing. Your parent needs a system that makes locating those papers easy. If a parent plans to move, converting paper to electronic files or creating a new portable file system brings smoother paper management. If those problems have already become an issue, take the time to merge, purge, and automate.

## Special Note
When someone dies, unique state laws and bank protocols determine how money is released to family members. First, you may want to ask your bank to release all joint bank account funds to your parent. In some states, joint bank accounts are automatically frozen upon the death of one spouse. You may also have to request authorization needed for family members to access accounts. If your parent has any problems accessing jointly held accounts or questions regarding bank laws, consult an estate attorney.

## Resources and Options
Purging, merging, and automating Mom's paperwork, files and accounts worked for us. If our system doesn't suit you or your family, a bookkeeper or a professional organizer might be a good option, or ask your CPA or your **AARP local office** (p. 165) for a referral. See the previous section for more information if you want to hire assistance. You and your parent must spend either time or money. First ask your parent what he or she prefers. When you and your parent establish new systems, it is worth your time. Order online office supplies from **Office Max** (p. 225), **Office Depot** (p. 226), **Staples** (p. 226), or **Discounted Office Supplies** (p. 225). See Part III: Resources for more merging, purging, and automating resources. See appendix C for a general list of filing categories.

## Special Note
Before you get started, check with your accountant and lawyer to find out what the current rules are for saving financial or legal paper or electronic files. Determine what files your parent needs to keep and how long will they need to maintain a record of those files.

**Questions to Ask about Purging, Merging, and Automating your Parent's Files**

- Does my parent want my help with purging, merging, and automating paper files?
- If I spent time to aid my widowed parent, how could it save me time in the future?
- What sacrifices do I already have to make in my own life to accommodate my widowed parent's questions regarding paperwork and bills?
- Are bill paying and paperwork management pushing my widowed parent into further isolation away from supportive communities and friends?

To reduce future problems, take a day or two to assist your parent to merge, purge, and automate papers and files. If affordable, hire a professional organizer. It may be a good long-term investment. Your parent's new system doesn't have to look like Martha's, Peter's, or a Pottery Barn catalog office. A simple, easy-to-use individualized system for your parent will allow you and your parent to reduce unnecessary panic and stress.

> *The man who removes a mountain*
> *begins by carrying away small stones.*
>
> **CHINESE PROVERB**
>
>

## CREATE A NEW BUDGET

When a widowed parent faces finances alone, possibly for the first time, the many decisions can be shocking. However, to avoid future decision paralysis and maintain momentum, a widowed parent needs to face the financial reality as a newly single person and consider changes.

## Three Budgeting Factors

When you discuss the sensitive area of money with your parent, remember three important factors:

1. Women who outlive their husbands still pay 80 percent of the expenses they had when they were two people living under one roof, according to **WISER, the Women's Institute for a Secure Retirement** [3] (p. 227). The widow or widower's expenses typically do not reduce to half, as many people might expect. Larger fixed cost—a person's mortgage, utilities, medical expenses, and health insurance—all stay the same after the loss of a spouse, while the reduction of Social Security or pension income may be reduced or regular income from a spouse's paycheck may cease.

2. The way your parents prioritized their expenses together will probably differ when one parent is alone, and a newly widowed parent needs to understand his or her relationship to money. Are they used to budgeting? Did they discuss a large household budget with their spouse? Are they a spender or a saver? Many times after the death of a spouse, the surviving spouse will become the opposite of what he or she was before. Savers go on shopping sprees and spenders refuse to spend a dime. As the surviving parent goes through the potential financial changes after the loss of a spouse, he or she needs to be mentally prepared to go through this process and acknowledge that everything is different.

   First encourage your parent to determine his or her current income, then budget in fixed costs. Once this is determined, stop and take a break. Keep in mind that if your widowed parent will still receive the same amount of income as before the spouse died, your parent may want to allocate the 20 percent excess income—if that is, in fact, the case—to a new financial priority, such as a new expense or investment. After creating an initial income and expense framework, encourage your parent to think about the things he or she might want to do or not do as a newly single person. Are they going to travel more or less? Are they going to move? Will they be paying for more or less entertainment or events outside the home such as movies or dinners out with friends? Encourage your parent to revisit these questions every three months or so until the budget is worked out.

3. Widows or widowers will be more or less comfortable with budgeting depending on how involved they were with the couple's finances. Some widows from traditional gender-role marriages who let their husbands manage the finances may feel less comfortable making financial decisions now that they are on their own. Other widows or widowers who managed the household budget or couple's investments may feel very comfortable making financial decisions.

## Our Story

In our situation, Mom understood she needed to make new financial choices. Self-restraint on her spending preferences required changing old habits. Mom was used to managing basic household expenses but not the mortgage, various insurance policies, or larger expenses. After paying all the bills, Mom realized the total income required to maintain her current lifestyle—and that number shocked her. Initially Mom tried to make a few small changes to reduce expenses. Over the next five years, Mom reevaluated memberships, subscriptions, credit cards, and insurance to decide if certain discretionary purchases brought substantial value to her new single life.

## Creating a New Budget May Take Time

Be forewarned. Your parent may not build a new working budget in one afternoon. The new budget process may take weeks, months, or even years for a widow or widower to let go of old lifestyle expenses or income levels. Let the financial transformation happen at the pace your parent can manage. Don't force the issue. Expense changes trigger large amounts of grief when a parent releases his or her past lifestyle. When some widowed parents evaluate their new income and expenses, current reality can hit hard; however, a widowed parent's acceptance of financial reality is critical to moving forward.

## Rebudget Early

If a widowed parent avoids reviewing their regular bills and spending habits, big problems may surface. Some widows or widowers can be incapable or afraid of handling their finances. When your parent's income is either reduced or increased through the payment or lack of payment of a large life-insurance inheritance, large or even smaller purchase decisions change. As a widowed parent overspends or charges large items and bills to credit card(s) without a way to pay them off, financial trouble brews. Budgeting or financial messes can be avoided if your parent addresses his or her own issues surrounding finances soon after being widowed. If your parent denies the financial reality, consult with a financial counselor.

## If Your Parent Managed the Financial Affairs

Regardless of your widowed parent's financial experience, after the loss of a spouse, he or she will need to possibly rebudget, seek financial assistance, and rework an investment portfolio. If your widowed parent was previously managing your parents' financial affairs, he or she may not seek advice from you. Keep in mind, however, even if your parent is a budgeting wiz, he or she may struggle with other financial decisions, such as buying, selling, or managing stocks, bonds, ETFs, mutual funds, or real estate assets and may require outside support and advice.

## Resources and Options

Talk to your parent to see if he or she needs budget assistance. If your parent requests assistance, divide expenses into three categories—simple survival expenses, little luxuries, and splurges—to clarify choices. Survival expenses are essential costs, such as rent or a mortgage, utilities, loans, insurance, or taxes. Little luxuries can be gym memberships, manicures, Starbucks coffee, or movies. Splurges can be vacations, shopping sprees, furniture, or a motorcycle. Little luxuries for some people may be survival for others. Budgeting and money-management choices are based on individual preferences. Encourage your parent to determine his or her own specific priorities, not necessarily the same choices made when part of a couple.

If your mother is your widowed parent, the **Women's Institute for Financial Education** (p. 227) has created local Money Clubs around the United States. In the clubs, women learn how to better understand and manage finances. Encourage your mother to read *Kiplinger's Money Smart Women* (p. 217), written by the executive editor of *Kiplinger's Personal Finance* magazine (p. 224) or join the **Women's Institute for a Secure Retirement** (p. 227).

If your widowed parent is age fifty-five or older, **Senior Discounts** (p. 228) lists discounts available to seniors. *Unbelievably Good Deals and Great Adventures That You Absolutely Can't Get Unless You're over Fifty* (p. 228) is another excellent discount resource for your parent.

For general budgeting information, grab a copy of the *Personal Budgeting Kit* (p. 222), *The Everything Budgeting Book* (p. 221), or the *Pocket Idiot's Guide to Living on a Budget* (p. 222). For more budgeting resources, review Part III: Resources (p. 155).

## Questions for Widowed Parents to Ask about Budgeting
- Do I have a good idea of my entire household budget?
- Is the budget written down?
- What things could I cut back on?
- How will I reduce my spending by 20 percent or whatever is needed to avoid going into debt or bankruptcy?
- Do I need budgeting advice or do I want to create a new budget myself?

Positive change can't take place until old blocks are removed. A few tweaks and your parent's new budget will allow him or her to keep moving forward. If your widowed parent reviews his or her finances early, future decisions are easier, confidence is boosted, and your parent's future financial security can be preserved.

> *Every worthwhile accomplishment,*
> *big or little, has its stages of drudgery and triumph;*
> *a beginning, a struggle, and a victory.*
>
> **ANONYMOUS**

# HOW TO SETTLE AN ESTATE

On Friday afternoon at the end of a hard workweek, you may want to go home and relax. What if your work required you to keep laboring through the weekend to prepare for a new client meeting Monday morning? After surviving the funeral and memorial service, the doors to settling your parent's estate open. Your free time or weekends may be filled assisting your parent with sorting through estate and legal paperwork. Before you and your widowed parent dig too deep into estate paperwork, talk about some critical questions.

## Four Estate Questions

Before beginning to settle an estate, know the answers to these four questions:

1.  Did the deceased leave a will?
2.  Is an executor of the estate mentioned in a will?
3.  If my parent is named as executor, does he or she want assistance from me or other family members in settling the estate?
4.  Should our family hire an estate attorney?

## The Role of an Estate Attorney

Estate attorneys can assist in many aspects of settling an estate, including explaining the will contents. Professionals with high ethics can prevent fraud or stealing from the estate from devious family members. If an executor is not named in a will, the estate attorney will consider the deceased's previous marriages, children, state laws, and other considerations before they approach the local court to obtain the required court order appointing an executor of the estate.

## The Role of an Executor

An executor, either named in a will or assigned by a court, is a person who accomplishes the wishes written out in a will. Spouses typically are assigned the executor role; however, some people choose executors other than spouses. The duties of an executor including regular estate attorney meetings, and sorting through legal paperwork can take a toll on a spouse along with his or her grief. An executor manages a lot of responsibility in the required tasks of administration of a large amount of legal and financial paperwork.

Unfortunately not everyone assigned to the position of executor has everyone's best interest at heart. When money is involved, illegal or unethical situations can occur. Sometimes, especially when large amounts of money are at stake, individuals and family squabbles get ugly. Sometimes greedy or squirrelly family members persuade the grieving spouse to allow them to step in and take over. When the role of executor falls into unethical hands, the assets of the estate can diminish overnight.

Sometimes the widowed parent may not able to perform the role of executor because of illness, impairment, or lack of interest in performing the job. If an alternate is needed, a trustworthy family member may have to be appointed. An ethical estate attorney can assist with sticky executor situations.

## How Long Does an Estate Take to Settle?

Typically, you send the final estate tax return to the Internal Revenue Service within twelve to eighteen months. An estate settlement time can be shortened or prolonged by many factors. Ask an estate attorney about your specific situation.

## Our Story

After my father's funeral and memorial service, Mom didn't want to deal with mountains of paperwork and attorneys; however, she was executor of Dad's estate. So Mom hired an estate attorney to assist her with her executor's job.

The estate attorney proved to be a stellar investment for Mom. The estate attorney facilitated paperwork and provided solid legal advice. The estate attorney brought trusted counsel into our chaotic world. She provided structure, logical thinking, and support.

Nevertheless, even with an estate attorney's assistance, Mom's executor job required her to make countless phone calls, take notarized documents to banks and investment companies, and photocopy various needed papers daily. In one of Mom's typical days during this time, she would photocopy Dad's death certificate, open or close accounts, deal with insurance companies, and look for papers in my father's old files. Because Mom did the executor's many meticulous tasks while isolated and grieving, she grew depressed. An executor's role can be a burden in many cases, especially when spouses carry their deep grief along on the job. Don't misjudge the power of grief.

Mom's daily life in the months after Dad died consisted of the tedious tasks of the estate work combined with managing all the unfamiliar household bills and chores. Across the country, my sister and I struggled to support Mom with her new responsibilities and put food on our own table. Unfortunately for us, we didn't have a good alternative for the executor role. Mom had no other choice.

Mom went to probate court, opened estate checking accounts, and renamed the retirement accounts. She kept an official log of all related death expenses for taxes. Mom created a personal inventory of my father's belongings and talked to insurance companies. She worked with her investment company to figure out date-of-death-cost basis of stocks Dad owned. She sent thank-you notes to friends who donated to charities in Dad's name. Even though some days were tougher than others, fifteen months later, Mom completed her executor's job. The estate settled. If Mom became an executor of an estate again, she would hire an organizer or paralegal or ask close friends for some assistance.

## A Personal Friend as an Estate Attorney

If your widowed parent or a family member is an attorney, his or her legal knowledge will be useful, but you may want to hire outside legal assistance to diffuse any potential family tension. A nonbiased legal opinion may maintain clear perspective on how to handle touchy situations.

## Resources and Options

If you can afford an estate attorney or extra assistance, the money is well spent. To find an estate attorney, contact **AARP Legal Services** (p. 219), the **American College of Trust and Estate Council** (p. 219) or online resources such as the **Lawyers** Web site (p. 219) or the **1-800Probate** Web site (p. 219).

Not everyone can afford an estate attorney or pay for outside paperwork assistance. If outside aid is unaffordable, ask honest and loyal friends to assist with some of the less sensitive nonfinancial tasks, such as making phone calls or addressing thank-you notes. Another resource for legal information is **Nolo Publishing** (p. 220), which produces a wide variety of legal reference books on wills, executor roles, and trusts. If your parent is a member of AARP, call its local office to ask for referrals for reduced-cost estate attorneys. Read *Facing a Death in the Family: Caring for Someone through Illness and Dying, Arranging the Funeral, Dealing with the Will and Estate* (p. 169) for details on administering an estate.

For other ideas on how to be an executor, locate a death certificate, find lost insurance policies or safe deposit boxes, or find an estate attorney, look over the Part III: Resources, under "Paperwork and Finances" for more estate and legal resources.

## Questions to Ask When You and Your Parent Sort Out an Estate

- If my parent is named as executor in the will, can he or she perform duties that could require eighteen months worth of work?
- Does my parent or I know a trustworthy estate attorney?
- Should my parent or I ask close friends or hire an organizer or paralegal to manage the estate paperwork?

When anyone settles an estate, no matter how much assistance a person has, an executor's duties can be extensive. If you or your parent understands the responsibilities of an executor, the estate's paperwork management will run smoother. You can prevent family members from overstepping boundaries and trying to control the estate distributions in their favor if you hire a professional estate attorney. Once properly executed, the estate settles, and the executor can spend more time on more uplifting activities.

> *One step and then another, and the longest walk is ended.*
> *One stitch and then another, and the longest rent is mended.*
> *One brick upon another, and the tallest wall is made.*
> *One flake and then another, and the deepest snow is made.*
>
> **ANONYMOUS**

## WHO WILL MANAGE THE INVESTMENTS?

After the loss of your parent's spouse, your widowed parent may need to decide if he or she wants to self-manage the finances, hire a financial planner or investment counselor, ask a family member to manage the finances, or stay with his or her current financial advisor. Your parent may make this decision based on his or her own views about how finances should be managed and how involved he or she was with your parents' finances before the loss of the spouse. When a spouse dies, the surviving partner may face many unfamiliar financial tasks if managing the couple's finances was not one of his or her roles in the marriage. If your widowed parent fears managing investments alone, financial planners or investment counselors can provide guidance.

## Four Investment Management Ideas

With all the financial management options available for your widowed parent, keep four ideas in mind:

1. If your parent has a professional financial planner or investment counselor who manages your parent's finances appropriately with success, a change in management may be unnecessary. After the loss of a spouse, many widowed parents will appreciate the security of discussing changing finances with a familiar advisor.
2. If your parent wants to hire a financial planner or investment counselor, find someone your parent can trust who has a similar investment philosophy. A professional financial manager should be able to advise your parent on a variety of options and provide advice based on your parent's comprehensive financial picture.
3. If your parent wants to manage his or her own finances, make sure he or she will have the time and energy needed to research investments, handle transactions, and track tax information.
4. Financial education is important to pursue no matter who manages your parent's finances. Your parent can make more educated money-management decisions if they read financial books, listen to financial audio tapes, attend financial seminars or conferences, review information on financial Web sites, and join investment associations and organizations.

 ## Our Story

My sister, Ivy, and I were raised and actively educated as children of a stockbroker. Fortunately for us, Dad believed that women, especially his daughters, should understand business and make their own stock-market investment decisions.

Regularly, my father took Mom, Ivy, and I to dinners at new restaurants with investment potential. Dad asked for our input on his possible stock purchases. He tested our investment choices with questions. My father encouraged us to think about the products we bought and the companies behind those products. We invested in the products and companies that made sense to us. Every day Dad discussed with us new products to test and companies to buy or sell.

Ivy and I placed our own stock trades when we were fifteen years old. Dad groomed us to depend on our own investment instincts. His stock-market and business teachings made a big and permanent impression on us both. Dad taught us investment tools to use for life.

His financially independent mind-set was enforced when, months before Dad died, he and I drove home from his unsuccessful stem-cell transplant in Washington D.C. He talked to me about what to do about investment advisors if something happened to him. He stared blankly out the window. He must have understood at that moment that the self-management philosophy of investments he encouraged in us would be implemented by his children and wife at his unexpected, early death. Dad counted on more time to make additional financial planning decisions in his retirement but ran out of time. I knew he didn't have a suggested advisor's name to tell me to contact if he died. Dad knew that if given a name, we would have followed that advice. Yet he trusted us to manage the investments more than any other advisor he could name, even after networking in the investment business for over forty years. The silence in the car clearly spoke his mind.

After Dad died, as Ivy and I juggled our own businesses and Mom struggled with being overwhelmed, we tried to use financial advisors. As time passed, we recognized that the advisors we chose charged high fees and produced low returns, invading Mom's principal. The three of us decided to tackle the investments on our own. We joined associations and groups, ordered newsletters, took investment classes to get additional perspectives, and took over the management of our futures.

Our choice to manage Mom's finances empowered us. After we looked at our talents and background, our management of Mom's investments was an obvious choice. We knew Mom's future financial security was in the hands of the people who cared most about her. We had not planned to manage Mom's investments, but considered our job another avenue for growth and education and, we hoped, success.

Our mother's choice to allow her adult children to assist her in managing her investments will not necessarily be the right choice for everyone. Carefully consider your own parent's situation and resources as well as your own and the resources provided in this book before making any new financial management decision. Monitor financial accounts closely to secure solid returns, whether you, your parent, or an advisor invests your parent's money.

## Financial Management Options

Before your parent decides which financial management choice he or she prefers, ask your parent what type of financial advice they need. Will your parent need the same or additional financial planning assistance because of the loss of his or her spouse? Does your parent need help with estate planning or stock-market investments or both? If your parent manages his or her finances, does he or she need additional resources? Once your parent has identified the need, then ask friends or other advisors, such as your accountant or attorney, for referrals to financial planners, investment counselors, or investment resources.

### FINANCIAL MANAGEMENT OPTION #1
*Your Parent Wants to Stay with His or Her Current Financial Advisor*

Many people hire a money manager to reduce their own worry over financial management. If your parent feels comfortable with his or her current advisor, don't force a change; instead, encourage your parent to meet with the advisor to discuss the financial implication of the loss of a spouse.

### FINANCIAL MANAGEMENT OPTION #2
*Your Parent Wants to Hire a New Financial Advisor*

Before hiring a new financial advisor, encourage your parent to consult the book *The Right Way to Hire Financial Help: A Complete Guide to Choosing and Managing Brokers, Financial Planners, Insurance Agents, Lawyers, Tax Preparers, Bankers, and Real Estate Agents* (p. 218). This book helps your parent prepare questions to ask any potential advisors—such as portfolio value requirements, services offered by an advisor, and an advisor's financial specialties. Your parent can then set up in-person meetings with a few advisors.

Tell your parent to ask any financial advisor they meet with to review their ADV. This document includes information about the advisor's education, disciplinary history within the last ten years, and professional designations such as Certified Financial Planner (CFP). This document also reveals how the advisor is compensated as well as business relationships they maintain with specific insurance or mutual-fund companies. These business relationships are legal, as long as the relationship is disclosed to clients.

Before your parent leaves a meeting with a potential advisor, make sure your parent understands how the advisor is compensated. Advisors can be fee-only, commission-based, fee-and-commission, or salaried. Ask for a written plan from each advisor on what it will cost to both create a plan and manage your parent's investments.

Financial planners and investment advisors work at full-service investment companies such as **Merrill Lynch** (p. 223), **Smith Barney** (p. 223), or **Edward Jones** (p .223). Your parent can find fee-only comprehensive financial planners through the **National Association for Personal Financial Advisors** (p. 226). To find a financial planner or advisor, consult the **Financial Planning Association** (p. 226) or the Personal Financial Planning division of the **American Institute for CPAs** (p. 226). Before your parent hands over his or her life savings, contact the **Financial Industry Regulatory Authority** (p. 227) or the **Securities and Exchange Commission** (p. 227) to make sure no disciplinary action has been taken against your advisor.

### Special Note

Before your parent chooses an investment advisor, suggest he or she research and investigate a handful of advisors. Some people prefer multiple advisors to reduce the risks of one manager, company, or person guiding all their investment choices, while other people prefer one manager.

### FINANCIAL MANAGEMENT OPTION #3
#### *Your Parent Wants to Self-Manage His or Her Finances or Learn More about Investments*

When your parent manages his or her own finances, he or she can save advisor management fees every year that can cost from 0.5 to 2 percent of your parent's total portfolio in some cases. Additionally, when your parent manages his or her finances, he or she alleviates the issue of discussing changes in a portfolio prior to placing trades. On the other hand, managing your own finances is stressful and time-consuming, and your parent will need to seek out information and do research. If your parent initially wants to manage his or her own finances but then gets overwhelmed, he or she can hire a financial manager later.

More companies and investment vehicles are available today than ever before through premium, full-service, and discount brokers. If your parent wants to buy mutual funds, **Fidelity** (p. 223), **T. Rowe Price** (p. 223), and **Vanguard** (p. 223) all offer low-cost, no-load mutual funds. **Morningstar** (p. 224) offers free information on funds and stocks as well as a fee-based service for researching mutual funds and stocks using their fully researched analyst reports. Discount brokers such as **Tradeking** (p. 223), **Firsttrade** (p. 223), or **OptionsExpress** (p. 223) all offer the least-expensive trading commissions. Review *SmartMoney* **magazine's annual broker survey** (p. 224) for detailed descriptions of the top premium, full-service, and discount brokers.

Index funds or ETFs (exchange traded funds) also offer other lower-cost investment options. These are passively managed and hold multiple stocks that track different sectors or indexes, such as the S & P 500, if your parent is uncomfortable picking individual stocks. Your parent can learn more about index funds or ETFs on many online financial Web sites and magazines such as **CNN Money Personal Finance** (p. 224), *Kiplinger's Personal Finance* **magazine** (p. 224), or **Yahoo! Finance** (p. 225). Your parent can also subscribe to business newspapers such as *Investor's Business Daily* (p. 220) or the *Wall Street Journal* (p. 220) to stay on top of current financial trends and gather new financial investment ideas. For additional information and rankings of online brokers and mutual funds, review the personal finance section of **Consumer Reports**'s Web site (p. 224).

Encourage your parent to join an investment group to share and learn investment ideas from other individual investors. **American Association of Individual Investors** (p. 226) and **Better Investing** (p. 226) are well-known independent investment educational associations. If your widowed parent is your mother, encourage her to seek out information from a women's financial organization such as **Women's Institute for Financial Education (WIFE)** (p. 227) or a national nonprofit such as **Women's Institute for a Secure Retirement (WISER)** (p. 227) and register for a newsletter or class. For more investment resources, thumb through Part III: Resources under "Paperwork and Finances."

## Questions to Ask about Your Parent's Investments

- What does my widowed parent want to do about financial management?
- Does my parent prefer someone else manage his or her investments or prefer to manage the investments himself or herself? Is my parent too overwhelmed to manage investments?
- Does my parent already have a trusted advisor who has performed well for him or her? Does my parent want to continue to work with that advisor?
- If my parent asks me to manage his or her finances, do I want the job and do I have time to educate myself about my parent's best financial choices?
- Should Mom or Dad hire a financial manager to invest money now and reconsider self-management of investments in the future?
- Could my parent find one investment resource listed in Part III: Resources that he or she wants to research further to aid in making a decision?

Support whatever financial-management decision makes your parent the most comfortable. Each possible choice has specific benefits and drawbacks. Whomever your parent initially chooses to manage his or her investments is not a permanent selection. If the relationship doesn't work out, your parent can make another choice.

---

*Only those means of security are good,*
*are certain, are lasting,*
*that depend on yourself and your own vigor.*

**NICCOLO MACHIAVELLI**

# CHAPTER FIVE

# TECHNOLOGY TIME-SAVERS

Technology today is designed to make our lives easier. You have likely adjusted to using it daily, even hourly, to manage your life, schedule, communication, and finances. Your newly widowed parent, however, may not be as comfortable with technology, or as confident in its ability to make his or her life easier. Helping your parent find ways to automate some of the paperwork and tasks of daily life can ease some frustration for them.

## AUTOMATE EVERYTHING

Your parent may face never-ending piles of paper without using technology. With free online bill-paying options at most banks and free shipping offered by many online delivery services, automating bills and tasks can free your time. Even monthly deliveries of groceries, drugstore items, or office supplies can be automated. Automation provides an extra set of invisible hands that reduce energy and attention on less important tasks.

### What Is Automation?
Automation is an electronic process created to deduct or move specific amounts of money in regular intervals (daily, weekly, monthly, yearly, etc.) with bank, investment, and other electronic accounts. Automation relieves individual management of recurring monthly bills, financial statements, and deliveries, providing more freedom for your parent. Automation also eliminates time and money spent on stamps to mail check payments.

## Three Benefits of Automation

Automation can benefit your widowed parent's situation three ways:

1. Your parent reduces time spent on isolating, unfulfilling, and monotonous tasks when he or she automates payments for regular bills, such as utilities, mortgage, insurance, and memberships.
2. When your parent does tasks such as bill paying and grocery or drugstore shopping, these activities may trigger memories of the deceased spouse and the spouse's past role. Your parent reduces these repetitive tasks when he or she elects to pay bills or receive regular drugstore and grocery deliveries automatically.
3. When a parent automates routine tasks, he or she creates more free time and spends less time alone without support.

## Our Story

Right before Dad was diagnosed in 2000, he entered a few accounts—also called payees—in an online bank bill-paying program. Before online bill pay was available, my father paid all the bills by check. After Dad died, the paper bills he had tried to reduce flooded Mom's mailbox daily. Mom spent many miserable days at home alone as she tried to sort through the paperwork and locate Dad's passwords for access to his online accounts. She wasn't prepared to handle the required volume of bill paying and paper management.

The more my sister and I unraveled our parents' bills and lifestyle, the more we knew Mom needed to automate. Mom focused on all the paperwork but neglected to see the more important big picture of her income and expenses.

## The Beauty of Technology

Technology eases widowed parents' financial accounting burdens when they are comfortable with computers and understand how to use their computer software. If you regularly download Quicken, pay your bills online, and check e-mail a few times a day, keep in mind those same activities may not be part of your parent's normal daily or weekly experience. For your parent, daily use of technology for common household duties may be outside the normal comfort zone. View the situation from your parent's perspective. Go slow and respect all small jumps forward. If your parent already uses automatic or online bill pay, be grateful for such organization; your parent's skill will save you time.

## Resources and Options

Initially, if you or your parent suffers from lack of computer experience or unease with the Internet and paying bills online, technology forces a vertical learning curve. However, the time technology saves is well worth the challenge. To automate monthly drugstore needs, go to the **Drugstore** Web site (p. 230). **Netgrocer** (p. 230) can automate you or your parent's grocery deliveries. **Efax** (p. 231) or **GoDaddy** (p. 231) can both set up faxes to be sent to you or your parent's e-mail address instead of fussing with a fax machine. Contact a financial organizer through the **National Association of Professional Organizers** (p. 164) to automate your bills or banking transactions. If your parent wants to save all online passwords for accounts in one place, go to **A1RoboForm** (p. 233), **Any Password** (p. 233), or **Splash Data** (p. 233). For more automation resources, check out Part III: Resources under the Technology section.

## Questions to Ask about Your Parent's Automation Possibilities

* Does my parent have regular income that provides a specific amount in a bank account every month? Is my parent comfortable with automatic payments deducted each month from that bank account?
* What other items, aside from regular bills or monthly deliveries, could be automated to reduce the workload?
* Has my parent automated membership dues, prescriptions, condo dues, investments, insurance payments, utilities, phone bills, or cell phone bills?
* How else could my parent and I simplify bill pay systems?

Automation of even a few bills or deliveries may relieve some anxiety. If used correctly and monitored well, technology will make both your and your parent's lives simpler.

> *Simplicity, simplicity, simplicity!*
> *I say, let your affairs be as two or three, and not*
> *a hundred or a thousand … Simplify, Simplify.*
>
> HENRY DAVID THOREAU

## ONLINE AND LOCAL TECH SUPPORT

Few stores are open twenty-four hours a day. Okay, maybe Waffle House, but how healthy do the customers and waitresses really look at 2:00 a.m.? I bet one night or two you will have no choice but to coach your parent through some kind of technology or computer issue. Things happen; however, make future plans to let the technology support companies that stay open for business twenty-four-hours a day, seven days a week be on call for your parent instead of you.

### Three Technology Support Questions

Before your parent hires online or local technology support, discuss the following three questions:

1. Is your parent computer proficient enough to use online tech-support tools like live chat, remote access software, and message boards?
2. Is your parent more comfortable learning from a technology support technician at home or at a local store?
3. Is your parent self-conscious about a lack of computer knowledge? Would he or she prefer to learn about computers in a group environment?

 ### Our Story

Mom normally used her Apple laptop computer and wasn't familiar with my father's Windows operating system. As the months progressed, Mom struggled with Dad's computer to locate files. Mom had technical problems and questions almost daily about both my parents' computers.

After I came home from a long day at work, Mom called me with a technical question she needed answered to make an important financial decision. Because of Mom's lack of knowledge about computers and my sister's and my more developed computer skills, technology support calls from Mom were frequent. That particular night I had plans for a long workout and dinner with friends to blow off stress, plans that ended up getting cancelled.

After months of similar weekly or even daily calls, my sister, Ivy, and I needed to hire outside technology support. Although qualified, Ivy and I grew frustrated with Mom's around-the-clock need for our technology support, but we weren't sure who else could answer Mom's computer questions late at night.

## Outsourced Technology Support Benefits

If Ivy and I had found Mom local technology support, or even online technology support, we all would have benefited. If Mom hired outside technology support, she could have called a hotline about her technology questions while my sister and I stabilized our lives and jobs. Mom would have indirectly benefited from human interaction at a local technology support store or from a technician who provided in-home technology support. Local computer training courses could have provided Mom additional support and a reason to get out of the home. Mom would have seen others struggling to understand with her in a class. We all would have been less frustrated if we had hired outside technology support for Mom.

## If Your Widowed Parent Is Computer Proficient

If your parent excels at computer troubleshooting, he or she may fix his or her own computer problems. A monthly or per-call technology support program is still an option if your parent gets frustrated regularly.

## Technology Support Costs Cash

Most technology support costs money. Lower-cost technology support is also offered at community centers, libraries, and churches. If those are unavailable and your parent is comfortable online, try online message boards.

## Resources and Options

If you or your parent is interested in online assistance for a monthly fee, investigate **PC Pitstop** (p. 232), **PC Pinpoint** (p. 232), **Plum Choice** (p. 232), or **Ask Dr. Tech** (p. 232). To find out more about local technology support, visit **Geek Squad** (p. 231) or **Geeks on Time** (p. 232). Review remote-access software companies online such as **GoToMyPC** (p. 234), **Mionet** (p. 234), and **Avvenu's Access n' Share** (p. 233). **GCF Global Learning** (p. 230) offers free online computer classes and its Web site locates local computer classes. If your parent needs a lighter and less-expensive laptoplike computer with wireless access, take a look at **Dana by Alphasmart** (p. 234). Browse Part III: Resources under "Technology" for more technology support ideas.

**Questions to Ask about Your Parent and Online or Local Technology Support**

- Does my parent need technology support?
- Do I want to be available to offer technology support for my parent? Is technology support better outsourced to someone else?
- Could I give more valuable advice to my parent in areas other than technology?
- What is the most effective tech support for my parent—online, in-person, or a combination of both?
- Could someone in my parent's community who charges less than other services assist him or her?
- What lower-cost technology support services are available in my parent's community—library, community center, or churches?
- Does my parent lack technical skills?
- Would my parent be more comfortable asking technology support questions in a computer class with others instead of alone?

As soon as possible, determine your tech support "office hours" available for your parent's technical questions. Stick to them. Twenty-five dollars a month for around-the-clock technology support may seem a high price to pay, but after one long day at work, a quiet phone may provide a million dollars' worth of peace and rest.

*The driver knows how much the ox can carry,*
*and keeps the ox from being overloaded.*
*You know your way and your state of mind.*
*Do not carry too much.*

ZEN SAYING

# CHAPTER SIX

# MOVING FORWARD

If you have moved past the crucial immediate days and weeks following your mom or dad's death, some tasks may be behind you now. Yet other challenges still lie ahead. As you walk through grief, it can become easy for each day to meld into the next, with no change and nothing positive to anticipate. Don't let yourself or your parent become paralyzed and listless, unable to move forward. At first you can't imagine life without your parent. Yet inevitably you must push forward with your life while you remember and honor the memory of your parent. Finding the motivation to move forward, one day at a time, will help you and your widowed parent find new life and energy again.

## CRITICAL MOTIVATORS

What motivates you? Travel inspires me. No matter if I walk down the street or fly to California, I escape my problems or daily work engrossed in the spontaneity of the outside world. When I encounter people or places that motivate me, I return to my regular life renewed and recharged.

As you and your widowed parent learn how to move forward in your lives after loss, carefully chosen motivators bring invigorating energy. When you take the time to change your environment, depleted motivation returns reactivated.

### Four Ideas about Motivation

Reflect on the following four ideas as you note your own motivators:

1. Get involved in motivating environments. Encouraging environments can

include work, church, volunteering, classes, book clubs, community gyms, small groups, or group therapy. When you surround yourself with uplifting experiences and people, you increase your energy, and new, hopeful attitudes attract new opportunities. If you choose to isolate, low energy and depression grow.

2. Absorb solution-based and positive thinking information in books, affirmation or meditation CDs, classes, or seminars. Those motivators encourage enthusiasm for self-improvement and attract interaction with others. When you read newspapers and the nightly news, an opposite and isolating effect occurs.

3. Get exposure to a world outside of your usual life and you'll create movement, perspective, energy shifts, and lifted moods. Even if you have time to do only something small, get out of your typical environment. You deplete yourself and lack motivation when you stay in the same environment without a break.

4. For many widows and widowers, regular interaction with their grown children and possible grandchildren may be critical motivators to move forward with life. Newly widowed parents make the choice to fight through their despair after loss to support their children or grandchildren. Adult children and grandchildren may give the widowed parent a reason to live, especially after the loss of a spouse from a long-term marriage.

 **Our Story**

After my sister and I returned home to California after organizing and supporting Mom during the month following my father's death, Mom talked to us on the phone about the same unresolved issues over and over again. Meanwhile we had to run our real estate and mortgage businesses. We jammed our days with work and little play. I tried to make life work, but over time, my motivation diminished, and I burned out from work overload. I craved rejuvenation but wasn't sure how to make time for play.

My motivation strategy, a combination of approaches, pulled me out of a burned-out state. I began individual therapy, read memoirs about loss, and listened to relaxation CDs to rejuvenate myself. I reduced my daily news intake and forced myself to create variety within my daily schedule. I also attended a long weekend certification training of the **Grief ❣ Recovery Outreach Program** (p. 236). During that weekend, I worked through my father's death as well as outstanding relationship issues. When I changed old habits, new positive energy invigorated me.

## Benefits of Motivational Environments, Books, and People

Optimistic and hopeful environments and people stimulated me to seek new directions. Old problems dissipated when new solutions surfaced. When I heard other people's stories, compassion filled my heart and loneliness left. When I altered my lunch routine or called an old friend, my energy changed and new environments or conversations inspired me. Small changes motivated me while we continued to tackle the big problems Mom, my sister, and I faced.

## If You Are Already Highly Motivated

I consider myself a motivated, driven personality; however, my constant tug-of-war between Mom's needs and my needs eroded my drive and motivation over time. Many people avoid their own feelings about their loss through working too much. Seek outlets that motivate you if you overwork and crave rejuvenation.

## Resources and Options

You must take action to create dynamic new energy in your daily life. Surround yourself and your parent with exciting environments and solution-based CDs, books, or classes to create new positive habits. Naomi Levy's book, *To Begin Again: The Journey toward Comfort, Strength, and Faith in Difficult Times* (p. 235), covers what brings comfort during grief; how to rebuild your life; and transformation after grief, prayer, and ritual. Relax to *Your Present: A Half Hour of Peace* (p. 235), an award-winning CD that fosters deep relaxation and reduces stress. Order the magazine *Living with Loss Magazine: Hope & Healing for the Body, Mind, and Spirit* (p. 237) to inspire you or your parent. You can find motivational speakers and their products in one place on the **Get Motivation** Web site (p. 238). **Achievement Radio** (p. 238), an Internet fee-based radio station, broadcasts motivational and inspiring broadcasts by speakers who focus on self-improvement topics to members. If you or your parent is interested in taking some adult education classes, try the **Learning Annex** (p. 236) or **Shaw Guides** (p. 210). Glance through Part III: Resources (p. 155), under "Moving Forward" for more motivation resources.

## Questions to Ask about Motivation

- In the past when I was stuck, what did I do? Did I go on a trip? Take a few days off work? Go fishing? Spend a weekend hiking in the mountains?

- Which of my environments motivate me?
- Who or what are great motivators in my life? How can I immediately spend more time around those people or activities?
- What classes, books, seminars, online workshops, or CDs could provide perspective and motivation after my loss?
- What could I do to change my normal routine?
- Before my loss, what used to motivate me?
- What or who drains me?
- What habits deplete my energy?

When you search for new motivating environments, remain open-minded and expect to be surprised. You shut yourself off from beneficial motivators when you sit at home or work in your office late at night. Seek motivation and see what surprises wait to encourage you and your parent.

> *Where the willingness is great,*
> *the difficulties cannot be great.*
>
> **NICCOLO MACHIAVELLI**

## THINK SHORT-TERM

When a parent dies, survivors experience a loss of long-term relationship security. The foundation upon which your security stood may seem to fall apart. Everything you built on that secure foundation may wobble and crumble. Short-term thinking may rebuild a new foundation.

### Three Concepts on Short-Term Thinking

When you shift to short-term thinking, keep three important concepts in mind:

1. If you build a daily or weekly structure after suffering a huge personal loss, you create consistency and stability. Without a structure, you or your parent may fail to gain momentum to move forward.

2. You or your parent can avoid pointless worrying about future events that may or may not happen when you maintain present-moment thinking.

3. Circumstances change daily. Small action steps push you forward in the direction of accomplishment. You change your circumstances by taking action.

 ## Our Story

When Mom settled into her new life alone after my sister, Ivy, and I went back home to California, her days lacked structure. Mom didn't work outside the home. During Dad's illness, she left her volunteer and community groups to care for him. Mom's home—surrounded by woods and off the beaten track from where her other friends lived—enforced her isolation from community. As her estate and household paperwork increased, Mom's isolation deepened as she worked at home, and Ivy and I worried about her. Initially, we suggested Mom balance her time between paperwork and community involvement. Because Mom was overwhelmed and worried about long-term situations, her focus on smaller goals and daily activity bred better results.

Mom worked on smaller achievements. She added simple things in her day to create routine. Morning jaunts to the gym grounded her in the day. After a few weeks, Mom attended church. Sunday church events surrounded her with friendly faces and pulled her out of isolation. Mom found a grief counselor who met with her weekly. Small activities built Mom an initial structure. Her small steps paved the way for bigger ones.

All three of us focused on what we could do in the present moment. During regular conversations on the phone, Ivy and I focused Mom on small steps, and she appreciated our support. After a year passed, the three of us talked about the upcoming summer or winter but still avoided discussions about next year or beyond.

When Mom talked about events beyond one month in the future, her brain stopped in "analysis paralysis." Mom settled Dad's estate with small daily steps. When she was ready to sell her home, she took small steps to decide where to move. Currently, several years after Dad's death, the three of us talk about and plan for next year.

When Mom used smaller action steps to make big decisions, she wasn't so overwhelmed. My sister and I supported Mom with deadline-based instead of emotionally based what-if scenarios. Speculative scenarios, for us, produced unnecessary fear and anxiety; short-term thinking created calm.

A simple structure created a foundation for Mom to rebuild her life and develop an identity as a newly single person. When Mom took and celebrated small action steps, all three of us saw her accomplishments multiply. Without small steps, we all spun in circles of worry. Mom listened to our suggestions and took action on many of them.

## If Mom Is Your Widowed Parent

If your widowed mother developed a strong sense of identity through work or community and avoided traditional gender roles, she may adapt and make choices alone better than a more traditional woman after the loss of a spouse. Regardless, if your mother is traditional or not, the death of a husband can devastate any wife.

Parents' financial knowledge as well as a support system outside the home may also play roles in their success after loss. Stay sensitive to your parent's situation and dramatic life change. Go easy.

## Resources and Options

Try short-term thinking in your own life. It can keep you balanced during the often emotionally turbulent first year after loss. Focus on what you can do in one day. Try not to worry about next year. Build a temporary structure for your life while you sort through your parent's and your own new problems and emotional issues.

According to Raphael Cushnir,[4] author of *Unconditional Bliss: Finding Happiness in the Face of Hardship*, when something negative happens in our lives, our usual response is to resist it. A better approach, Cushnir suggests, [iv]is to stay connected to the emotions and sensations that the situation evokes, moment by moment by moment. When we accept our painful emotions in this way, without analyzing, judging, or bargaining them, they dissipate quickly and easily, leaving a joyful peace in their wake.

When you seek outside perspective, you receive new insights. Call a friend or therapist, or join a support group to take small action steps. Read Eckhart Tolle's books *The Power of Now: A Guide to Spiritual Enlightenment* (p. 237) or *The New Earth: Awakening to Your Life's Purpose* (p. 237). Other books to encourage you to embrace short-term thinking include *Present Moment Awareness: A Simple Step-by-Step Guide to Living in the Now* (p. 237) or *Live, Laugh, and Be Blessed: Finding Humor and Holiness in Everyday Moments* (p. 237).

 ## Questions to Ask Yourself about Short-Term Thinking

* How has my parent's or my old security been shattered?
* What weekly or daily structure encourages short-term thinking?
* When we focus on what we can do one day at a time, do we accomplish more?
* Does anyone talk too much about next year or sometime in the future?
* Do we worry about events in the future too much when our circumstances could dramatically change at any moment?

One day can shatter long-term security. Grievers understand that fact better than most people. Stay in the present moment if your foundation is cracked and crumbled. Do small, manageable things. Each day provides small opportunities for success. Grab a jackhammer or some Crazy Glue and make your old foundation a little stronger for the future one step at a time.

> *The best thing about the future
> is that it comes only one day at a time.*
>
> **ABRAHAM LINCOLN**

## CELEBRATE MILESTONES

A star on the Hollywood Walk of Fame celebrates a person's success. Your version of success may be a dream home, a grandchild's birth, or enough money to retire. Your widowed parent may find success when making the first big decision on his or her own or when the deceased spouse's estate finally settles. Whatever success means to you or your parent, make sure you both celebrate the smallest of achievements.

### Three Milestone Celebration Ideas

Keep three points in mind as you celebrate successes:

1.  How you celebrate the small things doesn't matter; the celebrating matters most.
2.  Stay sensitive to a widowed parent's smaller achievements. When your widowed parent makes decisions alone, without his or her spouse available for discussion, your parent's self-esteem is tested and represents a huge step forward for your widowed parent.
3.  When you celebrate the little moments, you acknowledge small steps forward. Celebrations along the way boost energy and motivate you and your parent toward other future achievements.

 ### Our Story

Because I have been self-employed for a long time, certain financial tasks come naturally, such as downloading bank transactions into Quicken, paying bills online, and talking with my accountant about taxes. As for Mom, Dad handled all the financial tasks for their joint household for thirty-four years. After my father died, all those foreign tasks fell into my mother's lap. Initially we were frustrated that Mom didn't know how to handle everything, and my sister and I sorted out Mom's finances. As Mom gradually learned how to pay all the bills and understand financial choices herself, we checked that task off our list. When Mom accepted her responsibility and mustered the courage to try, she reached her first financial milestone. My sister and I saw the achievement but didn't celebrate her success.

As Mom continued to step outside of her comfort zone, she continued to blossom. My sister and I saw her change many old habits. My sister and I achieved small victories along the way. Over time, we celebrated all the small achievements each of us made along our recovery after Dad's death.

When you and your parent celebrate daily successes, fewer breakdowns occur over the what-ifs of the future. Celebrated milestones build self-esteem as you both identify your small steps of growth. You may think celebrations of small achievements may seem like a waste of time or silly. Do what pleases you, but celebrating milestones moves both you and your parent forward faster.

### Resources and Options

Go ahead and plan your next milestone celebration for when you succeed with a small step. Celebrations could be a day off, a night out, or a quiet night in. Get celebration ideas through the fun-filled card deck *52 Ways to Celebrate Life* (p. 236). Send you or your parent an e-card through the **Blue Mountain** (p. 235) or **Hallmark** (p. 236) Web sites. Read *Wow! Celebrations for the Successes of Life* (p. 236) for lists and enjoyable stories about celebrating. Make your celebration count. Check out Part III: Resources under the "Moving Forward" section for more celebration resources.

### Questions to Ask about Milestone Celebrations

* What are some recent small accomplishments I achieved that went unnoticed?
* What has my parent accomplished that I can celebrate?
* What can I do to recognize any accomplishments?
* Do I stop to celebrate? If celebrating is difficult for me, what can I do to change that behavior?
* When I celebrated events in the past, did I relax?
* What are the top three celebrations I will put into practice in my life to recognize small feats?

As you determine what milestones to celebrate, encourage your parent to do the same. Put on your party hats from time to time and watch your self-esteem rise and your and energy reemerge.

> *No matter what looms ahead, if you can eat today,*
> *enjoy the sunlight today, mix good cheer with friends today,*
> *enjoy it and bless God for it.*
>
> **HENRY WARD BEECHER**

# CHAPTER SEVEN

# HOLIDAYS AND ANNIVERSARIES

Ask anyone who has lost a loved one and they'll likely tell you that the most difficult times in the following months and years are the holidays and anniversaries that inevitably come. Instead of dreading these days as they approach, learn how to find ways to honor your loved one on these occasions, perhaps even bringing some relief and renewal to yourself and your widowed parent as well.

## RETHINK YOUR HOLIDAY ROUTINE

When you think about Christmas, Thanksgiving, or Hanukkah, what comes to your mind first? Eggnog? Christmas trees? Turkey? Menorahs? Presents? Or maybe difficult relatives or hectic plane travel? Whatever your past holiday memories, the first holidays after the death of a parent create challenges. The year you lose a loved one, rethink your holiday routine. You or your parent may or may not want to make changes, but if you need to make changes to make the holidays work for both you and your newly widowed parent, that's okay.

### Four Holiday-after-Loss Issues

When you plan the first holidays after the loss of a parent, think about four holiday realities:

1. Tension, emotional anxiety, and grief may run high with all or various family members.

2. Holiday ads that showcase the perfect American family and the gifts they give each other explode in malls, on TV, in magazines, and newspapers during the holiday season.

3. Everyone may not remember your deceased parent in the same way.

4. You can decline holiday invitations if you don't want to attend.

 ## Our Story

In the past, we alternated Thanksgiving and Christmas holidays in various locations where we had family members. We dreaded our first Thanksgiving without Dad, packed with memories of Thanksgivings past. Our family of three chose to be with some family members, but not at our typical holiday location. We spent that week with Dad's brother and his family in Arizona.

The first Christmas after my father's death, we vacationed in an unfamiliar but interesting city with nearby access to pampering options. We didn't exchange gifts but decided our vacation was our gift to each other that year. This way we avoided the retail Christmas barrage.

Because we spent the holidays in a new environment, we distracted ourselves for four days with new stimulation and conversation instead of old memories. This was what we needed to do to cope. We allowed others to care for us awhile, which brought us comfort and conserved our energies. We ate out without worrying about coordinating or creating meals, which lowered our stress. Because we stayed at a hotel with different activities available, each of us could do what we wanted. We could have a massage, relax, or read by the pool. Because we couldn't offer much support for each other the first holiday after loss, the combination of interacting with family members and staying at a nurturing hotel retreat was the best way for us to minimize the effects of the first holidays without Dad.

## Rethink the Holidays at Home

If you share the holidays in your typical location, determine if any holiday routines need to change or not. Holiday memories of the loved one who died can be both comforting and distressing to different family members. Everyone in your family will handle their grief differently. Some people stay strong to keep the holidays the same as usual. Others will break down and need to leave. It's all okay.

## Low-Cost Holiday Routine Changes

Under many circumstances, a week-long holiday away from home isn't necessary or affordable. Yet you can change your holiday routine without travel or high costs. Ask close family friends if your family can join theirs in celebrations during the holiday season. Contribute food or drink to celebrations but place someone else in charge of the holiday meals. Some funeral homes or various places of worship offer holiday remembrance services. Go to your local day spa and get a massage. Go to a midnight holiday mass or other spiritual event that brings you comfort. Volunteer to serve holiday meals to the homeless or deliver presents to less fortunate children on the holiday which can take the focus off your own troubles. Sometimes simple changes to your normal holiday routine can make the holidays more tolerable.

For some ideas on managing grief during the holidays, read *Healing Your Holiday Grief: 100 Practical Ideas for Blending Mourning and Celebration During the Holiday Season* (p. 239).

## Out-of-Town Holiday Resources and Options

If you are stuck on what to do, plan a holiday trip outdoors, on a cruise, or at a ranch. Your holiday can stretch the full holiday week or a two- or three-day weekend depending on what you can manage. Check out travel companies such as **Iexplore** (p. 242), **Cruise411** (p. 241), and **RanchWeb** (p. 243). Other options include an RV trip with family on **GoRVing** (p. 245). Search for bike trips on **Mike Bentley**'s Web site (p. 240). Use **SpaFinder** (p. 213) online to find a relaxing spa or rent a villa in an interesting destination by using **Homeaway** or **VRBO** (p. 244). **Tennis Resorts Online** (p. 245) and **Travel Golf** (p. 243) offer tennis and golf vacation options. If you want to splurge, rent a villa in the Caribbean or South America through **Turquoise Net** (p. 240). **Club Med** (p. 241) offers package vacations for their worldwide resorts. For families with young children, review the **Family Travel Network** (p. 241) or **Family Travel Files** (p. 241) Web sites.

Whether you stay close to home or take a trip away, don't wait to make plans for the holidays. Create a game plan and talk to other family members. Review Part III: Resources for other holiday-planning help, as well as the book *The Empty Chair: Handling Grief on Holidays and Special Occasions* (p. 239) and a book from a Christian perspective, *A Decembered Grief: Living with Loss while Others Are Celebrating* (p. 239).

## Questions to Ask about Holiday and Anniversary Plans

- How do I want to change my family holiday plans for the current year if at all?
- What have my family or I always wished our family did for the holidays?
- Where are family members we have not seen for a while that might be interested in visiting with us?
- How can my parent and I nurture and comfort ourselves to make the holidays a little more tolerable?

Open your mind to new possibilities. You might develop a better holiday routine than you and your family created before. Don't wait too long to decide. As you explore new holiday ideas, build in comfort and nurturing activities for you and your parent. Listen to what your bodies, minds, and spirits need most.

> *Do what you can, with what you have, where you are.*
>
> THEODORE ROOSEVELT

# CREATE A YEARLY MEMORIAL

Personal yearly rituals can take many forms. Whether you clean out your closet in the spring or take a summer beach trip, yearly rituals ground us in time. A yearly memorial ritual to honor your deceased parent's memory can mark an important relationship in your life.

## Three Yearly Memorial Strategies

Before you commit to a yearly ritual, keep three strategies in mind:

1. Choose a time of year you associate with good memories about your deceased parent. Birthdays, anniversaries, favorite annual trips, or Mother's or Father's Day may stand out.

2.  Commit to a written plan. A memorial may be as simple as a visit to the grave with flowers, a yearly trip, or a day with your widowed parent. Create whatever memorial works for you.

3.  Plan to do the same activity every year. You maintain a deep, continuing connection with your parent through a repeated ritual.

 ## Our Story

Every spring, I loved the celebrations surrounding Dad's birthday. I scoured stores for the perfect card and present to make Dad smile. On his birthday, Dad allowed others to dote on him. Because Dad's birthday marks an important date in my life, I celebrate Dad's yearly memorial on his birthday. Every year I browse through a scrapbook with pictures, letters, e-mails, and cards my father sent me over many years. My spring ritual connects me to reminders of my father's advice, wisdom, and friendship every year.

I began this annual ritual the second year after my father died. The first year after Dad's death, Mom, my sister and I prepared Mom's home for a spring sale. As time passed, I missed my father's friendship. When I created a scrapbook of my best memories of Dad, my bond to my father was reconnected. Through Dad's written words and my memory, he retains a strong presence in my life.

## Do What Works for You

A yearly memorial trip or a visit to your parent's gravesite may not work for you. That's okay. Do what reconnects you to your parent. For some people, a yearly event may be too infrequent. Regular gravesite visits, especially soon after your parent's death, may be what you need most. Or maybe that's too tough. Revisit the idea of a yearly ritual after some time has passed. In some cases, no memorial works best. That's fine. If you had a negative or abusive relationship with your parent and don't want to honor them with an ongoing celebration, engaging in one final ritual that feels comfortable to you may provide closure on the relationship. The need for memorial rituals varies for everyone. Again, do what brings you comfort—nothing more or less.

If you want to share a yearly ritual with your family and everyone lives far apart, one option is to set a date and time for everyone to do something in memory of your parent at the same time. You can create an annual event in which all family members can participate, such as releasing balloons in the air, raising a glass in a toast, or whatever activity is personal for your family. When you coordinate a yearly event for everyone to share, your family members create annual connection with each other while honoring the deceased parent.

## Resources and Options

When you create your own yearly memorial, only your imagination limits you. You could create a scrapbook of personal letters and photos or post a memorial Web site. See **Scrapbooking** (p. 246), **Personalized Memorial** (p. 246), or **Memory-Of** (p. 168) for scrapbook and memorial ideas. If your parent passed away of a disease such as leukemia or lymphoma or another disease for which marathons or walks raise funds, you could run, walk, or bike a half or full marathon to raise money for other patients. **Team in Training** (p. 246) raises money through sports events for leukemia or lymphoma research. To support others with a similar loss, research **Fundraisers** (p. 246) for more ideas. Check out Part III: Resources for more ideas on memorial rituals.

## Questions to Ask about a Yearly Memorial

- Is a yearly ritual a comfortable way for me to remember my parent?
- What other ways could I remember my parent through the year if a yearly ritual sounds too far away in the future?
- Was my parent someone I want to celebrate and remember?
- What is the best way to remember my parent: create a scrapbook, take a trip, go to the cemetery, bring flowers, talk to him or her aloud, or bring a piece of cake?
- What works for me?
- What date works best for me to create or celebrate a personal memorial to my parent?

Once you figure out what fits best, you may be grateful for your ritual. When you choose to remember your parent, you weave the loss into your life story and benefit from the ritual's healing nature. When the time is right, create a small ritual to remember your parent. Through tears or grief, a good memory may make you smile.

> *Praising what is lost makes the remembrance dear.*
>
> **WILLIAM SHAKESPEARE**

# CHAPTER EIGHT

# MOVING MOM OR DAD

Perhaps the most emotional decision a widow or widower can make in the weeks and months following a spouse' death is whether to stay in the home he or she shared with that partner. Decisions about staying or moving, where to go, when to go—all are filled with emotional attachments. As the adult child of a recently widowed parent, you will likely be a part of these decisions. Prepare yourself and your parent with the suggestions that follow.

## SUGGEST MOM OR DAD WAIT TO MOVE, IF POSSIBLE

If your parent faces the choice of staying in his or her current home or moving after the loss of a spouse, the right decision may not be immediately clear. Florida may sound like the perfect place for your widowed parent. Days filled with golf, tennis, or walks on beaches or palm tree–lined streets may lift your parent's spirits. With succulent mango, calamari, and fish caught fresh that morning and beautiful cluster homes and condos available, how could Mom or Dad not love fresh food and a beautiful environment? What more could they want in retirement? Your parent may love Phoenix; the dry, desert environment surrounded by interesting western states and attractions, golf, and tennis available at every turn entices him or her. You may think your widowed parent should try Florida or Phoenix and build a new life in a new environment. Yes, many retirees relocate South or West, but those places don't fit everyone's needs. When a widowed parent makes an impulsive choice to move too soon after the death of a spouse, the decision may be a huge mistake.

## Five Points about Possible Moves

If your parent asks you to assist him or her in deciding about a move, mull over the following points:

1. A newly widowed parent's main support network centers around his or her current home. If your parent moves, he or she might lose critical support. Local support is vital during the first year after loss.
2. A newly widowed parent's home provides comfort and stability when everything else in your parent's life turns upside down.
3. If a parent relocates, the move forces him or her to rebuild a new community as a single or widowed person.
4. A parent's identity is forced to change after the loss of a spouse. Where a parent lives creates an aspect of his or her identity.
5. Easy access to household files and legal papers shifts to a higher priority in the twelve to eighteen months after the loss of a spouse.

 ## Our Story

The first six months after our loss, many decisions swirled around all of us. Everything changed for Mom, my sister, Ivy, and me overnight: life without a father, an unexpected widowhood, and the family roles we each played. The thought of selling, packing, and moving Mom's home exhausted us; however, nine months after my father died, the three of us agreed that Mom should sell her home to allow her more flexibility in future choices. Mom wanted to sell the home when she had the opportunity. She said, "I don't know where I want to live yet, but I don't want to be stuck in a lonely big home in the woods." Mom could rent or buy, stay in Richmond or move to other cities. She eventually settled on Atlanta because of previous history and family in the area.

The over-five-hundred-mile move from Richmond to Atlanta presented more challenges than the sale of the home. Because of the large amount of furniture and breakables my parents' owned, Mom hired a large national moving company to pack and move her. The moving company, with two to three of its packers at work daily along with all three of us, packed Mom's belongings and furniture in three days. The two weeks prior to her move, we all had dropped off donations, consigned unwanted possessions, and packed and taped hundred of boxes.

On moving day, Mom said good-bye to her home by herself. After she closed the front door, Mom joined us in her car packed to the ceiling for the ten-hour drive. Mom was filled with conflicting emotions as she permanently left the only life she ever knew in her adulthood—a life as part of a couple. The gravel popped beneath our car tires as we drove out of my parent's driveway for the last time, headed to Mom's three-bedroom apartment in Atlanta. We had not seen the apartment that would serve as our "family home" for our newly altered family. We arrived late at night in Atlanta after the ten-hour drive.

The next morning, Mom, Ivy, and I drove together to her apartment. Ivy and I walked up one flight of stairs to see our new family home. One-eighth the size of my parents' home in Richmond, the small apartment sat dark and empty. Mom followed us into her new home. The apartment's small dining room overlooked a parking lot. A narrow galley kitchen hosted black-and-white linoleum floors. Small windows blocked the light from outside. Views of restful woods from the living room created the one upside. Our new reality hit us all hard.

The apartment provided Mom a temporary living solution. I pondered if everything in the moving van would fit in the apartment and the unit at the storage facility. Mom's new apartment was a shock; however, the apartment was safe, affordable for Mom, and available.

We quietly unloaded the valuables from Mom's car and drove to meet the movers at the self-storage facility. After they moved the last box into the unit, we drove back to the rental apartment and waited for the movers to unload furniture, beds, and boxes.

Throughout the day, old friends of ours from Atlanta delivered food, plants, well wishes, and hugs. Those drop-bys brought comfort. After a few hours, the truck was empty, and we crashed on the sofa, bleary-eyed and exhausted. The move took us more than two weeks and plenty of elbow grease and patience, but Mom successfully sold her home and moved to another city.

After the move, Mom questioned if she left too soon. She missed her friends. She sat in an unfamiliar apartment with only a few familiar comforts around her. She had moved back to Atlanta where we all used to live. Now, as a widow, she saw the city and her old friends who still lived in Atlanta with changed eyes. Old friends with whom she raised her children and organizations she belonged to as part of a couple didn't fit her anymore. For the three years after the sale of her home, Mom rented in two different cities. She felt unsettled and directionless as her social identity changed.

Because Mom delayed moving, even for nine months in her case, she reaped worthwhile benefits. She experienced the reality and cost of all the household bills. She took time to weigh all the possibilities instead of acting on impulse. As the months rolled on, Mom gained confidence when she made decisions. She saw some friends act awkwardly while others provided great comfort. Mom received invitations for social activities with other divorced, widowed, or single women. She could search for legal files in one familiar place during those first months. Because Mom delayed her purchase of a home, she made better long-term decisions.

After renting for three years, Mom bought another home. Mom chose, by herself, the home to buy and the city to move to as my sister coached her on mortgage options. A permanent home purchase grounded Mom as she committed to a new life. Three years of renting allowed Mom time to figure out where she wanted to live. The new home solved many problems. The decision gave her clarity for the immediate future. The home provided a permanent location for Mom's files and bills. A new neighborhood of potential friends awaited her. The purchase of the home marked the first big financial decision Mom made alone as a widow.

## If Your Widowed Parent Wants to Move

If your parent's home contains many memories of happier days or if the spouse died at home, living in the home may intensify sad memories. Your parent's new life labeled as a widow or widower in the community may result in fewer or no social invitations. Friends may act odd or avoid contact. Encourage your parent to not pack and leave but delay a move for at least a year and you could avoid disaster. After a year, a widowed parent often builds enough perspective to choose better options; however, everyone's situation is different and some people who choose to move within twelve months after loss find the move made the most sense for them.

## If Your Parent Has To Move

Sometimes, soon after the loss of a spouse, a widowed parent can't afford to stay in their current home. If your parent faces this situation, decide if your parent will sell the home himself or herself or use a real estate agent. If you choose to use an agent, contact one with the **Senior Real Estate Specialist** (p. 253) designation to find out about the current real estate market. Consider contacting the **National Association of Senior Move Managers** (p. 250) to find a senior move manager to talk with about the realities and implications of your parent making a move. If you need to research potential assisted-living communities for your parent, go to **Care Pathways** (p. 252). Order and read *Moving Mom and Dad: The Stress-Free Guide to Helping Seniors Move* (p. 247) in preparation for the move. Call **Aging Network Services** (p. 207) for information on housing options. When you reach out for professional advice, your parent's undesired move might be easier for everyone.

## Resources and Options

If your parent is considering moving to a retirement community, encourage him or her to spend some time reviewing the **Retirement Living Information Center** Web site (p. 252) or read about various locations in *Where to Retire* magazine (p. 250). For more moving ideas and resources, thumb through Part III: Resources.

## Questions to Ask about Moving Mom or Dad

* Can Mom or Dad afford to stay in his or her home?
* Does my parent have access to a large support network where he or she currently lives?
* If my parent did not move, would his or her home provide some stability?
* Is my parent ready to go through the stressful and emotional process of the sale of his or her home?
* Is my parent ready and equipped with the energy required to rebuild a new community as a single person in a new place?
* Does my parent have a strong identity outside of his or her life as a couple?
* Was my parent's entire identity associated to his or her spouse and children?
* Does my parent think a move will solve all his or her current problems?
* Does my parent view costs realistically?
* Where are all the legal and important papers filed in my parent's home? Are they paper or electronic?
* Could my parent create a portable file system to access while in transition?

The new Florida or Arizona life works for some people, but not all. A move to another community may only delay your widowed parent's reality. Discuss all your parent's options with him or her. After you both weigh all the factors, your parent can make the best decision for his or her current circumstances. Before your parent grabs the mango-coconut-shrimp lifestyle, he or she may want to rent or visit before making a permanent move.

> *No matter how far you have gone on a wrong road, turn back.*
>
> **TURKISH PROVERB**

## WHERE SHOULD MOM OR DAD RETIRE?

How do people pick out a college or university? They research the school's majors, extracurricular activities, sports teams, social life, and campus location. Eventually they visit the school and spend the weekend with a current student. After an initial evaluation, a handful of schools are chosen and ranked and applications sent. In the end, hopeful attendees cross their fingers and hope their number-one choice school accepts them. Widowed parents might choose a retirement location in a similar way.

### Three Retirement Issues

When you and your parent discuss his or her retirement options at the appropriate time, explore three thoughts:

1. An easy-to-build friend network may be critical for your parent's happiness in a new location.
2. The best place for your widowed parent to live may not be the city you live in.
3. Don't count on your Mom or Dad's current friends to stay where they currently live.

### Our Story

Mom sold her home the first year after my father died. The decision for Mom to buy a home took three more years. Before Mom purchased a new home, Mom tested different lifestyles when she rented apartments in three states. Initially Mom believed if she moved to a retirement community, a new environment might solve her loneliness, lack of companionship, and grief. As Mom visited various retirement options, the reality of particular communities became clear. When she spent time within those communities, they lost their initial glitter and allure. Where Mom chose to live needed to suit her personal daily needs and interests, regardless of how her neighbors spent their time. When Mom experienced day-to-day living in retirement communities, she knew a retirement community didn't solve all of her problems. No matter where she traveled, she faced widowhood.

## Retirement Community Illusions

Many retirement communities create a false illusion. New retirees buy into retirement communities when they assume legions of comparable-aged people float around in abundance within the community. Retirees think they bought a new reliable community. Unfortunately new homeowners in the communities often are disappointed. Many retirement community homeowners travel, spend time at clubs with established networks, visit children and grandchildren, and spend six months of the year somewhere else.

## A Supportive Community

When your parent is ready to discuss retirement options, examine the distance and cost required to visit supportive friends and family from various choices. If a newly widowed parent moves closer to you, stronger dependency on you results, because he or she has been uprooted from familiar support. A parent's hobbies or interests could determine the best place to relocate. Keep in mind if your parent is a younger widow or widower on the verge of retirement in his or her fifties or sixties, friends may not sit home all the time. Friends may try out their own retirement options. Keep the location of a parent's friends a secondary consideration. Focus on how your parent plans to rebuild a new support system without you at its central core. Encourage the parent to put new roots in a place with a variety of support options.

## Plan and Avoid the What-ifs Later

Encourage your parent to get an early taste of various retirement communities of interest. If your parent samples retirement communities, he or she makes an educated decision on where to live and diverts the what-if's that may surface later. After the right choice is made, everyone sleeps better.

## Resources and Options

When your parent is ready, build with your parent a top-ten list of retirement possibilities within his or her budget and rank them. Next your parent should make a list of hobbies, interests, or fields of work desired in a new community. Review the two lists together and brainstorm. If your parent is interested in retirement communities, he or she may want to look at the **Retirement Living Information Center** (p. 252) or *Where to Retire* magazine (p. 250) for ideas. *AARP The Magazine* (p. 249) has an online questionnaire called "Location Scout" to narrow down choices. If your parent needs assisted living, go to **Care Pathways** (p. 252) to find local choices. Explore Part III: Resources for more ideas about retirement communities.

Some parents are happy with their current location and may not move. That's fine. Everyone saves energy, time, and money when a parent doesn't move. If you don't live in the same city as your parent, make sure you jointly create a **Community Extra-Hands List** (see appendix C for a worksheet), for future needs and both you and your parent keep copies handy.

## Questions to Discuss with Your Parent about Retirement Options

- Do you want to stay where you are or move?
- What places offer the most opportunities for your interests?
- Do you want good medical facilities nearby?
- Are retirement communities affordable on your budget?
- Do you want to live near a university or community college to take classes or get a degree?
- Do you need to be in a community that creates activities for homeowners?
- Can you meet people on your own, or do you need scheduled activities?
- Do you want to buy or rent?
- Do you prefer a low-maintenance condo over a higher maintenance home? What can you afford?

If your parent wants to move to a retirement community, encourage him or her to make plans to visit or stay with friends in retirement communities of interest. With plans in place, you avoid a parent's long-term, flip-flop thinking. Applaud definitive choices. Well-researched decisions bring your parent the best choice.

> *To know what you prefer, instead of humbly saying "Amen" to what the world tells you you ought to prefer, is to keep your soul alive.*
>
> ROBERT LOUIS STEVENSON

## HOW TO HELP A PARENT PREPARE FOR A MOVE, GIVE AWAY BELONGINGS, OR CLEAN OUT A HOME

Sometimes, after the death of a spouse, your parent may need your assistance giving away personal belongings or cleaning out the home to prepare for a move or an upcoming sale of the house. When you and your parent sort through possessions, the decision of what to keep, donate, sell, or liquidate will be easier if you both prepare ahead of time.

Your parent's home, condo, or apartment holds many memories; possessions remind Mom or Dad of bad, good, and possibly unfinished discussions, histories, or relationships. When you or your parent returns to the family home after the loss of a parent, past memories bubble to the surface. A lifetime of possessions to sort through can challenge anyone, but the task can be completed. Tackle each task one small step at a time. If your parent doesn't have to meet a moving deadline, he or she can sort through or clean out personal belongings at a pace that feels comfortable. No rules exist that your parent must clean out the spouse's belongings in a certain number of months or even years.

## Five Ideas to Consider before Taking Action

Before your parent prepares for a move, gives away personal belongings of his or her spouse, or cleans out the family home, think about these five ideas:

1.  If you can, encourage your parent to postpone cleaning out the home, personal possessions, and clothing until at least six months after your parent's death. Suggest that your parent wait to implement any big changes until the initial chaos after loss settles. Certain belongings may offer stability and comfort during the first year after loss.

2.  Start with the emotionally easier rooms to maintain motivation and energy levels. You need to determine which rooms will be the least difficult to clean out. The choice is different for each family.

3.  Reward yourselves for achieving progress, no matter how small, with walks outside, take-out lunches, calls to friends, and coffee or water breaks.

4.  Don't expect to accomplish these tasks in one weekend. As you and your parent sort personal family belongings, you both get emotionally drained. Logically you may think you can complete the process in one weekend; however, delays are inevitable as you face unexpected emotional reactions from yourself or others.

5.  For the more difficult rooms and spaces, you may want to encourage your parent to hire a professional or gather a group of close friends to assist. When your parent involves others, additional support creates more steady progress. Friends that help may appreciate your parent giving them a small possession of the deceased such as a favorite book, sports equipment, or memento that may serve as a happy reminder of your parent.

 ## Our Story

Luckily for us, my parents lived in their last home together only twelve years. We moved and cleaned out my childhood home of eighteen years during my college years. My parents had amassed more stuff than they had in their previous home. At Mom's request, we started the home clean-out process the year Dad was sick. My sister, Ivy, or I spent at least an hour in the attic or basement each day. Every item brought back old memories, but the attic or basement provided a private place to go for some time alone after Dad was asleep for the night.

After my father's death, we stayed with Mom for the month after Dad's death to assist her with estate matters before returning to California. Mom planned on selling the home quickly. With Mom's approval, my sister and I started cleaning out Dad's possessions by throwing out his unimportant possessions, such as shampoo and old medicines, along with cleaning out the basement and attic within two weeks after my father's funeral. Because Mom was having difficulty sleeping in my parents' bedroom packed with reminders of Dad, we thought reducing visible signs of Dad would reduce Mom's deep grief. After cleaning out Dad's bathroom supplies, we made the mistake of cleaning out a very emotional area of the home—my father's closet. We considered which of his possessions to keep, give to his friends, or donate. We didn't know what else to do.

Instead of a garage sale, Mom consigned and donated unneeded items; the consigned pieces generated cash to assist paying for the expensive move and Mom received a tax deduction for donated items. When multiple charities refused to collect attic and basement items, Mom rented a truck and loaded items to take to a donation center with assistance from a few friends

Ivy and I worked feverishly to get everything done before we left to go back to San Francisco. We had selfish motives for our decisions after a two-month absence from our regular lives. We had come to a crossroads with no map to guide us in our next choices. Because we were unprepared for the uncharted territory, we acted on impulse. We were torn between assisting our mother and tending to our lives and careers in California, but we had to make choices. Either way, each choice had large side effects, good and bad. The pull between our lives and assisting our mother continued to create conflicts inside us.

During our feverish pace to complete many critical tasks, my sister and I rarely took breaks or rewarded ourselves for our accomplishments. We saw our tasks as small steps within one big project to complete. Needless to say, we burned out fast. The weeks after Dad's death were a time of whirlwind decision making and numbness for all of us. We found out later, through therapists, the impulsive choice to clean out the home soon after Dad's death might have been a mistake. At the time, we all did what we thought was the right thing to do. If Mom moved again, we would hire a **professional estate organizer** (p. 250) or **senior move manager** (p. 250) to assist in the move, planning, and tasks.

## If Your Parent Needs to Prepare for a Move

If your parent is moving to a smaller home, he or she needs to work through nine critical steps:

1.  Your parent needs to identify what to take to the new home. Ask your parent to consider how the current furniture, clothes, and other belongings match the weather, lifestyle, and space of the new residence.

2.  After your parent identifies items to move to the new location, family members need to identify which items they want to receive from what possessions remain.

3.  Your parent then needs to decide what to do with the remaining items—either sell them at an estate sale, donate them, or use a liquidator to sell them.

    Start by setting up an area in each room of the items to be moved to the new home. Then, place removable stickers on each item and write down a list of items to be moved if your parent chooses to hire movers. If your parent chooses to hire someone to sell the remaining items in an estate sale, the remaining items in each room can then be assessed by the estate-sale professional and you receive a quote to sell the items without having to unpack boxes. The online company **Estate Sales** (p. 249) lists many estate-sale companies.

    If your parent chooses to have his or her own estate sale, do research to understand values of items you plan to sell. You might suggest finding and hiring a personal-property appraiser through the **Appraisers Association of America** (p. 251) or the **International Society of Appraisers** (p. 252) prior to selling items. Also, take a look at **EHow**'s (p. 249) article on how to create a successful estate sale.

    If your parent chooses to donate everything that remains, call nonprofits that will come to the home and pick up items for donation, including the Salvation Army. If you have trouble finding non profits who are able to pick up donations, search for smaller, more privately run local non profits such as thrift shops, hospices, small cancer societies, or shelters who might be able to schedule a pick up. Use Turbo Tax's free online program **Turbo Tax ItsDeductible** (p. 248) to track household-item donations and generate the highest tax deductions for the estate tax return. Check out **Just Give** (p. 248) for ideas of charities and types of donations needed.

**Special Note**

Ask the charity's donation coordinator specifically what type of items they accept and the required condition (new, slightly worn, no stains, no damage, etc.). Certain charities accept only items within specific "acceptable quality" guidelines.

If your parent chooses to have a liquidator purchase the remainder of items instead of an estate sale, hire a personal-property appraiser to come appraise the items first. Ask the appraiser to price items at "independent family" values not "insurance" values. An appraisal will give you an idea of the real value of the items before the liquidator makes you an offer. You can find liquidators in your local phone book under "estate sale," "auctioneers," or "liquidators."

4. Decide if your parent will hire movers to pack and move the contents of the home. If the cost of hiring movers fits in your parent's budget, hire licensed movers. The charge for the packing is well worth the family not having to do it. Ask friends for personal referrals. Ask the movers to unpack and remove packing materials at the destination too. If you plan to do the work yourself, accumulate supplies in advance, such as boxes, dollies, bubble wrap, strapping tape, and special equipment to move heavy furniture. Hand pack and carry jewelry, silver, and other expensive items. File special papers and photographs in a portable filing system for long-distance moves. Pack breakables or heirlooms yourself or hire a qualified mover who specializes in antiques or delicate belongings.

5. Create a workable schedule for cleaning out the home. Be sure to include dates and times, friends or family involved, hired assistance, and scheduled breaks. When you take time to make a workable schedule, coupled with assistance from friends or professionals, the large task reduces to a more manageable one. If many people are involved, make sure one person, most likely your parent, is in charge of all final decisions to avoid chaos. Create a plan for everyone to work together in the same room. When everyone cleans out one room at a time, you will minimize distractions and questions about other belongings in other rooms of the home. A focused clean-out strategy maximizes support and dissipates stress. A schedule that tackles the emotionally easy rooms first keeps energy and motivation higher from the beginning.

6. Research your local approved facilities that accept toxic waste materials such as paint, metal items or computer equipment. Make arrangements for those facilities to pick up your toxic materials or drop off items at their location. See **Earth 911** (p. 252) and **My Green Electronics** (p. 252) under "Recycling Resources."

7. Finally, merge and purge paper files with your parent. Review "Merge, Purge, and Automate" from chapter 4 for more details. Together, create a mobile working file system for your parent to use daily. Your parent will need to use the mobile files before, during, and after the move.

8. Don't forget to buy or order your packing or cleaning supplies ahead of time. Check out **PacKing** (p. 249) for online packing supplies.

9. As you take small steps in packing and preparing, reward yourselves to prevent burnout.

## Helping Your Parent Clean Out a Home

If you need additional organizing strategies prior to a move or cleaning out a home, grab Peter Walsh's book, *How to Organize Everything* (p. 218) on how to handle organizing anything your parent might own. The book presents more than five hundred easy-to-follow organizing solutions created by the professional organizer of the TLC hit TV show, *Clean Sweep*. The book offers solutions and resources for storage, paper, home, e-mail, filing, financial, family affairs, and event issues.

## If Your Parent Plans to Give Away or Clean Out the Deceased's Personal Belongings

When you clean out the deceased parent's personal belongings, you may want to bring in more support. For each room with the deceased person's possessions, put together six boxes and label them: keep, sell, toss, donate, give to friends, and reconsider in one year. The six-box system creates a simple structure for what to do with each item.

Another option is to have the person who holds legal control and fiduciary power for the deceased's estate—usually an executor or trustee of the estate, a trust officer, a conservator, or a private professional fiduciary—hire a professional estate organizer such as **Exit Stage Right** (p. 250) to aid the family with sorting out estate issues. Estate-organizing companies like Exit Stage Right work closely as the agent of the estate administrator to organize the contents, information, and records of the home for the estate administrator to review. For example, an estate organizer might gather all the family memorabilia or old personal files together in one place for the family to then make decisions on what to keep or shred. Additionally an estate organizer may take digital photographs of household items that correspond to a spreadsheet with descriptions and appraised value of items to help an executor make decisions about estate goods. If you hire an estate organizer, the cost is tax deductible on the estate tax return. I wish we had known about this service. If we had hired an estate organizer, Mom's estate work, move, and cleaning out process would have been simplified.

For other resources, thumb through Part III: Resources under the section "Moving Mom or Dad" for more ideas on estate sales, auctions, and cleaning out a home.

 ## Questions to Ask about Helping Your Parent Prepare for a Move, Give Away Belongings or Clean Out the Home

* Does Mom or Dad have the energy required to prepare for a move, give away belongings, or clean out his or her home now, or is it better for me to encourage him or her to wait?
* What completion deadline does my parent need to meet such as a real estate closing date or moving date?
* How does Mom or Dad prefer to clean out his or her home?
* Which rooms will be the easiest for my parent to clean out first?
* Do I see any items I could encourage my parent to sell that they may not need? Could the sale of these unneeded items substantially reduce the moving costs for my parent?
* Does Mom or Dad have supportive family or friends who can give their time and energy when they are needed?
* Could Mom or Dad afford a professional organizer to sort out and categorize household items?
* What rewards will my family members give ourselves when each of us completes small tasks?

Encourage your parent to take advantage of all the packing, moving, or organizing support available. Relatives and friends can provide more hands and support to create lighter work. With a plan and extra hands, preparing for a move or cleaning out your parent's possessions changes from a daunting task to a manageable spring cleaning.

> *Little strokes fell great oaks.*
>
> **BENJAMIN FRANKLIN**

## WHEN AND HOW TO SELL YOUR PARENT'S HOME

When your parent weighs the pros and cons of selling his or her home, emotional comfort plays a large role in any decision. Do I want to move? Where will I move? Do I need to stay near my friends? Will my friends move to retirement homes soon and leave me here alone? Will I stay in the same city I live now or move to another city? I love my home. Will I find a new home that brings me as much comfort as this one? For many widows or widowers, a home creates a predictable place to be when chaos from the loss of a spouse affects all the other areas of their life.

Finances also play a large role in determining if your parent sells his or her home. Real-estate agents are readily available to assist your parent when he or she is ready to sell the home, however, the current real estate market may not be a seller's market. Your parent may wonder about the following: If I sell the home, will I buy another home or rent? Can I sell my home in the current market at a fair price? If I stay in my home, can I afford it? Can I afford to pay movers? If I can't sell my home, should I rent it out? For many widowed parents, finances determine the final decision to sell their home.

As you assist your parent in answering all the different questions about a home sale, include a discussion about the energy and time required from your parent and other family members to prepare for a move. Multiple meetings with a real estate agent, stager, or organizer will take time and energy. The best time to sell your parent's home is when your parent is both emotionally and financially ready.

## Five Selling-the-House Issues

As you talk with your parent to determine the best decision about selling the home, discuss five issues:

1. Your parent is forced to make numerous decisions regarding the sale of his or her home that may create months of erratic and unpredictable emotions.
2. When your parent waits until a year after the loss of the spouse to sell the home, time provides clarity and perspective to make the best decision instead of a forced decision.
3. The real estate market where your parent lives changes. If the local market favors buyers and your parent wants to move, you can suggest your parent rent out the home, if financially feasible. When your parent chooses to rent out the home, he or she can still move to a new environment and possibly create rental income. If so, keep in mind the high potential for property destruction and wear and tear.
4. If your parent can't sell the home, another option to consider is a reverse mortgage.

## Special Note

A reverse mortgage loan—available to people sixty-two years old or older that own their own home—allows either a single lump sum of cash, a consistent monthly payment, or a line of credit that lets the homeowner decide when to take the cash and how much. When the owner dies, permanently moves out of the home, or sells the home, a reverse mortgage loan becomes due.

5. You or other family members may need to schedule travel, take time off work, or coordinate child or pet care to assist your parent with the preparation before or after the sale of the home.

**Our Story**

During the twelve years Mom lived in Richmond, Virginia, my parents enjoyed many friendships and cherished their home. After Dad's death, Mom's social interactions evaporated when her network of single female friends in Richmond refused to drive at night. The combined loss of her husband, reduced social invitations, and isolation of the location of her home sent Mom into a negative spiral.

After the first winter alone in her home, Mom felt quarantined. She wanted to sell the home and move back to Atlanta, Georgia, where she had spent eighteen years prior to the move to Richmond. Mom believed Atlanta provided old friends, more opportunities for educational advancement, more organizations and groups to join, and more like-minded single and divorced women to build her social network.

After her experience with Dad's cancer treatments, one of the reasons Mom chose Atlanta was because of its better hospitals and doctors in case she required future medical care. My sister and I worried about the massive change of Mom's move, but her decision didn't surprise us.

Mom signed a lease on an apartment in Atlanta. She rented because she couldn't decide if she wanted to make Atlanta her permanent home. One of Mom's friends cautioned her to wait a year before instigating a move, but Mom feared the loss of the opportunity to sell her home for a top price in a sellers' market. Mom chose financial freedom over the stability of living in her home. Because spring is usually the best time to sell a home, Mom put her home on the market in April.

Mom never considered selling the home herself. She determined that her investments, executor work, and managing her bills required her focused attention. So she interviewed three real estate agents from three competing brokerage firms in her area. Mom selected a listing price positioned in the middle of the comparable sales of the neighborhood, with hope for a quick sale. A two-woman real estate team won the listing. They referred Mom to a stager who prepared the interior of the home for upcoming showings. Mom's choice to hire a team worked well; when one agent was unavailable or on vacation, the other, who knew the property well, answered questions or calls.

Before the first ad hit the local newspaper, agents presented multiple offers to Mom's agent. The successful bidders were represented by one of the realtors Mom interviewed who did not get the listing. One condition the buyers offered in the contract, a sixty-day closing period, gave Mom the breathing space she needed to stay in her home longer to pack. Nine months after Dad died, Mom sold her home.

## HOW TO SELL THE HOME OPTION #1
### Hiring a Real-Estate Broker

Before you hire anyone to sell your home, you need to understand certain industry terms: real estate broker, real estate agent, and a Realtor.

A real estate broker is a real estate company licensed by the state. The brokers buy and sell real estate and handle all aspects of real estate transactions for themselves as licensees, as well as any independent real estate agents or salespeople. Brokers take additional training beyond the requirements of an agent or salesperson and take on a great deal of risk and liability for any independent real estate agents or salespeople they hire to work under their brokerage. Because real estate brokers take on additional risk for the independent agents or salespeople they hire, they receive a percentage of each agent's buying and selling transactions. A real estate agent works under a licensed real estate broker and buys and sells property for clients for a percentage of the typical 2 to 3 percent—per selling or buying side—commission.

Every state has unique laws for real estate brokers and agents. The more reputable brokers require their agents or salespeople to join local real estate boards, which require membership in the **National Association of Realtors** (NAR) (p. 253). NAR membership gives real estate agents the Realtor credential; that designation holds them to a higher ethical standard. You and your parent should review the real estate laws for your parent's particular state before you decide whether to use a real estate broker or sell the home yourself.

### What Do Real-Estate Agents Do for Your Listing?
No matter which real estate broker or agent you hire to sell your parent's home, a good real estate salesperson can save you time, energy, and money. Professional real estate agents attend to the many details of a selling transaction, which provides the sellers time to focus on transitioning their lives.

Initially real estate agents advise the seller how to make the property most attractive to a targeted buyer through repair, advertising, listing price, design, and clutter removal. An agent prepares all the legal paperwork, takes photos of the home, and uploads the information to the local Multiple Listing Service (MLS). Agents prepare flyers for open houses and office distribution as well as announce your home for sale at company meetings. Many times other agents in their office represent potential buyers. A good agent's ability to market property well makes the agent a valuable asset.

## Special Note

Many agents prefer to work with agents they know. Agents know other agents' abilities and reliability based on past transactions and the ability to represent qualified buyers who will follow through on the purchase of a home. Respected agents manage many issues that arise during the transaction with little drama and usually close on time. An agent's connections in the real estate community offer an essential perk a smart seller should require when he or she hires an agent. An agent's experience can be especially important when the seller's finances are tight and homes are on the market longer.

Agents negotiate the details of any purchase offers the seller receives with the seller's best interest in mind. During the selling transaction, a good agent attends home inspections and monitors repairs. Real-estate closing practices vary from state to state; therefore, the agent's role changes depending on the state in which your widowed parent purchases or sells a home. For example, California uses title companies to facilitate closings, while Georgia uses closing attorneys, not title companies. The seller saves themselves many headaches if they find a professional and honest real estate agent.

### *If You Decide to Hire a Broker*

With all the other difficulties a parent faces after a spouse's death, the decision to hire a Realtor or real estate agent may be worth the commission. Encourage your parent to interview at least three agents from competing real estate companies to receive different perspectives on pricing the home and gain understanding of the buying demand. When your parent exposes his or her home to three brokerages, that strategy may bring in more buyers, as those agents can talk about previewing the new listing at their firms' company meetings. When your parent interviews real estate agents, ask if they have the designation of **Senior Residential Specialist** (p. 253). The Senior Residential Specialist designation shows the agent's advanced level of training to work with senior lifestyle issues and relocation concerns and questions.

When your parent meets with an agent, ask for comparable sales—homes in the neighborhood with same number of bedrooms and baths and square feet as your parent's home—from the previous six months. The comparable sales list gives a good view of current demand to aid in picking the best price to list the home. If you price your parent's home for sale accurately from the beginning, the home sells faster.

## Special Note

The real estate agent who pitches the highest listing price for the home may not prove to be the best choice. Why? Many agents may want to use a high listing price as a way to broker the listing and persuade their client later to reduce the listing price.

### HOW TO SELL THE HOUSE OPTION #2
#### *For Sale by Owner*

If your parent wants to sell the property on his or her own, weigh four issues:

1. For a majority of home buyers, for-sale-by-owner properties create fear or distrust of the seller's disclosures about the property problems. If your parent sells the home, he or she may reduce the potential of a fast sale and limit buyer interest.

2. For-sale-by-owner properties tend to take longer to sell and may create legal problems for both buyer and seller because of the seller's lack of knowledge about appropriate disclosures, inspection requirements, and required closing paperwork. Generally, unless you or your parent holds a real estate license or builds homes, the choice to list a home for sale with a real estate broker may create a faster sale at a better price, with repair and legal considerations brokered instead, reducing potential problems.

3. You or your parent will spend time and energy to market the property, handle showings, and answer phone calls from interested buyers.

4. If your parent successfully sells the home without a broker, he or she will save money by not paying 5 to 6 percent of the listing price of the home in broker commissions.

If your parent decides to sell the home himself or herself, many Web sites exist to make the process easier, such as **For Sale by Owner** (p. 253) and **Homes by Owner** (p. 253). Current books describe techniques for owners to sell his or her home, including *The For-Sale-by-Owner Handbook: FSBO FAQ's: From Pricing Your Home Right and Increasing Its Curb Appeal to Negotiating the Contract and Hassle-Free Closing* (p. 253) or *How to Sell Your Home without a Broker* (p. 253).

## Resources: Senior Moving Organizers

Many memories rest in the rooms and possessions of a family home. When a widowed parent prepares a home for sale alone, the isolation and memories personal possessions create can be devastating. If you or your siblings are unavailable to help your parent prepare the home for sale, hire a professional organizer through the **National Association of Professional Organizers** (p. 164) or a moving company that specializes in senior relocations such as **Moving Solutions** (p. 250) or **Ultimate Moves** (p. 251) that supplies alternative packing assistance. The **National Association of Senior Move Managers** (p. 250) or **Exit Stage Right** (p. 250) can connect your parent with a senior move manager or an estate organizer in his or her area. If you hire a resourceful real estate agent, he or she will provide local moving resources.

If your parent wants to move himself or herself or can't afford the fees of larger moving companies, **Uhaul** (p. 251) and **Budget** (p. 250), among other companies, provide low-cost rental vans, trucks, and dollies for short or cross-country journeys. Portable storage container companies such as **PODS** (p. 251) or **Door-to-Door** (p. 250) provide an alternative to traditional van or truck moves. Those companies deliver portable storage containers to clients' homes or offices for the client to pack themselves. After a storage container is filled, a transport truck collects and delivers the container to the client's requested destination.

In addition, the book *Moving Mom and Dad: The Stress-Free Guide to Helping Seniors Move* (p. 247) is a good resource to consult. Written by the owner of a senior transition specialist moving company based in Northern California called Ultimate Moves, *Moving Mom and Dad* offers information on how to choose where to move a parent, housing options, and how to avoid the moving problems. The book also includes a cost worksheet. For more home-selling resources, go to Part III: Resources under "Moving Mom or Dad."

## Resources: Repairmen and Stagers

When you prepare a home for sale, you need to make small repairs and organize items, even if the home has been maintained well. If your parent hires an unknown handyman, it can create a safety issue, especially for widows who might be more vulnerable when strangers enter her home. Consult with your real estate agent for recommendations for a repairperson as part of the prelisting repair part of the agent's services. To find a local handyman, look at **Angie's List** (p. 249).

Some people hire stagers—professionals who make homes look cozier through design techniques—to wow home buyers. Although staging can be expensive, staging sometimes brings more profits or a quicker sale. To find a professional stager consult the **International Association of Home Staging Professionals** (p. 251).

## Resources: Garage and Estate Sales

Your parent may want to purge excess possessions prior to the marketing of a home for sale. When you reduce or downsize possessions, five choices are available: (1) donate them to a charity such as Salvation Army or Goodwill—to find other charitable organizations, go to **Just Give** (p. 248); (2) have a yard or garage sale to sell the goods—see **EHow** (p. 249) or read *The Great Garage Sale Book: How to Run a Garage, Tag, Attic, Barn or Yard Sale* (p. 248), *The Complete Guidebook to the Business of Tag and Estate Sales* (p. 247), or *The Pocket Idiot's Guide to Garage and Yard Sales* (p. 248); (3) hire an estate or auction home to sell the goods—the *Antiques Roadshow* Web site (p. 251) is a good place to start to look for one; (4) sell the items online on a Web site like **Ebay** (p. 248); or (5) take them to the local recycling center or landfill.

If you or your parent needs outside appraisals for items you intend to sell, contact the **International Society of Appraisers** (p. 252) or **Appraisers Association of America** (p. 251) or search the *Antiques Roadshow* Web site (p. 251) for sources.

## Special Note

Keep con artists—people who appraise possessions at low prices to buy an antique or valuable item for less than the item's worth—and safety in mind when your parent allows personal-property appraisers into the home to evaluate goods. Find a personal-property appraiser through a respected appraiser organization to reduce risk.

## Questions to Discuss with Your Parent about Selling the Home

* Do you want to move?
* Who could you hire to assist with all the moving tasks?
* Do you want to hire a Realtor or sell the home yourself?
* Do you know any handymen, stagers, or organizers?
* Do you want to hold a garage or estate sale?
* What could you donate and receive tax advantages?
* Do you want to hire a moving company or move yourself?
* Do you want to use traditional moving trucks or an alternative portable storage company?
* Who will assist you at the destination location?

If you prepare ahead of time for pitfalls and problems, everyone saves time and money. Talk to your parent to see when is the best time to sell the home, and don't forget the most important planning task—stock cold drinks for moving day.

---

*Start by doing what's necessary, then what's possible,*
*and suddenly you are doing the impossible.*

**SAINT FRANCIS OF ASSISI**

# CHAPTER NINE

# CHANGES IN FAMILY DYNAMICS

Change is inevitable after your parent's death—changes in your widowed parent's living situations, changes in how your family relates to one another, changes in family responsibilities. Navigating these family challenges in positive ways can keep your relationships from eroding and help lay the path to a hopeful future for you, your parent, and your entire family.

## EVERYONE NEEDS A NEW FAMILY JOB

After a parent dies, family dynamics shift. Your deceased parent left behind certain tasks or roles he or she performed or filled. Your widowed parent may not be able to handle or manage those tasks or roles alone. Other family members, especially those who live closest to the widowed parent, step in—sometimes volunteering and sometimes appointed by other family members due to proximity—to fill needed family positions. Jobs such as accounting, investment and financial management, technology support, paperwork management and organizing, planning for a move, and many others leave vacancies for family members to either fill or assist the parent in hiring outside help.

Along with new family jobs, you and your family members juggle new expectations of each other, resentments, or gaps in family duties. The challenges a death creates for family members force change. Critical questions arise, such as: How can other family members support the family member who handles the majority of a widowed parent's regular needs? How can other family members who live far away lend a hand? Does your widowed parent's professional advisor(s)—certified public accountants, money managers, or lawyers—fit with your family's new roles? These questions provide the initial discussion points for dividing new family jobs and roles.

## Five Issues Surrounding New Family Jobs

When you discuss new roles or jobs for family members, keep in mind five potential issues:

1. The absence of one parent creates new family roles or job openings.
2. Old family resentments, sibling order, and gender-role expectations can emerge or be challenged. Traditionally minded female family members might be forced to fill roles outside of their normal habits, preferences, or roles, such as the management of finances or investments.
3. Family members may grieve at alternating times; some members jump to offer their time and energy, while others avoid the reality of their parent's death. Some family members struggle with limited energy or intense grief.
4. Past family advisors, such as certified public accountants and money managers, who advised your family or parents for years, may not be the preferred advisors with new family member roles. Female family members who take on financial roles may or may not experience opposition from long-standing family male advisors. However, if a male advisor views women in unhealthy ways, and his ego is threatened by women in control of financial choices, be prepared for disagreements or hostility. When you hire advisors who fit in with family members in new roles, then better communication and understanding of your widowed parent's financial situation result.
5. Relationships with extended family and close friends of the deceased parent may change or end.

## Our Story

In my parents' marriage, my father played the traditional male role of the money and investment manager. After Dad's death, all his duties shifted to his wife and indirectly to his two daughters. When the three of us interviewed financial managers, we discussed investments and financial choices for Mom. Many of the men said directly or indirectly, "You ladies don't worry about things; your father didn't want you to worry. I'll take care of you." Dad never acted condescending to us when we discussed financial choices. He left big shoes to fill.

Dad taught Mom, my sister, Ivy, and me to manage our own investments by his example. After his death, Mom wrestled with what to do with the investments my father left her to manage. Mom asked us for advice. Initially Ivy and I considered managing the money ourselves, but we got nervous and suggested Mom talk to money managers suggested by friends.

Many of the fifty- or sixty-something financial managers we interviewed acted days away from retirement. Their attitude suggested a lack of interest or motivation in taking Mom on as a new client. Mom didn't know whom to trust, and our extended family presented no alternative options. For the next five years, Mom hired and dissolved two financial-manager business relationships. Eventually the three of us determined we cared the most about Mom's investments. We trusted each other's decisions. Dad had trained Ivy and I, over several years, how to buy various stock market investments.

When we finally accepted the fact that a traditional financial manager didn't fit our new female family of three, we adapted. Luckily for us, past experience in investing, mortgages, and real estate built a strong foundation for us to make solid financial decisions. Along the way, we had both investing mistakes and successes. More importantly, our futures rested in our own hands, as Dad taught us.

Initially our roles organically grew until clear delineations emerged. As Mom gathered more energy, she took an active part in more financial decisions. Because of our small family, we each played more roles. My sister and I zapped resentments by airing our irritations with each other early. We lacked time for disagreements; our ability to communicate and cooperate as a team determined our survival.

### Benefits of New Family Jobs

When you assign new roles in your family to cover new needs, you spread out responsibilities and create a structure of support. As jobs and roles sort themselves out, open and honest communication with your family members provides the best solutions. Leave your old role and fill a new one if you are the best person for the job. Maintain your boundaries and say no if your family violates them.

Shifting roles can create discomfort, but change is necessary. New roles take years to iron out. Don't expect new family roles to fall into place overnight. You accomplish tasks faster and reduce resentments toward other family members when everyone takes on roles that suit their unique talents.

 ## Resources and Options

For a list of typical family jobs or roles that are created after the loss of a parent, see appendix C: New Family Jobs worksheet (p. 289). Use this worksheet as a starting point to determine who among your family members can handle what job and share support roles for your widowed parent. If you handle most of the responsibilities assisting your parent, talk to your family about creating a caregivers contract (see "Should We Create a Caregivers Contract?" in chapter 3) if finances permit. As families see members' income and personal time reduced by caregiving for parents, many agree to compensate the participating family members.

As you put together new family roles and jobs, review the books *Living beyond Loss: Death in the Family* (p. 255) or *In the Presence of Grief: Helping Family Members Resolve Death, Dying and Bereavement Issues* (p. 255). Both offer solutions for common family dynamics problems, issues, and concerns. Also use Part III: Resources for more resources on how to handle elderly parent issues and changing family dynamics, especially the **Sandwich Generation** (p. 255).

 ## Questions to Ask about Family Roles and New Jobs

- What duties did my deceased parent do?
- Does my parent need assistance with certain jobs?
- Who lives closest to my parent? How can other family members support the family member who handles the majority of my parent's regular needs?
- How can other family members who live far away lend a hand?
- Who in the family understands investments? How about accounting? Is anyone knowledgeable in technology? Who excels in paperwork management or organizing? Who has experience with moving or real estate? Who does my parent prefer to have in those roles?
- What duties is my parent uncomfortable managing?
- Do my parent's advisors—certified public accountants, money managers, or lawyers—fit with my family's new roles? Can my parent and I communicate easily with them?

New puzzles challenge everyone. As time passes, your parent and other family members will bring their own unique talents and skills to vacant roles and jobs and family life and relationship stabilize within the new framework.

> *If you have no will to change it,*
> *you have no right to criticize it.*
>
> **ANONYMOUS**

## STAY SENSITIVE TO BIG CHANGES

You breathe fresh energy into your soul when you drive to the countryside for the weekend. While you cruise along, your tire suddenly blows out. Your car rolls to a stop. You search for your cell phone, but it's nowhere to be found. You open the trunk of your car to find no spare tire. The next gas station sits miles away. Your good spirits and sense of security sink. Nightfall comes. You sit all alone against whatever lies ahead in the darkness.

Many widows and widowers experience similar fear and loneliness—but a thousand times stronger and deeper emotions, when their spouse dies. Embrace compassion and sensitivity to your widowed parent's tremendous daily life change.

### Three Ideas about Sensitivity to Big Changes
Keep these three ideas in mind when considering the effects of change on both your parent and yourself:

1. Widowed parents suffer their own kind of death when their spouse dies. Past familiar companionship and routines evaporates. Self-esteem sinks. Money concerns take center stage.

2.  You and your parent must swallow the painful finality of death and the abrupt halt of communication with your deceased parent. Life continues but changes for both of you. Your view of your parent's situation and your parent's view of the same situation can differ, though.

3.  Be patient; a newly widowed parent experiences a massive change and may suffer from indecision or overwhelm. If your parent appears embarrassed or acts frustrated when he or she does a task, reassure or calm him or her. Everyone fights through undesired change in his or her own way.

## Our Story

Dad orchestrated all his and Mom's finances during their marriage. For the longest time, my sister and I questioned why our mother barked at us when we reminded her of unpaid bills or decisions about investments.

One day Mom voiced her dread about spearheading her personal financial decisions and tasks; she felt too embarrassed to tell us before. She said, "Dad made all our big financial choices because he knew more about investments than I did." After Mom's revelation, we encouraged her to enroll in some computer classes to learn software and online bill-paying options. She subscribed to financial newsletters and registered for financial education classes. My sister and I facilitated new paperwork systems for Mom that matched her lifestyle and needs.

Because we empowered Mom through financial and computer education, her frustration left and her self-esteem rose. Sensitivity toward Mom's daily life changes brought us compassion and patience with her progress.

## Resources and Options

Your circumstances swirl around issues particular to your widowed parent. If your widowed parent paid the bills himself or herself, sparkles with high self-esteem, or enjoys monitoring finances, he or she may experience more of an emotional loss than a practical loss. Because every relationship and its loss are unique to the individuals involved, that loss evokes unexpected and differing reactions and emotions—even among family members.

Read *Living beyond Loss: Death in the Family* (p. 255) to learn more about the effect of death on various types of families and how they handled it. Another book that offers advice about survivor problems and issues is *In the Presence of Grief:*

*Helping Family Members Resolve Death, Dying, and Bereavement Issues* (p. 255). If your father is your widowed parent and you are a woman, you can read *When Men Grieve: Why Men Grieve Differently and How You Can Help* (p. 171) to understand the unique issues men face during grief. *Life after Loss: A Personal Guide Dealing with Death, Divorce, Job Change, and Relocation* (p. 254), written by a pastor with twenty-five years of grief-support-group and counseling experience, offers advice about intense feelings after loss and a chapter on sudden loss versus prolonged loss.

If you struggle with unresolved issues with your deceased parent, read *She Loved Me, She Loved Me Not: Adult Parent Loss after a Conflicted Relationship* (p. 255). Use Part III: Resources to find more help on how to gain sensitivity to grief, loss, and change.

## Questions to Ask about Your Sensitivity to Change

* What areas of life—spiritual, personal, business, finances, relationships, or relaxation—will my parent struggle with after the loss of his or her spouse?
* What boosts my parent's self-esteem in those difficult areas?
* Does my parent push back when I ask him or her to do certain tasks?
* How could I facilitate easier decision making for my parent?
* How has the loss of my parent affected my life?
* Do I enjoy new tasks created because of the death of my parent or do they make me vulnerable or nervous?
* Am I the right person in my family to take on those tasks?

One day you might be the person in that car alone. Shift gears and think of your parent in that vulnerable position. In time, all tasks will be done. Stay patient and give your newly widowed parent space to breathe in this new foreign life.

> *Happy the man who early learns*
> *the wide chasm that lies between*
> *his wishes and his powers.*
>
> **ANONYMOUS**

## UNBLOCK, CHANGE, AND BOOST ENERGY

Change is never easy; however, if you fight it, you create blocked energy. As your family processes the diverse seasons after loss, some people, jobs, or things don't fit anymore. You or your parent may experience blockage in one or more areas of your lives. As you release old routines, emotions, people, or habits, you increase your energy and make room for new opportunities.

### Three Ideas to Boost Your Energy

As you determine your own blocked areas, utilize these three ideas:

1.  Find your energy drains. Examine the seven areas of your life—spiritual, personal, career, finances, relaxation, relationships, or routine life-maintenance errands—for energy drains. What area(s) exhaust you? Create energy-boosting solutions. Could you rearrange furniture, throw out clutter, or move? Current homes, possessions, friends, files, or holiday plans can block energy.
2.  Watch out for consistent frustration. When you or your parent experiences continued irritation as you engage in a new activity or task, devise a way to unclog the block.
3.  When you hold on to unresolved emotions such as anger, bitterness, and blame, this negativity can block rejuvenating life-enhancing energy. If you struggle with negative emotions, professional therapy can help you work on forgiveness and release unsettled destructive emotions. Read "Individual Therapy: Is It for Me?" in chapter 2 to learn more about various therapy options.

### Our Story

Paperwork and chaos in Mom's home created by clutter and losing Dad blocked all of our energy. Since Dad's death in 2001, we have all overhauled our energy drains. Healing changes were needed for new energy to flow again.

Three big energy drains for Mom were financial systems, budget, and lifestyle changes. With time and effort, we transformed my father's old file system into a better system to fit Mom's needs. The three of us renovated Dad's old budget for Mom to fit her new financial reality. Mom's identity changed from an executive wife who entertained constantly at home to a single woman who attended more social events outside her home. Over time, Mom changed her living spaces from formal to casual. One by one, Mom released her energy drains.

Big energy drains for Ivy and me included lack of exercise, unhealthy eating, toxic friendships, unfulfilling careers, and lack of fun-filled personal time. My sister and I released our energy drains by regular workouts, eating well, severing unhealthy friendships, pursuing new careers, and making time for fun-filled activities. At first all the change spun us in circles, but after time, we adapted. When we avoided change, we only frustrated ourselves and stopped the flow of good energy into our lives.

## Resources and Options

First, unblock a few minor frustrations. **Professional organizers** (p. 164) can offer you unblocking assistance and advice. Thumb through the books *Soaring through Setbacks* (p. 254) and *When Life Changes or You Wish It Would: A Guide to Finding Your Next Step Despite Fear, Obstacles, or Confusion* (p. 254) for more ideas on how to deal with change. Check out interior-design books such as *Six Steps to Design on a Dime* (p. 256) or *Feng Shui Dos and Taboos: A Guide to What to Place Where* (p. 256) for ideas on clearing out bad energy in a home. If your friendships shift, take a look at the book *When Friendship Hurts: How to Deal with Friends Who Betray, Abandon, or Wound You* (p. 254) for more insight on how to unblock.

## Natural Remedies for Low energy

Read books on alternative medicine that provide natural energy solutions, such as *Natural Health, Natural Medicine* (p. 256) or *Prescription for Nutritional Healing: A Practical A-to-Z Reference to Drug-Free Remedies Using Vitamins, Minerals, Herbs & Food Supplements* (p. 256) or *Perfect Health: The Complete Mind/Body Guide* (p. 256). Always consult a doctor before you take any new medicines or herbal supplements. Check Part III: Resources for more ways to unblock and ideas on increasing energy.

## Questions to Ask about Energy Blocks
* Do I have a strategy in place for adapting to change?
* Does my parent or I suffer from depression or low energy?

* Does the energy feel unbalanced in my home or office?
* What trips or celebrations does my family participate in every year? Does my parent or I enjoy those times? Do I want to continue to take trips or have celebrations as we did before, or do I want to change gears and do something else?
* Are my feelings toward friends changing? What friends have moved in an opposite direction in their lives? Should I end any toxic friendships?
* Is my current budget representative of my priorities? What services or products does my parent or I pay for that are underused or not used?
* Does my lifestyle still fit my newly changed world? Does my parent's fit his or hers?
* What issues do my parent and I constantly fight over that needs to be examined?

When you don't declutter and unblock, low energy runs rampant. You appear stuck and tired. As you take time to figure out what needs work, you release blocks. Actively seek ways to bring good energy back into your life and the life of your parent. Stay open to things or people who don't appear to fit you or your parent's changed lives. When you derail the blocked energy, you make room for new potential, sparkle, and zing.

> *Self-knowledge is the beginning of self-improvement.*
>
> **SPANISH PROVERB**

# CHAPTER TEN

# COMMUNITY

No one walks through life alone. You and your widowed parent are surrounded by people in your family, work lives, neighborhoods, and friendships. How you let these communities help you during your life after losing your parent can make a huge difference in the present and the future. Be willing to seek community, and encourage your parent to do the same, as you move forward into this new phase of your lives.

## DON'T UNDERESTIMATE THE POWER OF COMMUNITY

What do church congregations, the G8 Summit, and the Rolling Stones have in common? They all formed groups because they knew they would be more successful together than apart. As you guide your widowed parent through new life changes, don't underestimate the power of community and groups.

### Three Benefits of Community

Community resources and groups can provide three huge benefits to you and your widowed parent:

1. Groups brainstorm new solutions to problems that you might not have thought of on your own.
2. Other people know of local resources that could be useful to you or your parent.
3. New community can provide unexpected support.

**Our Story**

Initially my sister, Ivy, and I sought solutions to everything ourselves. Our communities were scattered in distance and limited in scope. Eventually our resources and own energies became depleted, and we needed to delegate. After our mother moved to a new city, she needed new therapists, new loss-support groups, a new CPA, and a new lawyer. Ivy and I were tapped out. Mom needed a new list of local community services (see "Community Extra-Hands List" in appendix C). She updated her list with new local vendors for when she needed outside assistance.

Because we stayed open to new resources, we reaped the rewards of fresh ideas, support, and community. As outside assistance grew, Mom felt less like a burden to her children. She also felt less alone and more assured she could find assistance. The responsibilities my sister and I carried lessened. Mom hired others or asked friends for advice to avoid her dependence on us too much. She empathized with our own struggles. With Mom's new local handyman, housekeeper, and accountant, she accomplished tasks that before had created arguments between the three of us, though we all did the best we could at the time.

## If Your Community Is Strong

Your family may not need to unearth new resources. If your extended family includes a doctor, an investment advisor, or a handyman, outside assistance may be unnecessary or minimal. Your parent may have lived in the same location for years and may have a solid list of resources and contacts. If your parent has good local support, encourage him or her to use those contacts.

 **Resources and Options**

Your or your parent's community creates a powerful and supportive force. Ask for assistance from others and let some things go. If your parent has recently bought a home, a Realtor can be a great source of local contacts. Your parent can explore **Meetup** (p. 264) or audit university classes for free or a low-cost (see **universities offering class discounts to seniors** [p. 257]) as avenues to meet new people with similar interests. If your parent is interested in volunteering, try **Senior Corps** (p. 265) or **VolunteerMatch** (p. 265). When and if your parent is interested in socializing in mixed-gender environments in the future,

Match (p. 264) or **Eharmony** (p. 264) provide online options. See appendix C for a sample local "Community Extra-Hands List" and Part III: Resources (p. 155) for other community ideas.

### Questions to Ask about Your or Your Parent's Community

* Am I too overwhelmed with responsibilities and duties?
* Does my parent worry about being a burden?
* What family members can I place on my parent's Community Extra-Hands List, and what duties need to be filled by other community members?
* Who could my parent or I call in my parent's or my community who seems to know who to call for anything?
* If my parent has moved to a new city, has my parent called the local Chamber of Commerce for local resources or referrals? Has my parent contacted local newcomer resources?

Two or more brains together come up with many more ideas than just one. Build a strong local extra-hands list with your widowed parent for when he or she needs extra help or advice, and sit back and watch the power of community go to work.

---

*Everything that lives, lives not alone, nor for itself.*

WILLIAM BLAKE

---

## FIND OUT WHO YOUR REAL FRIENDS ARE

When you come back from a vacation, your real life looks different. If you visited an exotic locale, the customs, attitudes, or foods may be in stark contrast to your own neighborhood. After the loss of your parent, you experience an internal transformation similar to the après vacation experience. You return from the experience of loss a changed person; some of your friends will not like the change.

## Four Ideas about Changing Friendships

As you sort through friends supporting and abandoning you after loss, keep these four ideas in mind:

1. When you leave old friendships, the foundation you built around those relationships shakes and unnerves you. The friends who stick around might surprise you. The friends who leave might shock you.
2. Don't carry any guilt when those friendship turning points occur. After the loss of a parent, your widowed parent's situation and your new family responsibilities rise to a higher priority. Your choice to assist a newly widowed parent could create extra stress, money issues, or volatile emotions, depending on your relationship with each parent.
3. Your relationships—including spousal or friendships—change because of your limited energy and your change in priorities. The management of your own energy becomes critical and your weaker relationships unravel.
4. Friends can be sympathetic to your situation but limited in understanding your daily struggles, especially if they haven't experienced a difficult loss. In addition, many people don't know how to react to death or grieving. Old losses of their own may surface that make them uncomfortable. Don't take their reactions personally. As your new world and interests form, some friendships may not survive.

 ## Our Story

The first three years after my father died, my friends supported me much more than I was able to support them. One newer friend I'd only known a few years, who had large losses from her past, offered regular advice and a listening ear to my many questions about pending decisions. After awhile, she needed to leave the friendship. I let her friendship go, but the loss tore my heart wide open. Her abrupt departure from my life left me shocked and vulnerable. As time went on and I moved out of state, my life moved in a contrary direction from when I knew her. The loss stung, but with time and distance, the parting made sense. Our friendship didn't fit anymore.

Friends who had known me for over fifteen years jumped to provide support. They tolerated the endless questions and discussions. They told me I wasn't a burden, and they said they enjoyed lending support. I'm sure they grew tired of the topic from time to time, but they never let me know. Many of my old friends stood by my side, but it is common for old friends to abandon those who experience the death of a parent or spouse after the initial time after loss passes. When friendships end unexpectedly, the griever faces an additional loss.

Without Dad around, our relationships with his old friends and family, former sources of support, disappeared. At Dad's memorial service, many of his friends and work associates, whom I had spoken to many times, awkwardly avoided talking to me, while other parental acquaintances I'd never met told me how they lost their parent at a young age. Death is a touchy subject for people; you never know how anyone will react until the time comes.

## What to Expect
Friendships are hard to make and break. The friends that stick by you soothe your heart and give you strength to keep going. When old friendships end, unsettling emotions persist. It's normal. Expect casual or work relationships to change. Everyone reacts to death based on their own personal issues. As you evolve, your friendships will either grow with your change or end. If you lived in the same city for a long time, your older, more stable friendships may survive. If you are new to an area or live in a transient big city, expect some reshuffling.

## Resources and Options
If you think your friendships will not change after the loss of a parent, don't be fooled. Friendships change because you change. You can hope your friends stick around through the difficult times, but prepare yourself for some shake-ups. If friendships shift, take a look at the book *When Friendship Hurts: How to Deal with Friends Who Betray, Abandon, or Wound You* (p. 254) for more insights.

As your friendships get tested, seek out new friends who have lost parents or experienced large losses. They may relate better to your situation and give sound advice based in experience. Parental loss support groups offer a good place to start. You can review Part III: Resources for more resources on parental-loss support groups.

### Questions to Ask about Your Friendships

- Have any of my close friends lost parents?
- Who is the best person to ask advice about my dilemmas with regard to my newly widowed parent?
- How can I find a local parental-loss support group?
- Does an online group work better with my schedule?
- Which of my weak friendships may not survive?
- What unhealthy friendships, partnerships, or work relationships do I need to end to protect my own health?
- Is my spouse or significant other prepared to support me as I go through the various aspects of the loss of my parent? Do I need to let him or her know how to support me?
- Do I need to have an open and honest discussion with my spouse or significant other about needing more time alone?
- Do I have any friendships that don't work anymore?

Good-byes challenge everyone, but they can release you from negative to more positive relationships. Stay open to your friends as they choose to stay or leave the friendship. As you blend old and new friendships after loss, new stability supports you.

---

*Things do not change; we change.*

**HENRY DAVID THOREAU**

---

## GROUP TRAVEL OPPORTUNITIES

If you attend your high-school reunion alone, standing alone can be awkward. You bolt over to a group of old friends while conversations around you strain for common ground after years, or possibly decades, have passed. You've changed, while others stayed the same. You bump into an attractive classmate you passed in the hall in high school, and after a lengthy conversation, receive an offer for a date in return. One connection legitimizes the new shoes you bought or the ten pounds you lost for the occasion. Your risk and nerve to attend the event alone garnered a reward. High-school reunions unnerve you, but can also inspire you. Group travel for your widowed parent can work the same way.

## One Travel Solution: Groups

When you suggest group travel to your parent, start by explaining some of the benefits. When you travel on group trips, especially group trips for singles, everyone enjoys other people, no matter if they are widowed, divorced, or married. Group trips based around your parent's hobby also can be a great way to build a new community, and many trips are affordable for all kinds of budgets.

## Our Story

Mom traveled frequently with Dad on business trips. As a widow, she faced the choice of either traveling alone or not at all. Familiar with the group-trip concept, Mom selected a biking trip run by a familiar company. She knew what to expect from the company, enjoyed traveling with the group and felt less alone. Because the trip provided for varying skill levels, fellow bikers of her skill level were always available. When she researched other trips after she returned, she discovered trips involving her hobbies of golf, learning, and wellness. When Mom takes trips—mostly with groups—she enjoys traveling. As she travels and changes her environment, she thinks less about her widowhood.

## The Benefits of Group Travel

Widows or widowers experience belonging instead of being ignored or avoided when they take trips with social, welcoming people in a group. Hobby-based vacations work well, as everyone immediately has a common ground that trumps marital status. Group travel is affordable to almost everyone. Churches, **AARP** (p. 165), and **Elderhostel** (p. 261) also provide low-cost group trips.

## Hobby-Based Travel Groups

If your parent likes to travel, encourage him or her to get involved in local groups organized around a favorite hobby. Local groups have day trips, conferences, or field trips that may interest your parent. Take a look at **Shaw Guides** (p. 210) for ideas on local art groups, cooking schools, golf or tennis, photography, or writing and language classes in the United States and abroad. When your parent stays connected to inclusive, not exclusive, groups or communities, he or she builds a village of support.

## Resources and Options

Encourage your parent to go online and explore travel options. With the growth of the group-travel business, many organizations offer opportunities. If your parent is adventurous, encourage him or her to look at **Specialty Travel Index** (p. 259) or **Fifty-Plus Expeditions** (p. 260). Religious group trips are available through **Globus Journeys** (p. 260), **World Mission Tours** (p. 260), or **Adventures in Missions** (p. 260). If your mother is your widowed parent, **Gutsy Women Travel** (p. 262), **Gordon's Guide** (p. 262), or **Transitions Abroad** (p. 262) trips may suit her needs. If your father is your widowed parent, he and his friends can plan a trip or get trip ideas using the Web site **Mancations** (p. 261). The **Groople** Web site (p. 260) creates an easy way for your parent and his or her friends to plan their own group trip. Check Part III: Resources for more ideas on available group trips.

## Questions to Ask about Your Parent and Travel

- Does my parent want to travel? Is he or she open to a group trip?
- Is my parent ready to travel?
- What is my parent's budget for a vacation?
- Has my parent been on any group trips before with an organization or company he or she liked?
- What hobbies does my parent pursue? Do those hobbies have a national organization with a national conference, group trip, or local organization? Golf? Tennis? Collectibles? Biking? Learning? Women's or men's groups?

Without new avenues for friendships and community, your parent is reminded his or her old world of living as part of a couple doesn't fit anymore. Persuade your parent to try a group trip. Your widowed parent will love being included and not avoided or left out. You never know what a group trip may lead to a new romance, a lifelong friendship, or a new attitude toward widowhood.

> *Nothing ventured, nothing gained.*
>
> ANONYMOUS

## LET MOM OR DAD TRY ANYTHING

Everyone fantasizes about an alternative life. Sail around the world on a yacht. Spend more time with your family. Start a nonprofit. Join the circus. Play golf every day of the year. Volunteer to serve others every day. Sleep until noon every day. Live without a budget. Become a self-made millionaire. Live in Paris. Your parent fantasizes too. When it's time, no matter how crazy the idea seems, encourage your parent's pursuit.

### Four Ideas for Encouraging Your Parent

As you coach your parent regarding his or her career, volunteer work, education, or new life choices, keep these four ideas in mind:

1. A career counselor may be a great resource and advisor to present your newly widowed parent with multiple possibilities.
2. If a parent volunteers, takes a new job, or goes back to school, he or she is choosing excellent ways to build a new community. Your parent may want to go back to school to pursue an interest or investigate a new career field.
3. When your parent moves in a new direction, he or she becomes receptive to fresh relationship, career, and learning possibilities.

4.  After facing the death of his or her spouse and the intense awareness of his or her own limited time on earth, your parent may be interested in pursuing a new or reinvigorated spiritual path or better physical health.

 ## Our Story

In our case, Mom never expected to be on her own at age fifty-six, but luckily Dad made good investments so Mom could take some time to figure out how to create an income and life that worked for her as a single widow. She had acquired a degree in interior design but wasn't interested in beginning a design business. When she asked our advice, Ivy and I suggested career counselors and talks with her friends. The best approach was to explore her options.

Mom visited friends in contrasting retirement towns. She took workshops, conferences, and seminars. She brainstormed with career counselors. She wrestled daily to figure out the second life she never expected. She explored her options while she and the estate attorney settled my father's estate and got used to new household and financial systems. We knew she was overwhelmed, but we needed to rebuild our own lives too.

At the end of five years, Mom embraced a new life that blended pursuit of a master's degree and PhD in nutrition, renovating rental properties, and travel. Her current choices are not permanent, but work for now and constantly evolve. Her choice was not one main interest but a blend of several smaller interests pursued together.

## Career Counselors and Classes

A career counselor may suggest plausible options that your parent had not considered. Career counselors have local connections that can open doors for your parent. If your parent has a scattered resumé or limited work experience, career counselors can restructure your parent's resumé to match current job opportunities.

Because your parent took time off work or reduced activity in organizations before or after the death of the spouse, free time may be available for your parent to try something new. Many universities offer low-cost or free classes for senior citizens to audit. These classes allow your parent to test the idea of going back to school or build a community of like-minded people.

### If Your Parent Doesn't Want to Try New Things

Some parents do not want to change. They find comfort sticking to the same old routine they have followed for years. That's okay. A familiar world in the middle of big personal changes brings comfort. Yet don't be surprised if one day they announce out of the blue they are going back to school in, say, theater.

### Resources and Options

A widowed parent who explores new options is healthy. Your parent may overlook opportunities he or she never knew existed if new options are not investigated. Your parent may want to read *Too Young to Retire: 101 Ways to Start the Rest of Your Life* (p. 263) or *Unbelievably Good Deals and Great Adventures That You Absolutely Can't Get Unless You're over Fifty* (p. 228) for inspiration. If your parent wants to try a career before committing, have him or her research **Vocation Vacations**'s (p. 264) career vacations. To investigate job opportunities, guide your parent to **Seniors for Hire** (p. 263), **Workforce 50** (p. 264), the **Senior Community Service Employment Program** (p. 263), or **AARP's Best Employers for Workers over 50 list** (p. 262).

The **Learning Annex** (p. 236) offers low-cost classes in many major cities on various hobbies and careers. If your parent lives in North Carolina, contact the **NC Center for Creative Retirement** (p. 257) in Asheville. The center offers workshops and life-transition classes. Review Part III, Resources (p. 155), for a list of other volunteer, work, and education resources.

### Questions to Ask about Your Parent's New Experiments

* Am I preventing my parent from trying new things?
* Did my parent have to sacrifice a career or volunteer opportunities to care for his or her family?
* Does my parent want to go back to school and earn another degree?
* Does my parent live near local universities that offer senior citizen low-cost classes?
* Should I encourage my parent to talk with a career counselor?
* Would my parent enjoy a blend of many interests in his or her new life or a focus on one?
* Is my parent concerned about his or her outdated or unimpressive resumé?

* How can my parent find a local writer to produce a stronger resumé for himself or herself?

Old fantasies can come true. Encourage your parent to stay open to new adventures and experiences even though he or she may be uncomfortable at first. Whether your parent pursues volunteer, work, or education opportunities, pursuit of an interest is vital.

> *Hope is grief's best music.*
>
> **ANONYMOUS**

ENDNOTES

[1] Dr. Jeff Brantley in discussion with the author, October 2007.

[2] Dr. Jeff Brantley in discussion with the author, October 2007.

[3] Edited by Jeffrey R. Lewis and Cindy Hounsell. *What Women Need to Know About Retirement*, (Washington D.C.: A joint project of the Heinz Family Philanthropies and The Women's Institute for a Secure Retirement.), P6.

[4] Raphael Cushnir in discussion with the author, October 2007.

**PART III**

# Resources

# RESOURCES CONTENTS

The majority of the listings below refer to the resources named in Part I and II of the book. Additional resources may be included. Listings include relevant books, Web sites, companies, people, nonprofits, national U.S. laws, and retail stores. All information listed here was accurate at the time of writing, but due to constant informational changes, some Web links or information may have changed.

## CHAPTER 1: FIRST WEEKS AFTER LOSS

## CHAPTER 2: BUILD YOUR SUPPORT TEAM

## CHAPTER 3: TAKING CARE OF YOURSELF

## CHAPTER 4: PAPERWORK AND FINANCES

## CHAPTER 5: TECHNOLOGY TIME-SAVERS

## CHAPTER 6: MOVING FORWARD

## CHAPTER 7: HOLIDAYS AND ANNIVERSARIES

## CHAPTER 8: MOVING MOM OR DAD

## CHAPTER 9: CHANGES IN FAMILY DYNAMICS

# CHAPTER 10: COMMUNITY

# APPENDIX B: LEGAL CONCERNS AND DIRECTIVES

# FIRST WEEKS AFTER LOSS

## BEREAVEMENT AND LOW-COST, LAST-MINUTE AIRFARES

### About

Many airlines offer 50 percent discount off tickets purchased the same day as travel at the airport counter, or "walk up" rates. Funeral homes can obtain copies of the death certificate or provide a letter stating a death has occurred, which may be required for bereavement rates to be offered. The About Web site weighs the pursuit of a bereavement airfare rate versus an online low-price ticket.

**WEB SITE:** www.airtravel.about.com/cs/airtravellinks/a/bereavement.htm

### Last-Minute Travel Web Sites

Some travel Web sites specialize in low fares for last-minute travel plans. Below are the most popular ones.

www.lastminutetravel.com
www.priceline.com
www.expedia.com/daily/deals/lastminute_deals
www.lastminute.com
www.skyauction.com
www.travelocity.lmdeals.com
www.11thhourvacations.com

## Smartertravel

The Smarter Travel Web site posts an article outlining various airlines and its bereavement fare options.

WEB SITE: www.smartertravel.com/travel-advice/Bereavement-fares.html?id=323904

## ENERGY TEAM EXAMPLE

**Capossela, Cappy and Sheila Warnock.** *Share the Care: How to Organize a Group to Care for Someone Who Is Seriously Ill.*
Rev. ed. New York: Fireside, 2004.

*Share the Care* shows you how to turn a group of friends, neighbors, family members, or volunteers into a powerful and balanced caregiving team for someone with a serious or chronic illness, those in rehabilitation from surgery or an accident, or to fill the needs of an elderly parent.

WEB SITE: www.sharethecare.org

## FLOWERS

### 1-800-Flowers (U.S. and international flower delivery)

This thirty-year-old flower company sells and delivers flowers, plants, gift baskets, and food. The Web site offers an extensive section filled with information about grief, sympathy and funeral flowers, and funeral flower etiquette articles from the Emily Post Institute.

U.S. orders:

PHONE: (800) FLOWERS   WEB SITE: www.1800flowers.com

International orders:

PHONE: (800) 858-5039   WEB SITE: www.1800flowers.com/international

### Calyx and Corolla

The company sells high-end flower arrangements available to be shipped within the continental United States. If you need international delivery, contact their partner Gifts for Europe.

PHONE: (800) 800-7788   WEB SITE: www.calyxandcorolla.com/calyx.storefront

WEB SITE: www.giftsforeurope.com/CalyxCorolla/welcome.htm

## Just Flowers

A Los Angeles-based flower company, Just Flowers sells flowers, balloons, plants, and gift baskets. Domestic and international deliveries are available.

PHONE: (800) 597-4489  WEB SITE: www.justflowers.com

## FOOD, MEALS, AND MEAL DELIVERY

## Big City Chefs

Prepared food can be a thoughtful and useful gift for a griever from friends or family, especially during the first few months after the loss of a spouse or loved one. In most major cities, Big City Chefs, a national company, prescreens and staffs qualified personal chefs to provide specific food needs for families and individuals.

PHONE: (866) 321-2433  WEB SITE: www.bigcitychefs.com

## Diamond Organics

Diamond Organics sells fresh organic foods from California with nationwide overnight home delivery. During a parent's or a family's early grief, easily available healthy foods offer comfort.

PHONE: (888) 674-2642  WEB SITE: www.diamondorganics.com

## Dinewise

This food delivery company offers gourmet frozen meals for healthy eating, seniors, diabetics, and many other specific food needs. Nationwide delivery and gift certificates are available.

PHONE: (800) 749-1170  WEB SITE: www.dinewise.com

## Fresh 'n Fit Cuisine

Available in Atlanta, Fresh 'n Fit Cuisine offers a five- and seven-day prepared meal plan that meets the guidelines of the American Diabetes Association, the American Heart Association, and the American Cancer Society for nutrition. Meals are available in 1200- or 2000-calorie-a-day programs and are available for local pickup or delivery for an extra fee.

PHONE: (877) 363-2572  WEB SITE: www.freshnfitcuisine.com

## Gourmet Grocery Online

This online grocer offers gift baskets and prepared meals and soups, among many other food options. Each meal notes the number of people it serves. Sampler meals can serve up to twelve people. Nationwide delivery available.

**PHONE:** (866) 682-1052   **WEB SITE:** www.gourmetgroceryonline.com

## Harry and David

Known for its gourmet gift baskets, Harry and David offers fresh fruits, vegetables, gourmet hams, turkeys, and seafood to ship to grievers and their families.

**PHONE:** (877) 322-1200   **WEB SITE:** www.harryanddavid.com

## Home Bistro

Fresh meals are made in New England's Lake Champlain Valley using local ingredients, then vacuum-sealed and flash frozen. Meals are designed for one person and will stay fresh in the freezer up to one year. Special diets such as low-fat, low-carb, low-sodium, and diabetic meals are offered. No preservatives are added. All orders are shipped in an insulated cooler filled with dry ice. Nationwide delivery available.

**PHONE:** (800) 628-5588   **WEB SITE:** www.homebistro.com

## Magic Kitchen

The chef-prepared gourmet frozen meals at Magic Kitchen are made to serve two to four people. They also offer senior, heart-healthy, low-fat, and low-carb meals as well as gift certificates. Nationwide delivery available.

**PHONE:** (877) 516-2442   **WEB SITE:** www.magickitchen.com

## Takeout Taxi

Takeout Taxi, a national home delivery service, delivers takeout food from local restaurants in various cities.

**WEB SITE:** www.takeouttaxi.com

## FUNERAL AND MEMORIAL SERVICE ASSISTANCE

## Chamber of Commerce

To find your local Chamber of Commerce, use the national Web site. Call your local chamber and ask for referrals to special-event planners or professional organizers to assist with a memorial service, funeral, or general organizational support.

**WEB SITE:** www.chamberofcommerce.com

## National Association of Professional Organizers (NAPO)

The National Association of Professional Organizers operates as the national association dedicated to the field of organizing and provides referrals to local organizers. On its Web site, you will find local organizers to assist with memorial service planning or general organizing assistance. You can find a referral to a local organizer for short-term or long-term projects or a part-time personal assistant on the Web site. The organizers are either generalists in the field of organizing or specialists in particular areas, such as cleaning out garages/attics/basements, working with seniors, electronic and paper organization, estate sales, and moving and relocation.

**PHONE:** (847) 375-4746  **WEB SITE:** www.napo.net

## FUNERAL PLANNING WEB SITES AND SERVICES

### American Association of Retired Persons Grief-and-Loss Program (AARP)

AARP, with more than thirty-five million members, is a highly respected nonprofit organization for people age fifty and older in the United States. The AARP Web site packs the grief-and-loss section with useful checklists, local and national resources, articles, funeral and memorial service ideas, grief-and-loss message boards, and publications on grief. The "Ways to Remember" article lists ideas you can incorporate into a memorial service. AARP supports the newly widowed and their families through support groups, educational meetings and online assistance.

Since 2004 AARP's Grief-and-Loss program is not a national AARP program. In some states, local AARP grief-and-loss bereavement support programs and Widowed Persons Services (WPS) programs will continue to be affiliated with AARP and will be managed by the appropriate AARP state office.

**PHONE:** (888) 687-2277  **WEB SITE:** www.griefandloss.org

### AARP Grief-and-Loss Article/Publication Section

The grief-and-loss section of the AARP Web site is the best place I have found on the Internet for estate and paperwork checklists you need quickly when assembling information after a death. Useful lists include Final Details, Urgent Details, Steps to Take, Necessary Papers, and Claiming Benefits. Final Details includes a list of documents you will need to organize for an estate attorney.

### Your local AARP office

Use the AARP direct link below to connect your to a local AARP office.

**WEB SITE:** www.aarp.org/states

## Costco

Costco, a wholesale and retail corporation with far-reaching businesses and products, offers eight different caskets for sale at reasonable prices on its Web site. Some caskets cost less than half of what an average funeral home charges. Costco can ship caskets to twenty-six U.S. states with expedited overnight shipping available. Casket prices on its Web site range from $924 to $2,999.

**PHONE:** (800) 774-2678 (general member services) **WEB SITE:** www.costco.com

## Cremation Association of North America

Founded in 1913, the Cremation Association of North America is an organization of more than 1,500 members composed of cemeterians, cremationists, funeral directors, crematorium industry suppliers, and consultants. The organization provides a searchable database of members, information on how to pick a crematorium, and links to a variety of companies providing services or products related to funerals.

**PHONE:** (312) 245-1077 **WEB SITE:** www.cremationassociation.org

## Eternal Reefs

Eternal Reef offers a unique environmentally friendly memorial service for your loved one. You can create an eternal reef designed out of cast concrete to commemorate a deceased parent or loved one. The concrete eternal reef can include the remains of a loved one and is placed in the ocean. After the reef cures for a month, the reef is placed in a designated body of water—the area must be preapproved and permits received—that requires new reefs to protect the environment. The Eternal Reef staff helps family members and/or friends cast the loved one's memorial reef, imprint handprints, or provide a rubbing of the loved one's bronze or other type of memorial plaque. After the memorial is cast, the Eternal Reef team lowers the memorial reef into the ocean and inspects the memorial periodically. The Eternal Reef memorial is particularly appropriate for a loved one who loved the sea, animal life, or the environment. A unique memorial, such as an Eternal Reef, might be selected as a place of remembrance to visit instead of a headstone. Reef locations are available from Atlantic City, New Jersey, to South Padre Island, Texas. Future upcoming locations include the Pacific Northwest.

**PHONE:** (888) 423-7333 **WEB SITE:** www.eternalreefs.com/index.html

## Federal Trade Commission's Funeral Rule Law

The FTC Web site describes the United States Funeral Rule enforced by the Federal Trade Commission. The Funeral Rule law requires funeral homes to offer consumers a general price list upon first entering a funeral home to plan a funeral. The Federal Trade Commission has two informative brochures: "Paying Final Respects: Your Rights When Buying Funeral Goods and Services" and the more-detailed guide "Funerals: A Consumer Guide."

**PHONE**: (877) 382-4357 (Consumer Response Center of FTC)
**WEB SITE**: www.ftc.gov/funerals

## Funeral Consumers Alliance

The Funeral Consumers Alliance, a nonprofit, protects consumers from funeral industry abuse. The alliance offers guidance to consumers about funeral-related questions.

**PHONE**: (800) 765-0107  **WEB SITE**: www.funerals.org

## Funeral Depot

Funeral Depot sells a range of funeral products and services and offers discounts to AARP members.

**PHONE**: (800) 318-8707  **WEB SITE**: www.funeraldepot.com

## Guidestar

Sometimes your family may prefer friends or family give donations to charitable causes instead of sending flowers for the memorial service or funeral. Guidestar provides lists of a variety of nonprofit organizations in the United States and abroad interested in receiving donations. You should mention the chosen recipient for donations in all funeral or memorial notices, including the newspaper obituary.

**PHONE**: (757) 229-4631  **WEB SITE**: www.guidestar.org

## Funeral Help Program

The Funeral Help Program offers budget-minded advice about funeral planning. The book *The Affordable Funeral: Going in Style, Not in Debt* provides dozens of tips on arranging for a sudden death or an anticipated funeral as well as preplanning a funeral service, which can save you money on expensive funeral costs. The book includes helpful funeral resources and a detailed funeral checklist. Additionally the companion software program (on CD) *Going in Style: A Funeral Planning Program for Families* is available to aid families in preplanning estate issues.

**PHONE**: (877) 427-0220  **WEB SITE**: www.funeral-help.com

## Funeral Planning 101

The Funeral Planning 101 Web site offers a variety of informational and useful links on planning funerals. The Web site covers numerous religious traditions, eulogies, costs, and memorials.

**WEB SITE:** www.funeralplanning101.com

## Memory-Of

Memory-Of provides a place to create a memorial Web site with photos and thoughts of the deceased parent or loved one. A memorial Web site can offer comfort, provide a place for family members to pay tribute, and celebrate the loved one's life. You can upload video and audio files, create a family tree, and provide an area for others to post comments. Hosting is free for two weeks.

**WEB SITE:** www.memory-of.com/

## National Funeral Directors Association (NFDA)

The NFDA is the world's largest funeral service association. Its Web site provides links to state funeral associations, a searchable directory of NFDA-member funeral homes, and information about creating meaningful funeral and memorial services. Additionally the NFDA Web site provides information on grief, explaining death to a child, and advance funeral planning. See the "Types of Tributes" page for ceremony ideas.

**PHONE:** 800-228-6332 or 262-789-1880  **WEB SITE:** www.nfda.org

## Legacy

Legacy provides a nationwide resource for obituary sites for more than 175 national newspapers.

**WEB SITE:** www.legacy.com

## U.S. Department of Veterans Affairs

If a parent worked in the military, the Veterans Benefits Administration Web site provides benefits information and services available to both widowed spouses and dependents of military personnel who died while in active military service and also to the survivors of veterans who died after active service. Its Web site links connect you to other federal agencies and organizations offering related benefits and services. You can download forms from the Web site to start the benefit process.

**PHONE:** (800) 827-1000  **WEB SITE:** www.va.gov

**WEB SITE:** www.vba.va.gov/survivors/index.htm (survivors benefits)

## FUNERAL PLANNING BOOKS

**Brown, Adele.** *What A Way to Go . . . Fabulous Funerals of the Famous and Infamous.*
  San Francisco: Chronicle Books, 2002.
Various pop culture and political icons' deaths, funeral services, and burials are summarized, including Princess Diana Spencer, Muppet creator Jim Henson, Winston Churchill, Grace Kelly, and Martin Luther King Jr., among others.

**Carlson, Lisa.** *Caring for the Dead: Your Final Act of Love.*
  Hinesburg, VT: Upper Access Books, 1998.
*Caring for the Dead*, written by the executive director of the Funeral and Memorial Societies of America, explains death and funeral issues such as cremation, burials, cemeteries, caskets, and embalming. The book also discusses specific death and funeral practices for each state.

**Kerr, Margaret, and JoAnn Kurtz.** *Facing a Death in the Family: Caring for Someone through Illness and Dying, Arranging the Funeral, Dealing with the Will and Estate.*
  1st. ed. Hoboken, NJ: John Wiley & Sons, 1999.
If you need guidance on difficult death issues before or after a death, consult this funeral-planning book. *Facing a Death in the Family* spells out ways to prepare in advance for death issues, including how to find the right kind of care, administer an estate, plan a funeral, or hire workers for home care.

## GRIEF

**Centering Corporation and *Grief Digest* Magazine**
The Centering Corporation offers a quarterly magazine and books on grief.
**PHONE:** (866) 218-0101  **WEB SITE:** www.centeringcorp.com/catalog/index.php

**Edelman, Hope.** *Motherless Daughters: The Legacy of Loss.*
  2nd ed. Cambridge, MA: Da Capo Press, 2006.
*Motherless Daughters* covers grief, life, and identity issues for women who have lost their mothers. The author includes professional bereavement research and resources.

**Ellis, Thomas M.** *This Thing Called Grief: New Understandings of Loss.*
  Minneapolis, MN: Syren Book Company, 2006.

This book about grief, written by Thomas Ellis—a second-generation funeral director, licensed marriage and family therapist, and executive director at the Center for Grief, Loss, and Transition—walks you through different ways people grieve and offers advice on how you can use loss to heal and grow.

**Hickman, Martha Whitmore. *Healing after Loss: Daily Meditations for Working through Grief.***
New York: Harper Perennial, 1999.
A small meditation book, *Healing after Loss* presents you with daily nuggets of encouragement after a death or loss.

**James, John and Russell Friedman. *The Grief ❣ Recovery Handbook: The Action Program for Moving beyond Death, Divorce, and Other Losses.***
Rev. ed. New York: HarperCollins, 1998.
*The Grief ❣ Recovery Handbook* explains grief and offers action-oriented recovery steps you can take to complete your grief.
**WEB SITE**: www.grief.net

**James, John, and Russell Friedman. *When Children Grieve: For Adults to Help Children Deal with Death, Divorce, Pet Loss, Moving and Other Losses.***
Reprint ed. New York: HarperCollins, 2002.
*When Children Grieve* aids parents in supporting their children through loss.
**WEB SITE**: www.grief.net

**James, John, and Russell Friedman. *Moving On: Dump Your Relationship Baggage and Make Room for the Love of Your Life.***
New York: M. Evans and Company, Inc., 2006.
*Moving On* shows readers how to work through debilitating old relationship issues in order to move on to a better life.
**WEB SITE**: www.grief.net

**Kübler-Ross, Elizabeth. *On Death and Dying: What the Dying Have to Teach Doctors, Nurses, Clergy, and Their Own Families.***
New York: Touchtone, 1969.
In this classic book about grief, Kübler-Ross explains the stages of grief that became widely used in the grief-and-loss field. The media's use of Kübler-Ross's stages—denial,

anger, bargaining, depression, and acceptance—created mainstream acceptance of Kübler-Ross's finding.

**WEB SITE:** www.elisabethkublerross.com/index.html

**Levang, Elizabeth.** *When Men Grieve: Why Men Grieve Differently and How You Can Help.*
 Minneapolis, MN: Fairview Press, 1998.
*When Men Grieve* explains how men's grief differs from women's grief. If you want to understand your male spouse, brother, or father's emotions or behaviors during grief, *When Men Grieve* might provide needed perspective.

**Noel, Brook, and Pamela D Blair.** *I Wasn't Ready to Say Good-bye: Surviving, Coping and Healing after the Death of a Loved One.*
 Belgium, WI: Champion Press, 2000.
An excellent book about grief and the different feelings you struggle with after a sudden death. Chapters include how to handle the first few weeks, awareness of the emotional and physical effects of grief, both the loss of a parent and partner, grief recovery exercises, and resources.

## GRIEF-AND-LOSS BOOK PUBLISHERS

### Compassion Books

Compassion Books offers more than four hundred books, videos, and audio products for adults and children from various publishers about grief and loss.
**PHONE:** (800) 970-4220  **WEB SITE:** www.compassionbooks.com

### In-Sight Books

In-Sight Books produces books, audio cassettes, greeting cards, gifts, videos, and framed art to aid children, teens, and adults who experience grief and loss. In-Sight Books products apply most to caregivers of elderly parents and grief and loss.
**PHONE:** (800) 658-9262  **WEB SITE:** www.insightbooks.com

### Roberts Press

Roberts Press, a Canadian publisher, produces books and videos for children, teenagers, and adults on topics about grief and loss.
**PHONE:** (866) 582-5558 (Canada)  **WEB SITE:** www.robertspress.ca

## GRIEVING AND CONDOLENCE PROTOCOL

**Post, Peggy. *Emily Post's Etiquette: The Definitive Guide to Manners.***
    17th ed. New York: HarperCollins, 2004.
*Emily Post's Etiquette*, a well-respected book on manners, includes a chapter called Grieving and Condolences that addresses protocol. The chapter covers topics such as notifying others of a death, funeral and memorial-service arrangements, eulogies, online memorials, flowers and donations, guest registers, appropriate clothing for funerals, various religious customs, and sympathy notes.

## INVESTIGATING THE AFTERLIFE (OR LIFE AFTER PHYSICAL DEATH)

**Chopra, Deepak. *Life after Death: The Burden of Proof.***
    New York: Harmony, 2006.
Written by a medical doctor, *Life after Death* offers an Indian perspective on life after death.

**Coward, Harold. ed. *Life after Death in World Religions.***
    5th ed. New York: Orbis, 2001.
The varying beliefs of life after death of Chinese religions, Buddhism, Christianity, Islam, Hinduism, and Judaism are discussed in *Life after Death in World Religions* through insights from religious scholars and followers of the faiths.

**Kübler-Ross, Elisabeth. *On Life after Death.***
    Berkeley, CA: Celestial Arts, 1991.
*On Life after Death* discusses life after death from the perspective of Elisabeth Kübler-Ross, a pioneer in death-and-dying issues.

**Moody Jr., Dr. Raymond A. *Life after Life: The Investigation of a Phenomenon Survival of Bodily Death.***
    2nd ed. New York: HarperCollins, 2001.
A doctor wrote *Life after Life* after he studied one hundred people who experienced "clinical death" and returned to life. The findings in the book demonstrate a belief in life after physical death.

**Osis, Karlis, PhD and Erlendur Haraldsson PhD. *What They Saw... at the Hour of Death: A New Look at Evidence for Life after Death.***
    3rd ed. Norwalk, CT: Hastings House, 1995.

Originally written in 1977, *What They Saw . . . at the Hour of Death* reveals the findings of a four-year study of fifty thousand terminally ill patients right before death by one thousand doctors and nurses in the United States and India. The foreword to the book was written in 1977 by Elizabeth Kübler-Ross, a pioneer in studying death and dying. A new chapter was added in the 1995 edition with regard to life-after-death evidence.

## ONLINE GROCERY SHOPPING

A few grocery stores offer online shopping; the best-known online grocery stores include Peapod, Netgrocer, and Safeway. You can order groceries and have them delivered at your parent's or your home almost anywhere you have Internet access.

### Netgrocer

Netgrocer delivers groceries by FedEx about three to seven days after ordering. Netgrocer delivers to the forty-eight contiguous United States as well as Alaska and Hawaii.

**PHONE:** (888) 638-4762  **WEB SITE:** www.netgrocer.com

### Peapod

Grocery delivery is available from Peapod for personal residences and businesses in Chicago, Milwaukee, Southeast Wisconsin, Connecticut, Massachusetts, Rhode Island, New York, New Jersey, Maryland, Virginia, and Washington, DC. Delivery times depend on location.

**PHONE:** (800) 573-2763  **WEB SITE:** www.peapod.com

### Safeway

Safeway delivers groceries to Arizona, California, Maryland, Oregon, Virginia, Washington, and Washington, DC. Delivery times depend on location.

**PHONE:** (877) 723-3929  **WEB SITE:** www.safeway.com

## PAPERWORK

### American Association of Retired Persons' Grief-and-Loss Resources

See page 165 for full description

### American Bar Association

The American Bar Association is a large U.S. legal association. On its Web site under "Public Resources" you will find useful information and answers to common questions about probate, trustees, estates, and wills.

PHONE: (312) 988-5000  WEB SITE: www.abanet.org/public.html

## American Council of Life Insurance Policy

If you are looking for missing life insurance policies, click on "Missing Policy Inquiry" on the Web site for information and suggestions on finding policy information.

PHONE: (202) 624-2000  WEB SITE: www.acli.com/ACLI/Industry+Products/Life+
    Insurance/Locating+a+Missing+Policy/default.htm

## National Center for Health Statistics

The National Center for Health Statistics, a part of the Centers for Disease Control and Prevention, provides information and links to request birth, death, marriage, or divorce certificates.

PHONE: (800) 232-4636  WEB SITE: www.cdc.gov/nchs/howto/w2w/w2welcom.htm

## Social Security Administration

The Social Security Administration assists with eligibility inquiries for survivor benefits after a death in the family. When you apply for survivor's benefits, first gather birth, death, and marriage certificates; Social Security numbers; and a copy of the deceased's most recent federal income tax return.

PHONE: (800) 772-1213  WEB SITE: www.ssa.gov/ww&os1.htm

## Vitalchek

Vitalchek is a large supplier of certified birth, death, marriage, and divorce certificates in the United States. International document assistance is also available.

WEB SITE: www.vitalchek.com

## WORK LEAVE

### U.S. Department of Labor's Family and Medical Leave Act

The U.S. Department of Labor Web site outlines the federal U.S. law that provides a maximum of twelve weeks of legal unpaid, job-protected leave from work in a twelve-month period for eligible employees—state, or local, or federal government employees or employees of private-sector companies with over fifty employees—"to care for an immediate family member—spouse, child, or parent—with a serious health condition." A Wage and Hour District office can determine coverage and eligibility based on many different factors. Self-employed people or freelancers can take time away from their work, of course, but are not guaranteed work, projects, or income upon their return. You can obtain copies of FMLA Family and Medical Leave Act Fact Sheet (FS028); and FMLA Family and Medical Leave Act Regs 29 CFR 825 (WH1419); and FMLA Compliance Guide (WH1421) at the second Web site below.

**PHONE:** (866) 487-9243

**WEB SITE:** www.dol.gov/esa/whd/fmla/ (wage and hour division)

**WEB SITE:** www.osha.gov/pls/epub/owa_pub.pub_form (publications)

# BUILD YOUR SUPPORT TEAM

### (SUPPORT GROUPS, GRIEF-AND LOSS-CENTERS, AND INDIVIDUAL THERAPY)

The following list provides resources for finding individual therapy, parental-loss support groups, support for children, and widow or widower support groups in your own area. The resources are divided into seven sections: (1) support by resources covering multiple states; (2) support by location including countries outside the United States; (3) online parental-loss and widow or widower support groups; (4) association support groups; (5) grief-and-loss e-cards; (6) individual therapy; and (7) grief support for children.

If these groups are inconvenient, check local hospice, hospital, treatment centers, and church and religious programs for grief and loss support groups.

## 1. SUPPORT BY RESOURCES COVERING MULTIPLE STATES

### 2-1-1

Nonprofit and government agencies throughout the United States have created an easy-to-remember 3-digit phone number (2-1-1) to help people connect to local community resources such as support groups, family resource centers, and volunteering opportunities. Currently, more than 65% of the United States can dial 2-1-1 and gain access to those resources. The Web site shows which areas have services. The referral specialists can connect you with basic human needs resources; physical and mental health resources (including support groups); employment resources; support for older Americans and persons with disabilities; and support for children, youth, and families.

**PHONE:** Dial 2-1-1 **WEB SITE:** www.211.org/status.html

### Widowed Persons Service (WPS)

WPS provides one-on-one support for newly widowed individuals by volunteer widows and widowers. WPS also provides support through outreach programs, referrals, and financial and legal counseling services. Since 2004, WPS programs are not a national AARP program and may or may not be associated with your local AARP offices.

PHONE: (202) 434-2260  WEB SITE: Web sites available for specific cities' WPS programs

### Grief ❣ Recovery Institute

If you are ready to work through your grief, the Grief ❣ Recovery Institute has developed a successful program to assist you. Local Grief ❣ Recovery Specialists teach the twelve-week Grief ❣ Recovery Program in various cities. Call the main office for a local referral.

PHONE: (818) 907-9600 (Sherman Oaks, CA)  WEB SITE: www.grief-recovery.com

### Griefshare

Griefshare is a structured nondenominational thirteen-week support group with videos, workbooks, and discussions about grief and loss. The videos feature grief specialists talking about grief and recovery issues while telling real-life stories of others who have experienced a loss. Griefshare offers links to grief support in Australia, Hong Kong, Ireland, New Zealand, Philippines, South Africa, Tanzania, and the United Kingdom. Check the Web site to find a group starting in your local area. You can also sign up for daily e-mails on the Web site to aid in healing your grief.

PHONE: (800) 395-5755 (Wake Forest, NC)  WEB SITE: www.griefshare.org/findagroup

### Rural Assistance Center

The U.S. Department of Health and Human Services Rural Assistance Center offers assistance, resources, and information to people living in rural communities.

PHONE: (800) 270-1898 (Grand Forks, ND)  WEB SITE: www.raconline.org

### Vitas Innovative Hospice Care

Vitas, a national hospice company, posts a comprehensive list of community support grief groups available in California, Connecticut, Delaware, Florida, Georgia, Illinois, Kansas, Missouri, Michigan, New Jersey, Ohio, Pennsylvania, Texas, Virginia, Washington, DC, and Wisconsin.

PHONE: (305) 374-4143 (Miami, FL)

WEB SITE: www.vitas.com/bereavement/toc.asp#supportgroup

## 2. SUPPORT BY LOCATION

### ALABAMA

#### Alabama Grief

The Alabama Grief Support Foundation is a nonprofit organization that serves the central Alabama area and offers individual therapy and grief support groups.
**PHONE:** (205) 870-0336 (Central Alabama)  **WEB SITE:** www.alabamagrief.com

#### Griefshare  See page 177 for full description

### ALASKA

#### Tragedy Assistance Program for Survivors (TAPS)

TAPS, a nonprofit Veteran Service Organization-sponsored program, supports families of a loved one who died serving in the armed forces including families of veterans. E-mail or call TAPS to find local peer support groups after loss.
**PHONE:** (202) 588-8277 (Washington, DC)  **WEB SITE:** www.taps.org/home.aspx

#### Griefshare  See page 177 for full description

### ARIZONA

#### Find-a-Therapist

Find-a-Therapist, Inc assists in finding grief-and-loss support groups and individual therapists for unique needs such as finding Imago therapists, children's counselors, ethnic therapists, or Jungian therapists.
**PHONE:** (866) 450-FIND (Referral Line)  **WEB SITE:** www.find-a-therapist.com

### ARKANSAS

#### Arkansas Health Link

The Arkansas Health Link Web site is an excellent resource for various support groups throughout Arkansas. Click on "Grief and Loss" for loss-related support groups.
**PHONE:** There are many groups listed to call on the Web site.
**WEB SITE:** www.arhealthlink.org/arkansas/support/ARsupport.asp

### Arkansas Children's Hospital/Center for Good Mourning
The Web site lists a variety of support groups, including grief and loss, in all regions of Arkansas under "Good Mourning Grief Support Groups."
PHONE: (501) 364-1100 (Central Arkansas)
WEB SITE: www.archildrens.org/community_outreach/center_mourning/default.asp

## CALIFORNIA

### Kara
Kara, a thirty-year-old organization, offers grief support groups for children, teenagers, and adults, including spouse/partner loss, parent/caregiver loss, child loss, and suicide loss groups.
PHONE: (650) 321-5272 (Palo Alto)  WEB SITE: www.kara-grief.org

### Motherless Daughters of Los Angeles
Motherless Daughters supports adult women dealing with the loss of a mother. Individual therapy is available from a group leader who is a licensed psychotherapist. Find your local Motherless Daughter meeting on **Meetup** (p. 264).
PHONE: (310) 474-2208 (Los Angeles)  WEB SITE: www.motherlessdaughtersbiz.com
WEB SITE: www.motherlessdaug.meetup.com

### Our House
Our House is a Los Angeles–based grief-support center that offers age- and relationship-specific support groups to children, teens, and adults. Widows and widowers groups are available as well as groups for adults and children grieving the loss of a parent, close relative, sibling, or child.
PHONE: (310) 475-0299 (Los Angeles)  (818) 222-3344 (Woodland Hills)
WEB SITE: www.ourhouse-grief.org

## COLORADO

### Hospice of Metro Denver
Hospice of Metro Denver offers bereavement education; daytime and evening drop-in grief groups; newly bereaved groups; parental-loss groups; grief groups for children, women, and caregivers; and one-on-one individual counseling sessions.
PHONE: (303) 321-2828 (Denver)  WEB SITE: www.thedenverhospice.org

### Senior Answers

Senior Answers lists bereavement groups for seniors in Colorado.

PHONE: (303) 333-3482 (Denver)

WEB SITE: www.senioranswers.org/Pages/support.groups.htm

## CONNECTICUT

### Hartford Hospital Bereavement Support Guide

The Hartford Hospital Web site provides an excellent guide for finding local grief and loss support groups in your area, including groups for widows, widowers, and children. Yale-New Haven, Bridgeport, Bristol, Day Kimball, New Britain, and Rockville Hospitals' bereavement programs are also listed.

PHONE: (860) 545-2290 (Hartford)   WEB SITE: www.harthosp.org/bereavement/
    SupportServicesandPrograms/default.aspx

### Widowed Persons Service/Bridgeport

WPS offers one-on-one support for newly widowed people through trained male and female volunteers of all ages who have experienced the loss of a spouse. WPS services serve Bridgeport, Easton, Fairfield, Milford, Monroe, Shelton, Stratford, Trumbull, and Westport.

PHONE: (203) 381-9668 (Bridgeport)  WEB SITE: www.wpsbpt.org

## DELAWARE

### Griefshare   See page 177 for full description

### Supporting Grieving Children and Families

A Web site provided by Death Education Task Force of the Delaware End-of-Life Coalition lists many grief resources to be used by Delaware schools, children and their families dealing with grief and loss. Parent loss and widow/widower support groups are posted on this extensive list.

WEB SITE: www.udel.edu/DSP/SGCF/supportgroups.html

## FLORIDA

### Hospice of the Florida Suncoast

The Hospice of the Florida Suncoast offers a twenty-four-hours-a-day-seven-days-a-week

information and referral line. Individual, family, and bereavement support is offered.
**PHONE:** (727) 586-4432 (Clearwater)
**WEB SITE:** http://www.thehospice.org/resources_support/grief_counseling.aspx

### Miami Counseling and Resource Center

The Miami Counseling and Resource Center, a full-service mental-health treatment center, offers counseling on a wide variety of issues, including individual counseling for grief and loss. English and Spanish counseling is available.
**PHONE:** (305) 448-8325 (Coral Gables)
**WEB SITE:** www.miamicounseling.com/additional_services/grief_loss.asp

## GEORGIA

### Buckhead Church

Contact this church for referrals to Christian counselors who specialize in grief counseling in the Atlanta area.
**WEB SITE:** www.buckheadchurch.org/counseling

### Dekalb Medical Center

The hospital offers an adult grief group and a separate group for adolescents. Call ahead to register for the group.
**PHONE:** (404) 501-5701 (Decatur)
**WEB SITE:** www.dekalbmedicalcenter.org/ClassesEvents/tabid/54/Default.aspx

### Duluth First United Methodist Church

Duluth First United Methodist Church offers a bereavement support group the fourth Monday of every month. A Stephen Minister facilitates the meeting.
**PHONE:** (770) 476-3776 (Duluth)
**WEB SITE:** www.duluthumc.org/ministries/caring/support.html

### Front Porch of Atlanta

The Front Porch of Atlanta is an Atlanta-based organization for grieving children and their families, offering local support groups for parent loss.
**PHONE:** (770) 730-5858 (Atlanta)   **WEB SITE:** www.thefrontporch.org

### Griefshare   See page 177 for full description

### Link Counseling Center

The Link Counseling Center provides counseling services, support groups, and psychotherapy to all ages. The Link staff members are specialists in suicide bereavement.
**PHONE:** (404) 256-9797 (Sandy Springs)
**WEB SITE:** www.thelink.org/about_the_link.htm

### Perimeter Church

Perimeter Church offers local referrals to church members and the general public who seek Christian counseling. They also offer Griefshare, Rainbows, and widows groups listed under "Ministries—Support Groups."
**PHONE:** (678) 405-2000 (Duluth)   **WEB SITE:** www.perimeter.org

### WellStar Kennestone Hospital

Search here for information about the current Good Grief six-week-long adult bereavement support group led by the hospital chaplain.
**PHONE:** (770)732-3780 (Austell)
**WEB SITE:** www.wellstar.org/ws_content/ws_classreg.aspx?menu_id=46&link=contents

### Women Alone Together®

An Atlanta nonprofit started in 2002, Women Alone Together aims to assist single women with decisions about health, finances, and legal issues as well as community and personal growth, whether women are divorced, widowed, single by their own choice, or have a spouse with a chronic illness. They build a supportive community and facilitate knowledge through educational seminars, lunches, a book club, and special events. Fees vary for events.
**PHONE:** 404-769-3228 (Atlanta)   **WEB SITE:** www.womenalonetogether.org

## HAWAII

### Hospice Hawaii

Free bereavement groups at Hospice Hawaii are open to the public in Kailua and Honolulu.
**PHONE:** (808) 924-9255 (Oahu)   **PHONE:** (808) 553-4310 (Molokai)
**WEB SITE:** www.hospicehawaii.org/services/bereavement/groups/default.asp?PF=

### Hospice of Hilo

The Hospice of Hilo offers adult, widow, and youth grief support groups in Hilo.

**PHONE:** (808) 969-1733 (Hilo)   **WEB SITE:** www.hospiceofhilo.org

## IDAHO

### A Better Way Coalition

The organization offers a list of support groups available in Idaho.

**PHONE:** (208) 343-9735 (Boise)   **WEB SITE:** www.abetterwaycoalition.org/
resources/idaho-grief-loss-schedule.htm

### Kootenai Medical Center

The Kootenai Medical Center offers a weekly bereavement support group.

**PHONE:** (208) 666-3285 (Coeur d'Alene)   **WEB SITE:** www.kmc.org/awards.cfm?id=72

## ILLINOIS

### Center for Grief Recovery

The Center for Grief Recovery Web site connects you to many grief-and-loss resources throughout Illinois.

**PHONE:** (773) 274-4600 (Chicago)

**WEB SITE:** www.griefcounselor.org/grief-recovery-general-bereavement.html

### Family Service Self-Help Center

Family Service Self-Help Center lists various grief support options available in Champaign and surrounding areas, including death-of-a-parent groups, Griefshare groups, and children's groups.

**PHONE:** (217) 352-0099 (Family Service in Champaign)

**WEB SITE:** selfhelp.prairienet.org/groups.php?group=Bereavement+(General)&
parent=Bereavement

### Hospice of Northeastern Illinois

The hospice offers adult loss-of-a-parent groups and widow, widower, children, and junior-high-age classes on grief and loss.

**PHONE:** (800) 425-4444 (offices in Crystal Lake and Barrington)

**WEB SITE:** www.hospiceanswers.org/supportgroups.html

### Rush University Medical Center

The Rush University Medical Center offers a monthly bereavement-and-grief-support group in Chicago at the Anne Byron Waud Patient and Family Resource Center.

PHONE: (800) 757-0202 (Chicago)

WEB SITE: www.rush.edu/rumc/page-1124119164419.html

## INDIANA

### Bridges Center at Hospice & Palliative Care of Southern Indiana

Bridges Center is a resource for finding specific grief-and-loss programs and services for adults, children, and teens in southern Indiana and Kentucky.

PHONE: (812) 948-4862 and toll free (800) 895-5633 (southern Indiana)

WEB SITE: www.hospices.org/bridges

## IOWA

### Amanda the Panda

Amanda the Panda offers eight-week-long child, teen, and adult support groups continuously from September to May. They also offer weekend camps, fun days, and holiday grief support for both adults and children.

PHONE: (515) 223-4847 (Des Moines)

WEB SITE: www.amandathepanda.org

### Iowa Hospice

Iowa Hospice, a statewide hospice organization, offers a list of hospices all over the state.

PHONE: Specific phone numbers for each group listed on the Web site

WEB SITE: www.iowahospice.org/membershipdir/default.shtml

## KENTUCKY

### Bridges Center of Louisville

Bridges Center is a resource for finding specific grief-and-loss programs and services for adults, children, and teens in southern Indiana and Kentucky.

PHONE: (888) 345-8197 (Louisville) (800) 686-9577 (central Kentucky)

WEB SITE: www.hospices.org/bridges

## KANSAS

### Solace House

Solace House, a Kansas City grief resource center, offers individual and group support to grieving children, individuals, and their families who have lost a loved one. They also supply connections to other grief and support groups in the local Kansas City area.

**PHONE:** (913) 341-0318 (Shawnee Mission)   **WEB SITE:** www.solacehouse.org

## LOUISIANA

### Seasons Grief Center

The nonprofit Seasons Grief Center serves New Orleans for all types of loss. They offer parent, spousal, and child loss support groups as well as individual and family counseling.

**PHONE:** (504) 834-5957 (Metairie)   **WEB SITE:** www.seasonsgriefcenter.org

## MAINE

### Center for Grieving Children

The Center for Grieving Children offers teen, child, and adult bereavement support and information.

**PHONE:** (207)775-5216 (Portland)   **WEB SITE:** www.cgcmaine.org

### Grief Centers of Maine, New Hampshire, and New York

The Web site provides a comprehensive list of local grief centers.

**PHONE:** Specific phone numbers for each center listed on Web site

**WEB SITE:** www.cgcmaine.org/docs/subdocs/otherCtrs.htm

## MARYLAND

### Hospice Network of Maryland

The Hospice Network of Maryland Web site has a comprehensive list of local hospices in Maryland who may offer grief support groups or counseling.

**PHONE:** (410) 729-4571 (Millersville)

**WEB SITE:** www.hnmd.org/findinghospicecare.htm

### Hospice of the Chesapeake

The hospice program offers children, teen, and adult grief retreats as well as local support groups, including parental loss.

**PHONE:** (410) 987-2003 (Annapolis)  (301) 499-4500 (Landover)

**WEB SITE:** www.hospicechesapeake.org

## MINNESOTA

### Center for Grief, Loss, and Transition

The St. Paul, Minnesota nonprofit center provides grief therapy and education for people affected by various types of loss.

**PHONE:** (651) 641-0177 (St. Paul)  **WEB SITE:** www.griefloss.org

## MISSISSIPPI

### First United Methodist Church of Gulfport

The church offers an eleven-week grief-recovery workshop.

**PHONE:** (228) 863-0047 (Gulfport, MS)  **WEB SITE:** www.fumc-gulfport.org/index.html

### McClean Fletcher Center

Associated with Hospice Ministries, the McClean Fletcher Center offers grief support groups to children and their families who have experienced the death of a relative.

**PHONE:** (601) 982-4405 (Jackson)  **WEB SITE:** www.hospiceministries.org

## MISSOURI

### Armbruster-Donnelly Mortuary

The St. Louis funeral home, Armbruster-Donnelly Mortuary, has a Web site with a comprehensive list of Missouri-based grief support options under "Resources."

**PHONE:** Specific phone numbers for each group listed on Web site

**WEB SITE:** www.ambruster-donnelly.com

### Boone Hospital Center

A chaplain and social worker hold a monthly grief support group at the Boone Hospital Center.

**PHONE:** (573) 875-0555 x 5250 (Columbia)  **WEB SITE:** www.boone.org

### Sibling Connection

Based in St. Louis, the Sibling Connection is a resource Web site for anyone who has lost a brother or sister.

WEB SITE: www.counselingstlouis.net

## MONTANA

### Good Lives and Goodbyes Healthy Grieving Resource Guide

The Good Lives and Goodbyes Web site is a joint effort with the Missoula Demonstration Project: The Quality of Life's End and the *Missoulian*. The Web site lists the following local support groups: hospice bereavement, Garden City Funeral Home bereavement, and "Seasons" family grief support and education. For more details visit its Web site.

PHONE: (406) 523-5200 (the *Missoulian* in Missoula)

WEB SITE: www.missoulian.com/specials/dying/grieving.html

## MASSACHUSETTS

### Community Nurse and Hospice Care

Community Nurse and Hospice Care offers various bereavement support groups in six-week sessions. The groups are open to all members of the Fairhaven community regardless if your loved one received hospice services from them. The groups are open to the public.

PHONE: (508) 992-6278 ext. 2531 or 508-992-6278 ext. 2529 (Fairhaven)

WEB SITE: www.communitynurse.com/support.htm

### Hospice and Palliative Care Federation of Massachusetts

To find the closest hospice to you, click on "Hospice Locator" on its Web site. Many Massachusetts hospices offer grief support to hospice families and the local community.

PHONE: Specific phone numbers for each hospice listed on Web site

WEB SITE: www.hospicefed.org

### Newton-Wellesley Hospital

The Web page lists support groups at the Wellesley Hospital including spousal-loss and young widow and widower groups.

PHONE: (781) 899-7434 (Spousal Loss)

WEB SITE: www.nwh.org/itemDetail.asp?categoryID=24&itemID=17364

### UMass Memorial Medical Center

The UMass Memorial Medical Center Web site lists its bereavement groups available to the public.

PHONE: (508) 754-0052 (Worcester)

WEB SITE: www.umassmemorial.org/ummhc/hospitals/med_center/events/support/ bereave.cfm

### Young Widowed Group of Greater Boston, MA

The Young Widowed Group of Greater Boston meets monthly at the Beth Israel Deaconess Hospital in Needham.

WEB SITE: widow.meetup.com/38/about

### Young Widows & Widowers, Ltd.

Young Widows & Widowers holds weekly and bimonthly nightly meetings in Andover. The meetings are attended by widows and widowers between the ages of twenty and fifty-eight. The group also includes a qualified facilitator.

PHONE: (978) 979-8993 (Andover)  WEB SITE: www.youngwidowsandwidowers.org

## MICHIGAN

### Arbor Hospice

The Arbor Hospice offers loss support groups for loss of a parent, spouse/partner, and loss of adult children. They also have a Survivors of Suicide group.

PHONE: (800) 997-9266 (southeastern Michigan–Ann Arbor)

WEB SITE: www.arborhospice.org/services/GriefSupport/braveheartofmichigan.html

### *Marquette Monthly*

The *Marquette Monthly* Web site lists local events and various groups for the Upper Peninsula—scroll down toward bottom of page for various grief support groups.

PHONE: See specific groups for phone numbers

WEB SITE: www.mmnow.com/z_current_a/b/c/gallery_guide.html

### New Hope Center

The New Hope Center is a Christian-based center offering support groups in the Southern Michigan area.

PHONE: (248) 348-0115 (Northville)

WEB SITE: www.newhopecenter.net

### Therapeutic Resources

The Therapeutic Resources Web site lists various support groups in Michigan including bereavement, spousal-loss, and grief-recovery groups for adults and children.

PHONE: (888) 331-7114 (Cleveland, OH)

WEB SITE: www.therapeuticresources.com/supportmichigan.html

## NEBRASKA

### Nebraska Medical Center

The hospital Web site lists grief support groups in the Omaha area.

PHONE: Web site lists phone numbers for the groups

WEB SITE: www.nebraskamed.com/patients/pastoral_care/com_support_groups.aspx

## NEVADA

### Griefshare   See page 177 for full description

### Jewish Family Service Agency

The Jewish Family Service Agency has a weekly bereavement support group available.

PHONE: (702) 732-0304 (Las Vegas)   WEB SITE: www.jfsalv.org/supportgroups.htm

## NEW HAMPSHIRE

### Concord Regional Visiting Nurse Association

Adult grief support groups and lectures on bereavement are available from the Concord Regional Visiting Nurse Association.

PHONE: (800) 924-8620 (Concord)

WEB SITE: www.crvna.org/services/community-grief.php

### Grief Centers of Maine, New Hampshire, and New York

The Web site presents a comprehensive list of local grief centers.

PHONE: Specific phone numbers for each group listed on Web site

WEB SITE: www.cgcmaine.org/docs/subdocs/otherCtrs.htm

## NEW JERSEY

### Family Support Center of New Jersey

Family Support Center of New Jersey is clearinghouse for a wide variety of referrals and information for families and individuals with chronic or serious illnesses, disabilities, or grief issues in New Jersey. You can search the database under "Grief and Loss" or "Grief Support."

PHONE: toll free in New Jersey (800) 372-6510 (Manasquan) or (732) 528-8080
WEB SITE: www.fscnj.org

### New Jersey 2-1-1 Partnership   See page 176 for 2-1-1 description
WEB SITE: www.nj211.org/search.cfm

## NEW MEXICO

### Gerard's House
Gerard's House provides grief support for children and teens (ages three to twenty) and their families. Check the Web site for current group times.

PHONE: (505) 424-1800 (Santa Fe)   WEB SITE: www.gerardshouse.org

### Santa Fe Doorways
Santa Fe Doorways presents a well-organized Web site with links to grief counseling and related groups covering end-of-life issues.

WEB SITE: www.santafecare.org/resources.php

## NEW YORK

### Center for Loss and Renewal
A Manhattan-based center, the Center for Loss and Renewal offers individual therapy and workshops on grief and loss.

PHONE: (212) 874-4711 (New York)   WEB SITE: www.lossandrenewal.com

### Grief Centers of Maine, New Hampshire, and New York
Grief Centers of Maine, New Hampshire, and New York Web site lists a comprehensive list of local grief centers.

PHONE: Specific phone numbers for each group listed on Web site
WEB SITE: www.cgcmaine.org/docs/subdocs/otherCtrs.htm

### Hope for Bereaved
A Syracuse-based bereavement center, Hope for Bereaved offers support groups as well as other resources for widows, widowers, and individuals struggling with parent loss.

PHONE: (315) 475-9675 (Syracuse)
WEB SITE: www.hopeforbereaved.com/index.php?page=support-group-calendar

### Lifetime Care

The Lifetime Care Web site catalogues a list of grief support groups in Monroe, Wayne and Seneca counties in Rochester, New York.

PHONE: Specific phone numbers for each city listed on the Web site

WEB SITE: www.LifetimeCare.org

## NORTH CAROLINA

### Buddy Kemp Caring House

The Buddy Kemp Caring House offers support groups for adult survivors of family members who died of cancer.

PHONE: (704) 384-5223

WEB SITE: www.presbyterian.org/health_services/cancer_center/support_services/
    buddy_kemp_caring_house

### Hospice and Palliative Care-Charlotte Region

The hospice facilitates bereavement groups for Charlotte region residents who have lost a loved one as well as workshops on various aspects of grief.

PHONE: (704) 375-0100   WEB SITE: www.hospiceatcharlotte.com

### North Carolina 2-1-1   See page 176 for 2-1-1 description

WEB SITE: www.nc211.org

## NORTH DAKOTA

### Mental Health Association of North Dakota

Search the Mental Health Association Web site for local North Dakota grief groups

PHONE: (701) 255-3692 (Bismarck)

WEB SITE: www.mhand.org/support_groups/index.asp

## OHIO

### Fernside

Fernside, a nonprofit grief-support center for children and their families, is located in Cincinnati. Fernside provides free-of-charge peer support for children, teens, and adults in grieving families.

PHONE: (513) 745-0111 (Cincinnati)   WEB SITE: www.fernside.org

### Hospice Ohio

The Hospice Ohio program offers resources and support groups in the Cleveland area for adults, adolescents, and children dealing with grief.

PHONE: (216) 931-1327 (Cleveland)

WEB SITE: www.hospiceohio.org/bereavement_services.asp

### Ohio Funeral Directors Association

The Ohio Funeral Directors Association Web site, under its "Consumer Information" section, lists support groups in Ohio for various types of grief, including children and widows.

PHONE: (614) 486-5339 (Columbus)  WEB SITE: www.ohiofda.org/index.html

## OKLAHOMA

### 2-1-1 Oklahoma   See page 176 for 2-1-1 description

WEB SITE: www.211oklahoma.org

### Griefshare   See page 177 for full description

## OREGON

### Griefshare   See page 177 for full description

### Hospice of Sacred Heart

The hospice offers daytime and evening support for family, children, and friends after loss.

PHONE: (541) 242-8753 (Eugene)

WEB SITE: www.peacehealth.org/apps/course/CDetails.asp?CourseID=35

## PENNSYLVANIA

### The Good Grief Center for Bereavement Support

This nonprofit support center based in Pittsburgh offers peer support in person and over the phone as well as many online resources for people of all ages. Additionally the Web site lists specific support groups available for motherless daughters, young adults, and young widows and widowers. On the Good Grief Center Web site, you can order various types of high-quality sympathy care packages with or without an orchid or the book *Tear Soup*. The care packages include a journal with pen, a soothing music CD with guided

meditation, and thirty "quiet moment cards" that offer inspirational quotes for grievers on one side and helpful grief advice written by bereavement counselors on the other.
PHONE: (412) 224-4700 (Pittsburg) or toll free (888) 474-3388
WEB SITE: www.goodgriefcenter.com

### Taylor Hospice

The hospice offers three free support groups open to the public including: (1) a young widows/widowers group for people fifty-five and younger; (2) an adult bereavement group for adults who have lost a parent, grandparent, friend, etc.; and (3) a spouse bereavement group for widows/widowers age fifty-six and older. Ridley Park is located thirty minutes from the Philadelphia airport.
PHONE: (610) 521-5822 (Ridley Park)  WEB SITE: www.taylorhospice.org

### Wyndmoor Keystone Hospice

Wyndmoor Keystone Hospice sponsors a Younger Widows Group for ages thirty-five to sixty-five who have lost husbands or significant others. Contact Alix Amar MSS, LCSW, the director of bereavement, for more information. Groups are held the first Thursday of the month from 6:30 to 8:15 p.m.
PHONE: (215) 836-2440  WEB SITE: www.keystonecare.com/bereavment.html

## RHODE ISLAND

### Friends Way

Friends Way offers group support and grief information to children, teens, and their parents or caregivers after loss.
PHONE: (401) 921-0980 (Warwick)  WEB SITE: www.friendsway.org

### Lifespan

The Lifespan Web site indexes a variety of grief support groups in Rhode Island.
PHONE: Various phone numbers for each meeting on the Web site
WEB SITE: www.lifespan.org/services/support/bereave.htm

## SOUTH CAROLINA

### Cancer Society of Greenville County

The Cancer Society of Greenville County offers a bereavement support group and individual counseling for anyone grieving the loss of a loved one because of cancer.
PHONE: (864) 232-8439 (Greenville)  WEB SITE: www.cancersocietygc.org

**Griefshare**  See page 177 for full description

### St. Francis Hospital

St. Francis Hospital offers counseling and bereavement support for families of loved ones who received hospice care.

PHONE: (864) 688-1700 (Greenville)

WEB SITE: www.stfrancishealth.org/open_arms_hospice.php

## SOUTH DAKOTA

### South Dakota Council of Mental Health Centers

The Web site features a list of centers offering various mental-health counseling services, including grief issues.

PHONE: (605) 224-0123 (Pierre)  WEB SITE: www.sdmentalhealth.org/dir.htm

## TENNESSEE

### Angels of Alive Hospice Grief Center

The hospice center offers various grief support groups.

PHONE: (615) 327-1085 (Nashville)

WEB SITE: www.alivehospice.org/services-support.php

### Covenant Health Support Groups

Covenant HomeCare Hospice facilitates ongoing monthly grief support groups. Also, Peninsula, a division of Parkwest Medical Center, offers a six-week Solitary Men grief support group for men fifty and older.

PHONE: (865) 541-4500 (Knoxville)

WEB SITE: www.covenanthealth.com/events/listing.cfm?eventID=5#16

**Tennessee 2-1-1**  See page 176 for 2-1-1 description

WEB SITE: www.211tn.org/findhelp.html

## TEXAS

### Grief Resource Center

Grief groups, educational seminars, and creative workshops for all ages are available at the Grief Resource Center.

PHONE: (281) 292-6800 (The Woodlands)  WEB SITE: http://griefresourcecenter.org

**Griefshare**  See page 177 for full description

## Journey of Hope Grief Support Center

Grief peer-support groups for children and adults aged three to ninety-nine who are grieving a death or an impending death are available at the Journey of Hope Grief Support Center. Their services are free of charge, and the center offers a full meal to families prior to the group meetings.

**PHONE:** (972) 964-1600 (Plano)  **WEB SITE:** www.johgriefsupport.org

**Texas 2-1-1**  See page 176 for 2-1-1 description

**PHONE:** (512) 472-6267 (Austin)

**WEB SITE:** www.unitedwaycapitalarea.org/gethelp/index.cfm

# UTAH

**Griefshare**  See page 177 for full description

## Ogden Regional Medical Center

A six-week-long grief support group is available at the East Ogden Medical Center. Additional bereavement support groups are listed on the Web site.

**PHONE:** (801) 479-2074 (East Ogden)

**WEB SITE:** www.hopeguide.org/ResourceListCMD.jac?id=10367&type
    =topic&name=Grief%20and%20Bereavement%20-%20Adults#

## University of Utah/College of Nursing

Six specific types of grief support groups for adults and children are offered through the College of Nursing at the University of Utah.

**PHONE:** (801) 585-9522 (Salt Lake City)

**WEB SITE:** www.nurs.utah.edu/caringconnections/groups/grief.pdf

# VERMONT

## Hospice and Palliative Care Council of Vermont

The Hospice and Palliative Care Council of Vermont Web site lists information about various bereavement support groups in Vermont.

**PHONE:** Various phone numbers for each location on the Web site

**WEB SITE:** www.hpccv.org/bereavement.htm

## VIRGINIA

### Healing the Spirit

Healing the Spirit Web site, sponsored by the LifeNet Health Foundation, lists national and Virginia-based resources for grief support. LifeNet Health's Donor Family Services department offers support particularly for families of organ and tissue donors. Additionally the interactive grief Web page, the Healing Garden, is for grieving children and those who care for a grieving child.

**PHONE:** (800) 847-7831 (LifeNet Health Foundation, Virginia Beach)
**WEB SITE:** www.healingthespirit.org/support-groups.php
**WEB SITE:** www.healingthespirit.org/childs-place.php (The Healing Garden)

### Senior Navigator: Virginia's Resource for Health and Aging

The Web site lists many support groups—including grief support—in all areas of Virginia.

**PHONE:** (804) 827-1280 (Richmond) **WEB SITE:** www.seniornavigator.com/calendar.php

## WASHINGTON

### GriefWorks

The GriefWorks organization offers bereavement resources, information, referrals, and support for children, teens, adults, and families.

**PHONE:** (800) 850-9420 (toll-free in Auburn) or (253) 333-9420
**WEB SITE:** www.griefworks.org

### Jewish Family Service

Jewish Family Service offers individual grief counseling for the bereaved.

**PHONE:** (206) 461-3240 (Seattle) **WEB SITE:** www.jfsseattle.org

### Northwest Hospital and Medical Center

A weekly support group for anyone experiencing loss of a loved one is available at the medical center. Before you attend, call for a required phone interview.

**PHONE:** (206) 368-1891 (Seattle)
**WEB SITE:** www.nwhospital.org/classes/support_groups.asp

### Overlake Hospital Medical Center

The Overlake medical center provides a bereavement support group for adults coping

with the loss of a loved one through their Cancer Resource Center.
**PHONE:** (425) 688-5127 (Bellevue)
**WEB SITE:** www.overlakehospital.org/services/cancerservices/resources/support.aspx

### Whatcom Hospice Grief Support Group

The organization has two grief support groups for anyone in the community who is grieving a loss of a loved one.
**PHONE:** (360) 733-5877 (Bellingham)  **WEB SITE:** www.hospicehelp.org

## WASHINGTON, DC

### Widowed Persons Service (WPS)

WPS provides support through outreach programs, referrals, and financial and legal counseling services in certain cities.
**PHONE:** (202) 434-2260 (Washington)

### Loss Counseling Center of Washington

The Loss Counseling Center provides individual and group therapy led by a clinical psychologist.
**PHONE:** (202) 965-2764 (Washington) **WEB SITE:** www.losscounseling.com/services.html

### Wendt Center for Loss and Healing

A thirty-year-old organization, the Wendt Center for Loss and Healing offers grief-and-loss support groups, individual grief therapy, children's services, and grief-and-loss training and education.
**PHONE:** (202) 624-0010 (Washington)  **WEB SITE:** www.wendtcenter.org

### Widowed Persons Service (WPS)

WPS provides support through outreach programs, referrals, and financial and legal counseling services in certain cities.
**PHONE:** (202) 434-2260 (Washington, DC)

## WEST VIRGINIA

### Griefshare  See page 177 for full description

### Transitions Center

The Transitions Center offers grief support groups, education, and resources to

people who have lost a loved one.
**PHONE:** (866) 275-5677 (Morgantown)
**WEB SITE:** www.hospicecarecorp.org/transitionscenter

## WISCONSIN

**Griefshare**   See page 177 for full description

### Wisconsin Funeral Directors Association
The association for Wisconsin funeral directors provides a Web site full of useful
links to many Wisconsin grief support groups and related resources.
**PHONE:** (414) 453-3060 (Wauwatosa)
**WEB SITE:** www.wfda.org/public/links_public.html

## WYOMING

**Griefshare**   See page 177 for full description

### Cheyenne Regional Hospice
Adult bereavement groups are available through the Cheyenne Regional Hospice.
**PHONE:** 633-7016   **WEB SITE:** www.umcwy.org/Services/CalendarOfEvents.pdf

## ~ INTERNATIONAL ~

## AUSTRALIA

### Grief Link
The Australian Web site based in the southern region of Australia provides infor-
mation on grief and loss as well as support group referrals.
**PHONE:** 13 11 14 (in Australia)   **WEB SITE:** www.grieflink.asn.au

**Griefshare**   See page 177 for full description

## CANADA

### New Hope
New Hope provides online support for widows, widowers, and teens. In addition

New Hope offers a bimonthly newsletter, annual retreat, support groups, and local meetings in British Columbia, Canada.
**PHONE:** (250) 545-6004 or (250) 549-7273 (Vernon, British Columbia)
**WEB SITE:** www.newhope-grief.org/index.html

## FRANCE

### Kehilat Gesher

(English Language Jewish Synagogue)
Bereavement seminars are open to all English speakers. For the latest updates, check the Women of the American Church latest newsletter at the Web site listed below.
**PHONE:** 01 39 21 97 19  **WEB SITE:** www.woac.net

## UNITED KINGDOM

### Griefshare    See page 177 for full description

### London Bereavement Network

The British Web site provides information on available bereavement services in London.
**WEB SITE:** www.bereavement.org.uk/home/html_index.asp?p=1

### National Association of Widows United Kingdom

The British national charity is run by widows for widows. The association offers members local meetings, social events, seminars, an online bulletin board, and local assistance lines.
**PHONE:** 0845 838 2261 (Coventry, UK)  **WEB SITE:** www.nawidows.org.uk

# 3. ONLINE PARENTAL-LOSS AND WIDOW OR WIDOWER SUPPORT GROUPS

## BULLETIN BOARDS AND CHAT ROOMS

## GROWW

GROWW is a grief-recovery bulletin board (a place to post and read messages to encourage yourself and others through grief recovery) created by widows and widow-ers. The GROWW Web site has online chat rooms for adults facing parent or grand-parent loss as well as groups for the widowed.

WEB SITE: www.groww.org

## LISTSERV OR E-MAIL SUPPORT

### GriefNet

GriefNet offers sixty virtual-time e-mail support groups—including parental-loss and spousal-loss groups—that are monitored by GriefNet trained volunteers. The monitors make sure the groups are running smoothly and that the members stay within the GriefNet guidelines to ensure a safe environment for grieving. All members are screened before being allowed to join. GriefNet also offers grief resources, a library with reviews of books on grief, a section for vets and their loved ones, and virtual memorials.

WEB SITE: http://griefnet.org

### Sharegrief

Since 2000, Sharegrief has offered online e-mail bereavement support to people all over the world from a team of international grief specialists.

WEB SITE: www.sharegrief.com

### Yahoo Groups

Search here for worldwide widow, widower, or parental-loss online support groups.

WEB SITE: www.groups.yahoo.com

## MESSAGE BOARDS OR BULLETIN BOARDS

### AARP Grief-and-Loss Message Boards

The AARP Web site provides support for grief and loss through message boards. (Message boards, an Internet forum, are where members can read information posted by other members or post their own messages for others to read.)

PHONE: (888) 687-2277 (main general number)

WEB SITE: http://community.aarp.org/rp-griefnloss/start

### Beyond Indigo

Beyond Indigo offers message boards for loss of a parent, loss of a partner, losing family and friends, suicide, and many other topics related to grief and loss. The Web site is listed in *Forbes* magazine as "Best of the Web" for grief-support message boards and also offers articles on various grief topics.

**WEB SITE:** www.beyondindigo.com

### Grief Support Services

Grief Support Services, a national nonprofit, offers professionally moderated online groups and telephone support. They also offer teleclasses (online seminars you can attend from home when you call in to a designated phone number and log in to a specific Web site given out by the hosts) on grief topics. Grief Support Services also supplies other grief-related resources such as books, reports, journals, videos, and magazines.

**PHONE:** (818) 347-8955 (West Hills, CA)    **WEB SITE:** www.griefsupportservices.org

### Healthboards

Partnered with WebMD, the Healthboards Web site offers online patient-to-patient and caregiver-to-caregiver support for many diseases, conditions, and health topics, including parental loss, grief, and death and dying.

**WEB SITE:** www.healthboards.com/boards/showthread.php?t=208094

### Widow Net

The Widow Net Web site presents information about grief, bereavement, and recovery for widows by widows. An online bulletin board and chat is also available. (An online bulletin board is a place to read and post messages to others about a specific topic.)

**WEB SITE:** www.widownet.org

## ONLINE SAFETY

### OnGuard Online

This Web site combines government and technology industry information to protect your computer, your personal information and yourself against online fraud, scams, and viruses.

**WEB SITE:** www.onguardonline.gov

### Stay Safe Online

This Web site, created by the National Cyber Security Alliance, offers Internet safety education for users.

**WEB SITE:** www.staysafeonline.org

## 4. ASSOCIATION SUPPORT GROUPS

### American Cancer Society

Search the American Cancer Society's "In My Community" area to find local cancer patient, survivors, and loved ones support programs.

PHONE: (800) 227-2345 (main phone number)
WEB SITE: www.cancer.org/docroot/SHR/SHR_0.asp

### American Heart Association

Enter your zip code on the Web site to find your local American Heart Association (AHA) office. The American Heart Association's local office can offer suggestions for support groups in your local area through the Mended Hearts, Inc. program.

PHONE: (800) 242-8721 (AHA main phone number)
PHONE: (888) 432-7899 (Mended Hearts, Inc.)
WEB SITE: www.americanheart.org
WEB SITE: www.mendedhearts.org

### Leukemia & Lymphoma Society

The organization offers a list of free family support groups facilitated by two health/mental-health professionals for people affected by blood cancers.

PHONE: (800) 955-4572 (main phone number)
WEB SITE: www.leukemia-lymphoma.org/all_page?item_id=4388

### Survivors of Suicide

Sponsored by the American Association of Suicidology, the Web site lists links to Survivors of Suicide support groups across the United States.

PHONE: (202) 237-2280 (Washington, DC)
WEB SITE: www.suicidology.org/displaycommon.cfm?an=1&subarticlenbr=55

## 5. GRIEF-AND-LOSS E-CARDS

### Willowgreen

Willowgreen, a multifaceted grief-and-loss Web site, provides free e-cards focused on grief, illness, transition, caregiving, and encouragement—including gratitude themes—along with other grief-related products. If you are involved in caregiving, this

second Web site offers inspirational writings and images for caregivers.
**PHONE:** (260) 490-2222 (Fort Wayne, IN)  **WEB SITE:** www.willowgreen.com
**WEB SITE:** www.thoughtful-caregiver.com

## 6. INDIVIDUAL THERAPY

**2-1-1**  See page 176 for 2-1-1 description

### Association for Death Education and Counseling (ADEC)

ADEC is a professional organization promoting death education, bereavement counseling, and the care of the dying.
**PHONE:** (847) 509-0403 (Northbrook, IL)  **WEB SITE:** www.adec.org

### Hospice Foundation of America (HFA)

The nonprofit organization works to educate families in issues related to caregiving,
terminal illness, loss, and bereavement. Additionally, if you are a nurse, clergy or social
worker, HFA develops educational programs for health-care professionals designed to
maintain the quality of hospice care.
**PHONE:** (800) 854-3402 (Washington, DC)  **WEB SITE:** www.hospicefoundation.org

### Medicare Hospice Benefit, Section 40.2.3

The Medicare hospice benefit requires that bereavement counseling is made available
to family members up to one year after a patient's death in a hospice.
**PHONE:** (800) 633-4227
**WEB SITE:** www.cms.hhs.gov/manuals/Downloads/bp102c09.pdf

### National Association of Area Agencies on Aging/Eldercare Locator

The National Association of Area Agencies on Aging is the national umbrella organization for the more than 655 local area agencies on aging as well as 230 Title VI Native
American aging programs. These agencies assist older Americans who want to stay in
their own homes by offering supportive resources. The Eldercare Locator connects
older adults and family caregivers to these aging resources in their communities that
can help you identify  local widow and parental-loss support groups.
**PHONE:** (202) 872-0888 (Washington, DC)
**PHONE:** (800) 677-1116 (Eldercare Locator)
**WEB SITE:** www.n4a.org/default.cfm  **WEB SITE:** www.eldercare.gov

### National Board of Certified Counselors

Search here for a list of certified counselors.

**WEB SITE**: www.nbcc.org/counselorfind

### Network Therapy

Search here to find a therapist by location, treatment approach, or other criteria. Network Therapy also provides links to support groups and national hotlines.

**WEB SITE**: www.NetworkTherapy.com

### Phone Counseling.org

If you can only find time to talk to a counselor on the phone, phone-counseling.com offers immediate access to professional counselors licensed by the state where they live to offer counseling advice. This fee-based service charges you per minute or hour.

**WEB SITE**: http://phone-counseling.org

### *Psychology Today* Magazine Online
### Find a Therapist

The *Psychology Today* Web site offers information on how to choose a therapist and differentiate between types of therapists and their credentials. Insurance issues are also covered. The Web site also provides a nationwide database of therapists with its specialties, including grief and loss.

**WEB SITE**: http://therapists.psychologytoday.com

### National Association of Social Workers
### Find a Social Worker

The NASW Web site provides a national database of licensed social workers. In each individual social worker's profile, the Web site reveals fees for individual, family, and group therapy sessions; the free services offered; areas of expertise; and group support sessions available.

**WEB SITE**: www.helppro.com/aspdocs/naswbsearch1.asp?msta=1

### Society of Military Widows

The Society of Military Widows is a nationwide organization. The society's purpose is to assist widows of members of all branches of the uniformed services of the United States.

**PHONE**: (800) 842-3451 (Springfield, VA)   **WEB SITE**: www.militarywidows.org

### The Family and Marriage Counseling Online Directory
### Find Marriage and Family Therapists

To find a marriage or family counselor in your area, search this national directory.

**WEB SITE:** family-marriage-counseling.com/index.htm

### American Association of Marriage and Family Therapists' Therapist Locator

Search here for a list of members of the American Association of Marriage and Family Therapists.

**WEB SITE:** www.therapistlocator.net

## 7. GRIEF SUPPORT FOR CHILDREN

### A Little Hope

This organization provides grief counseling and bereavement peer-support groups to children and teens that have lost a parent or loved one.

**PHONE:** (516) 639-6727 (New York City)  **WEB SITE:** www.alittlehope.org

### Compassionate Friends

Compassionate Friends is a national organization with local chapters to support the grieving after the death of a child.

**PHONE:** (877) 969-0010 (Oak Brook, IL)  **WEB SITE:** www.compassionatefriends.org

### National Cancer Institute

The national organization offers assistance and information for dealing with grieving children.

**PHONE:** (800) 422-6237 (Spanish-speaking assistance available)

**WEB SITE:** www.nci.nih.gov/cancertopics/pdq/supportivecare/bereavement/
    Patient/page9

### National Institute for Trauma and Loss in Children

The organization's links page has many useful grief-and-loss resources for aiding grieving children.

**PHONE:** (877) 306-5256 (Grosse Pointe Woods, MI)

**WEB SITE:** www.tlcinstitute.org/links.html

## Rainbows

Rainbows is a twenty-year-old international nonprofit organization that provides free support for children who are grieving a loss.

**PHONE:** (847) 952-1770 (Rolling Meadows, IL)

**WEB SITE:** www.rainbows.org

## WARM Place

The WARM Place is a group-support center for grieving children and their families. Group night activities and discussions are determined by the children's age and the type of losses in the group. Support groups are available for children and young adults ages three to twenty-five and their parents or guardians.

**PHONE:** (817) 870-2272 (Fort Worth, TX)

**WEB SITE:** www.thewarmplace.org

# TAKING CARE OF YOURSELF

## BOUNDARIES

**Cloud, Henry, and John Townsend.** *Boundaries: When to Say Yes, When to Say No to Take Control of Your Life.*
Grand Rapids, MI: Zondervan, 1992.
*Boundaries* demonstrates what a life without boundaries looks like, how boundaries are lost, and how to set new boundaries with others.

**Lebow, Grace, Barbara Kane, and Irwin Lebow.** *Coping with Your Difficult Older Parent: A Guide for Stressed-Out Children.*
New York: HarperCollins Paperbacks, 1999.
*Coping with Your Difficult Older Parent,* written by the cofounders of Aging Network Services of Bethesda, Maryland, explores strategies for challenging mother or father behaviors. The book shows specific dialogues on how to handle difficult communication, such as telling your parent he or she cannot move in with you or how to deal with a parent who makes consistent unreasonable demands on your time.

## CAREGIVER CONTRACTS

### National Center on Caregiving/Family Caregiver Alliance
Caregivers who provide long-term care at home for loved ones can find support at the Family Caregiver Alliance. The Web site is packed with useful advice and tips on

caregiving. The alliance also offers local workshops in Northern California.

**PHONE:** (800) 445-8106  **WEB SITE:** www.caregiver.org

## National Academy of Elder Law Attorneys

A nonprofit, the National Academy of Elder Law Attorneys works with lawyers, bar associations, and others who aid older clients and their families. On its Web site you can review frequently asked questions about elder law attorneys as well as search the database of five thousand members for a local elder-law attorney.

**WEB SITE:** www.naela.com

## National Alliance for Caregiving

If you have questions about caregiving, the National Alliance for Caregiving—an alliance of many organizations—is the place to go for online brochures, tips, and advice. The Family Care Resource Connection Web site (www.caregiving.org/fcrc.htm) provides reviews of more than a thousand consumer products targeting the family caregiver.

**WEB SITE:** www.caregiving.org

## National Family Caregivers Association

The caregivers association educates, supports, and advocates for the more than fifty million Americans providing care to loved ones with chronic illness, disabilities, or difficulties caused by old age. The Web site offers many valuable resources, tips, and a link to online caregiver message boards.

**PHONE:** (800) 896-3650  **WEB SITE:** www.thefamilycaregiver.org

## DAILY INSPIRATION AND MEDITATION READERS

**Beattie, Melody. *Journey to the Heart: Daily Mediations on the Path to Freeing Your Soul.***
   San Francisco: Harper San Francisco, 1996.
*Journey to the Heart* is for people who want to connect daily with their heart and soul.

**Breathnach, Sarah Ban. *Simple Abundance: A Daybook of Comfort and Joy.***
   New York: Warner Books, 1995.
Read Breathnach's daily inspirational book for perspective and encouragement.

**Hickman, Martha Whitmore. *Healing after Loss: Daily Meditations for Working through Grief.*** See page 170 for full description

## GROUNDING ROUTINES OR PRACTICES

### Energy Grounding

**Choquette, Sonia.** *True Balance: A Commonsense Guide for Renewing your Spirit.*
New York: Three Rivers Press, 2000.
Sonia Choquette PhD, an intuitive and spiritual healer, offers many practical examples on how to balance energy through working on individual chakras.

### General Everyday Rituals or Practices

**Biziou, Barbara.** *The Joys of Everyday Ritual: Spiritual Recipes to Celebrate Milestones, Ease Transitions, and Make Every Day Sacred.*
Reprint ed. New York: St. Martin's Griffin, 2001.
Be inspired to create new everyday rituals or practices by reading Biziou's book.

## MINDFULNESS-BASED GROUNDING OR CENTERING PRACTICES

**Brantley, Jeffrey, and Wendy Millstine.** *Five Good Minutes in the Morning: 100 Morning Practices to Help You Stay Calm and Focused All Day Long.*
Oakland, CA: New Harbinger Publications, 2005.

**Brantley, Jeffrey, and Wendy Millstine.** *Five Good Minutes in the Evening: 100 Mindful Practices to Help You Unwind from the Day and Make the Most of Your Night.*
Oakland, CA: New Harbinger Publications, 2006.

**Brantley, Jeffrey, and Wendy Millstine.** *Five Good Minutes at Work: 100 Mindful Practices to Help You Relieve Stress and Bring Your Best to Work.*
Oakland, CA: New Harbinger Publications, 2007.

Each of these books offer a wide variety of mindfulness-based grounding practices that can be a foundation or support for personal rituals and ceremonies that can help with living a richer and more balanced life.

## HOUR-LONG VACATION IDEAS

### Bed-and-Breakfast Weekends

#### Worldwide Bed and Breakfast

Plan a quick weekend getaway at a charming bed-and-breakfast and let others pamper you.

PHONE: (800) 462-2632

WEB SITE: www.bedandbreakfast.com

### Cooking Classes

#### Kroger School of Cooking

Near Atlanta, Georgia, the Kroger School of Cooking offers a variety of cooking classes for adults and children by local known chefs. The classes cost between twenty-five and fifty dollars.

PHONE: (770) 740-2068

WEB SITE: www.kroger.com/mykroger/011/Pages/kroger_schoolof_cooking.aspx

#### Shaw Guides' Recreational Cooking Schools

Check Shaw Guides for local and international cooking school programs.

PHONE: (212) 799-6464   WEB SITE: www.cookforfun.shawguides.com

#### Sur la Table

Sur la Table offers affordable cooking classes in a variety of categories. Approximate class time is two-and-a-half hours. Sur la Table's cooking classes are available in Arizona, California, Connecticut, Florida, Illinois, New York, Ohio, Oregon, Texas, Virginia, and Washington.

PHONE: See Web site for local phone numbers

WEB SITE: www.surlatable.com/category/culinary.do

#### Viking Home Chef Cooking Classes

Viking offers affordable one- to three-hour cooking classes in Atlanta, Georgia; Cleveland, Ohio; Dallas, Texas; Northern New Jersey (Fairfield); Greenwood, Mississippi; Memphis and Nashville, Tennessee; New York, New York; Philadelphia, Pennsylvania; St. Louis, Missouri; and Walnut Creek, California.

PHONE: See Web site for local phone numbers

WEB SITE: www.vikingcookingschool.com

### Whole Foods Market's Cooking Schools

Whole Foods Market (at certain locations) offers a variety of cooking classes at various prices. Check the Web site to see if your local store currently offers classes.

PHONE: Various phone numbers for each location on Web site

WEB SITE: www.wholefoodsmarket.com/stores/index.html

## Crafts

### Michaels

Michaels is a craft store offering a wide variety of supplies, including scrapbooking supplies, silk flowers, paints, glitter pens, and other fun-filled crafty items.

PHONE: See Web site for local phone numbers

WEB SITE: www.michaels.com/art/online/home

## Food

### Farmers Markets

Search a state-by-state list of U.S. farmers markets to find a local market to tempt your taste buds.

PHONE: See Web site for local USDA service centers

WEB SITE: www.ams.usda.gov/farmersmarkets

## Gardens

### Online List of World's Botanical Gardens

This extensive Wikipedia list of the world's best botanical gardens includes links to their Web sites.

WEB SITE: en.wikipedia.org/wiki/List_of_botanical_gardens

## Journaling

### Center for Journal Therapy

The Center for Journal Therapy Web site offers another perspective on working with grief through journaling, plus related books and workshops.

PHONE: (303) 986-6460

WEB SITE: www.journaltherapy.com

### How to Journal through Grief Online Booklet

Click on the Web site to read a free four-page booklet about journaling and grief. The

Web site lists ideas on how to journal through grief and links to other journaling and grief Web sites and books.

**WEB SITE:** www.kporterfield.com/journal/Journal_Grief.html

## Laughter

### Comedy Day

Find a local comedy club from this Web site list of United States clubs.

**WEB SITE:** www.comedyday.com/world.php

### Laughter Yoga

Find a laughter yoga group (combining laughing exercises with yoga breathing for better health) using the Web site's searchable database.

**WEB SITE:** www.laughteryoga.org/index.php

## Movies

### Apple

You can rent movies from Apple's iTunes store and watch them on your computer, iPod, or iPhone. Apple allows you thirty days to start watching the movie and after you hit "play," you have twenty-four hours to finish watching the movie before it disappears. The per-use-rental fees are higher for new releases than older movies.

**WEB SITE:** www.apple.com

### Blockbuster Total Access

You can order movies and have them delivered free directly to your home with free shipping when you return the movies by mail. You can also return movies and exchange them in a Blockbuster store for a flat monthly rate.

**PHONE:** Specific phone numbers for local stores are listed on Web site

**WEB SITE:** www.blockbuster.com

### Netflix

You can join Netflix to have movies delivered directly to your home. Netflix sends easy-to-return mailers with the CDs.

**PHONE:** (800) 715-2135   **WEB SITE:** www.netflix.com

## Museums and Art Galleries

### Museums and Art Galleries Link

The Web site provides links to top museums and art galleries all over the world.
WEB SITE: witcombe.sbc.edu/ARTHLinks6.html

## Music/Audiobooks

### Audiobooks

Audiobooks users can buy, rent, download, or trade audiobooks in a variety of genres, from fiction to inspirational.
WEB SITE: www.audiobooks.com

### iTunes

ITunes is widely perceived as the largest online music store in the world. If you own an MP3 audio player (like an Apple IPod) you can download music, audiobooks, meditations, or podcasts to a MP3 device to listen to while at the gym, at work, or during personal time.
PHONE: (800) 692-7753  WEB SITE: www.apple.com/itunes

## Outdoors

### Gorp

The Web site lists all the national parks by region as well as best the biking, hiking, paddling, fishing, climbing, and wildlife-viewing spots in the country. Group trips are available under the "Active Vacations" tab.
WEB SITE: gorp.away.com/index.html

## Relaxation

### *Your Present: A Half-Hour of Peace* (CD)

Relax Intuit sells an award-winning guided meditation CD on their Web site.
PHONE: (888) 669-7352  WEB SITE: www.relaxintuit.com/main.asp

## Spa Treatments

### SpaFinder

The SpaFinder Web site connects consumers with resort, hotel, casino, cosmetic, medical, dental, day, mobile, and destination spas in the United States and Canada. The search feature allows clients to search categories such as specific types of spas, locations, cuisines, activities, facilities, amenities, and treatments and provides links to SpaFinder Japan and SpaFinder United Kingdom.

**PHONE:** (212) 924-6800  **WEB SITE:** www.spafinder.com

## Therapeutic Baths

### Burt's Bees Therapeutic Bath Crystals

Enjoy an all-natural soaking remedy of lemon oil, rosemary, and eucalyptus therapeutic bath crystals to relieve aches, pains, and stress.

**PHONE:** (866) 422-8787  **WEB SITE:** www.burtsbees.com

### Samantharoma

Samantharoma's all-natural mineral bath salts come in four scents: cleanse, love, balance, and peace.

**PHONE:** (843) 376-3008

**WEB SITE:** www.samantharoma.com/bath.htm

## Volunteer

### Habitat for Humanity

Habitat for Humanity organizes volunteers around the world to build houses for families in need.

**PHONE:** (800) 422-4828

**WEB SITE:** www.habitat.org/cd/local

### United Way

Search the United Way Web site for a list of volunteering opportunities in your local community.

**PHONE:** Your local United Way office phone number is listed on the national Web site.

**WEB SITE:** national.unitedway.org/volunteer

## Yoga

### Yoga Finder

Find yoga classes all over the world when you search this online database.

**PHONE:** (858) 213-7924

**WEB SITE:** www.yogafinder.com

## SLEEP

**Garber, Richard, and Paul Gouin.** *How to Get a Good Night's Sleep: More than 100 Ways You Can Improve Your Sleep.*
Hoboken, NJ: John Wiley & Sons, 1998.
The book offers practical advice to improve sleep.

## VIRTUAL ASSISTANCE

### AssistU

If you need a virtual assistant, contact AssistU. A virtual assistant is someone who has worked in a support position for a number of years and is interested in working "virtually" from a home office for a client anywhere in the world through exchanging files through the Internet. The company trains, coaches, and refers virtual assistants. Virtual assistants can provide affordable assistance with funeral and memorial-service planning, research on any topic, or make travel arrangements.
**PHONE:** (866) 829-6757  **WEB SITE:** www.assistu.com

## WORK

**Dlugozima, Hope, and James Scott and David Sharp.** *Six Months Off: How to Plan, Negotiate and Take the Break You Need without Burning Bridges or Going Broke.*
New York: Owl Books, 1996.
*Six Months Off* advises you how to figure out how or if you should take six months off work and examines the potential obstacles.

### Elance

Search the Elance Web site for freelance jobs in design, programming, writing, Web site design, accounting, research, or consulting.
**PHONE:** (877) 435-2623  **WEB SITE:** www.elance.com

### Guru

Guru lists jobs in creative, information technology, business consulting, and office and administration categories.
**PHONE:** (888) 678-0136  **WEB SITE:** www.guru.com

### Quint Careers

The Quint Careers Web site provides information and useful links about telecommuting, job flexibility, and working at home.

**WEB SITE:** www.quintcareers.com/telecommute_jobs.html

### Telecommuting Jobs

Telecommuting job opportunities for artists, desktop publishers, photographers, data entry, engineers, programmers, information technology (IT), sales, Web designers, writers, and other freelance projects are posted on the Web site. Users can post a resumé as well as accept temporary work from interested clients.

**WEB SITE:** www.tjobs.com

### U.S. Department of Labor's Family and Medical Leave Act

See page 174 for full description

# PAPERWORK AND FINANCES

## BOOKKEEPERS

### American Institute for Professional Bookkeepers

The national organization has more than thirty thousand bookkeeper members. Since 1998 the institute has offered a bookkeeping certification program available to members. The job-posting area allows you to post a job.

**PHONE:** (800) 622-0121  **WEB SITE:** www.aipb.org

### Bahr, Candace and Ginita Wall. *It's More Than Money—It's Your Life! The New Money Club for Women.*

Hoboken, NJ: John Wiley & Sons, *2003*.

This book was written by personal financial planners to help women better understand and manage finances. The Web site includes a section for widowed spouses with information about funeral and estate procedures.

**PHONE:** (760) 736-1660  **WEB SITE:** www.wife.org

### Bodnar, Janet. *Kiplinger's Money Smart Women: Everything You Need to Know to Achieve a Lifetime of Financial Security.*

New York: Kaplan Business, 2006.

*Kiplinger's Money Smart Women,* written by the executive editor of *Kiplinger's Personal Finance* magazine, advises women on financial choices throughout the various stages of the single life, marriage, divorce, children, investing, retirement, caring for your parents, and widowhood.

**Jaffe, Charles A.** *The Right Way to Hire Financial Help: A Complete Guide to Choosing and Managing Brokers, Financial Planners, Insurance Agents, Lawyers, Tax Preparers, Bankers, and Real-Estate Agents.*

2nd ed. Cambridge, MA: MIT Press, 2001.

Written by a *Boston Globe* columnist, this book offers assistance with understanding various aspects of hiring different types of financial advisors—including how to get multiple advisors to work together for your benefit.

**Walsh, Peter.** *How to Organize Just about Everything.*

New York: Free Press, 2004.

*How to Organize Just about Everything*, written by the professional organizer of the TLC hit TV show *Clean Sweep*, is an excellent book about organization. The book has more than five hundred easy-to-follow suggestions for storage, paper, home, e-mail, files, financial, family affairs, and event problems.

## CAREGIVING AND ESTATE ISSUES

**Kerr, Margaret, and JoAnn Kurtz.** *Facing a Death in the Family: Caring for Someone through Illness and Dying, Arranging the Funeral, Dealing with the Will and Estate.*

1st ed. Hoboken, NJ: John Wiley& Sons, 1999.

*Facing a Death in the Family* covers difficult death decisions faced before and after a death. The book explains what to do in advance of death, how to find the right kind of care, funerals, administering an estate, and hiring workers for in-home care.

## ShareTheCaregiving, Inc.

A nonprofit with a mission to educate people about group caregiving and how to turn offers of "What can I do to help?" into positive action. The comprehensive Web site provides information on the *Share the Care* model, resources, group stories, downloadable forms, and e-mail support.

**WEB SITE:** www.sharethecare.org

## DEATH CERTIFICATES

## Vitalchek

See page 174 for full description

## ELECTRONIC ORGANIZING

### Quicken

Quicken is a software accounting program used to manage personal finances. You can use the software to assist with budgeting, automatically track spending, download transactions from banks and credit cards, schedule and pay bills, and simplify tax preparations. Quicken also offers software for assistance with medical-bill management called Medical Expense Manager as well as Home Inventory Manager for home inventory issues for insurance claims.

PHONE: (800) 811-8766  WEB SITE: quicken.intuit.com

## ESTATE LAWYERS AND PROBATE

### 1800Probate

Review probate articles and search for local probate attorneys through their online referral system on the Web site.

PHONE: (800) 776-2283  WEB SITE: www.1800probate.com

### AARP Legal Services

If you are a member of AARP, call its Legal Services Department to find prescreened estate lawyers at discounted AARP rates. See page 165 for full AARP description.

PHONE: (888) 687-2277

WEB SITE: www.aarp.org/bulletin/yourmoney/Articles/a2004-03-17-estate_lawyer.html

### American College of Trust and Estate Council (ACTEC)

Research their list of ACTEC fellows in the United States through its Web site.

WEB SITE: www.actec.org

## LAWYERS

### Find an Estate Attorney

Search the database on the Web site to find specific kinds of attorneys as well as many articles on legal issues.

PHONE: Information for specific attorneys is on the Web site

WEB SITE: www.lawyers.com/Estate-Planning/browse-by-location.html

## ESTATE PLANNING

### Children of Aging Parents

Discuss the estate-planning questions listed on this Web site to better prepare you and your parent for the future. *The Capsule*, a bimonthly newsletter, is also available.
**PHONE:** (800) 227-7294  **WEB SITE:** www.caps4caregivers.org/guide.htm

### Estate Planning Links

The Web site, maintained by an elder law attorney, has an informative list of estate planning links connecting you to many of the best estate-planning Web sites.
**WEB SITE:** www.estateplanninglinks.com

### Find a Lawyer

See page 219 for description

### Nolo Publishing

Nolo is the leading U.S. publisher of do-it-yourself legal solutions for consumers and small businesses. Nolo has an entire section on its Web site about wills and estate planning.
**PHONE:** (800) 728-3555  **WEB SITE:** www.nolo.com

## FINANCIAL NEWSPAPERS

### *Investor's Business Daily*® (IBD)

Packed with investment ideas, *Investor's Business Daily* is written specifically for the individual investor. The paper simplifies investing in the U.S. stock market and offers unique stock screens and ratings with a record for identifying market leaders as they emerge. IBD also offers investing classes (introducing its CANSLIM® Investing System) from around the country. IBD's companion Web site Investors.com offers stock tools and research for investors of every level. Print and online subscriptions are available.
**PHONE:** (800) 831-2525  **WEB SITE:** www.investors.com

### *Wall Street Journal*

The classic business newspaper is a must to stay in touch with the stock market, business trends, and news. The *Wall Street Journal* has practical and useful articles on the topic of personal finance. Print and online subscriptions are available.
**PHONE:** (800) 369-2834  **WEB SITE:** www.wsj.com

## FINANCIAL PAPERWORK ASSISTANCE

### AARP Grief-and-Loss Article/Publication Section

See page 165 for full description

### American Institute for Economic Research's *How to Avoid Financial Tangles*

*How to Avoid Financial Tangles* is a paperback book produced and sold by this private educational charitable organization. The book includes a section for widowed spouses about what they need to know about funeral and estate procedures.

PHONE: (413) 528-1216  WEB SITE: www.aier.org

## INSURANCE

Search the Web site under "Life Insurance Articles" for information on finding and collecting life insurance.

PHONE: (866) 533-0227  WEB SITE: www.insurance.com/Life.aspx

## FINDING SAFE DEPOSIT BOXES

### Unclaimed Assets

You can hire Unclaimed Assets to search for an unclaimed safe deposit box and learn on its Web site how to reclaim items after you find the box. A special report, "Unclaimed Safe Deposit Box Search," is also available. They can also search for other abandoned property or unclaimed funds.

WEB SITE: www.unclaimedassets.com

## GENERAL FINANCE/BUDGETING

### American Association of Retired Persons (AARP) Finance Guide

AARP's Finance Guide leads you through decisions surrounding debt, employers for people over age fifty, Social Security, reverse mortgages, credit reports, and Medicaid. See page 165 for full description of AARP.

PHONE: (888) 687-2277  WEB SITE: www.aarp.org/money

**Drenth, Tere.** *The Everything Budgeting Book: Practical Advice for Spending Less, Saving More, and Having More Money for the Things You Really Want.*
Avon, MA: Adams Media Corporation, 2003.

The *Everything Budgeting Book* teaches you how to analyze your spending patterns, cut expenses and budget efficiently. Sample worksheets are included.

**Kim, Sylvia S. *Personal Budgeting Kit.***
>   2nd ed. with CD-ROM. Bellingham, WA: Self-Counsel Press, 2005.

The *Personal Budgeting Kit* covers everything you want to know to plan a solid budgeting strategy. Sample worksheets are included.

**Sander, Peter J., and Jennifer Basye Sander. *The Pocket Idiot's Guide to Living on a Budget.***
>   New York: Alpha Books, 2005.

This smaller-sized budget book is especially helpful for people working through a life transition such as loss with substantial financial effects.

## GOVERNMENT WEB SITES

### Internal Revenue Service (IRS)

>   IRS booklet #559, "Information for Survivors, Executors, and Administrators," offers information about estate tax returns and survivor tax benefits.
>   PHONE: (800) 829-1040   WEB SITE: www.irs.gov

### Social Security Administration

>   The Social Security Administration document, "How Social Security Can Help You When a Family Member Dies" (SSA Pub No. 05-10008), explains possible social security benefits after a family member dies.
>   PHONE: (800) 772-1213   WEB SITE: www.ssa.gov/pubs/10008.html

### Veterans Benefits Administration

>   See page 168 for full description

## INVESTMENT COMPANIES

Each of the companies listed below offer different investment advisors, products, and benefits. Review *SmartMoney* **magazine's** (p. 224) latest annual broker survey and rankings to choose these companies or other investment firms for a financial advisor or company to manage investment accounts.

## Premium Brokers

### Charles Schwab
PHONE: (866) 232-9890  WEB SITE: www.charleschwab.com

### Fidelity Investments
PHONE: (800) FIDELITY  WEB SITE: www.fidelity.com

### Vanguard
PHONE: (877) 662-7447  WEB SITE: www.vanguard.com

## Full-Service Brokers

### Merrill Lynch
PHONE: (800) MERRILL  WEB SITE: www.merrilllynch.com

### Smith Barney
PHONE: local branch numbers on the Web site  WEB SITE: www.smithbarney.com

### Edward Jones
PHONE: local branch numbers on the Web site  WEB SITE: www.edwardjones.com

## Discount Brokers

### TradeKing
PHONE: (877) 495-5464  WEB SITE: www.tradeking.com

### Firsttrade
PHONE: (800) 869-8800  WEB SITE: www.firsttrade.com

### Optionsexpress
PHONE: (888) 280-8020  WEB SITE: www.optionsexpress.com

### T. Rowe Price
PHONE: (800) 541-6066  WEB SITE: www.troweprice.com

## INVESTMENT RESEARCH

### American Institute for Economic Research
Since 1933 this independent research organization has provided useful pamphlets and books on various aspects of personal finance and global economics. As a member you

can receive additional pamphlets at half price, twenty-two issues of the twice-monthly *Research Reports* (with combined issues in January and August) and twelve issues of the monthly *Economic Education Bulletin*. The publications are meaty reading but contain current interesting economic information. The organization has been noted in *Reason, Newsweek, Barron's*, the *Wall Street Journal*, and *Fortune*.

**PHONE:** (413) 528-1216  **WEB SITE:** www.aier.org

## CNN Money Personal Finance/Money Magazine

Extensive personal finance and market research is available on this Web site.

**WEB SITE:** www.money.cnn.com/pf/index.html

## *Consumer Reports*

*Consumer Reports*, published by a nonprofit organization, produces ad-free reports featuring unbiased and objective opinions on consumer products. The *Consumer Reports* publication(s) can be useful for newly widowed parents not used to making purchasing decisions on cars, financial products, home appliances, insurance, or computers and technology products. Easy-to-understand rankings and comparison charts make purchasing decisions easier. Both print and online subscriptions are available, as well as an annually updated paperback book that is a compilation of articles and reviews published previously in past *Consumer Reports*. Both the paperback book as well as the current issue of *Consumer Reports* magazine are available in bookstores. The newsletters *Consumer Reports Money Adviser*™ and *ConsumerReportsHealth.org*™ are also available from *Consumer Reports*.

**WEB SITE:** www.consumerreports.org

## Kiplinger's Personal Finance Magazine

This magazine offers you easy-to-understand advice for managing various aspects of personal finances.

**WEB SITE:** www.kiplinger.com

## Morningstar

This fee-based service provides independent market research on various financial investment options. Morningstar is well known for its star ranking system on mutual funds.

**WEB SITE:** www.morningstar.com

## *SmartMoney* Magazine

This *Wall Street Journal* magazine offers award-winning personal finance advice. Check out their helpful annual broker's rankings of premium, full-service, and discount brokers.

**WEB SITE:** www.smartmoney.com

**WEB SITE:** www.smartmoney.com/brokers/index.cfm?story=august2007

    (Annual Broker's Rankings)

### Yahoo! Finance

Use this Web site to research stock market investments, the latest news and financial opinions, and personal finance questions, and to monitor your own stock, bonds, mutual funds, currency, or ETF portfolios.

**WEB SITE:** http://finance.yahoo.com

## LOCATE LOST LIFE INSURANCE POLICIES, U. S. SAVINGS BONDS, TREASURY NOTES, OR SECURITIES

### Medical Information Bureau Policy Locator Service

If your parent bought life insurance after January 1, 1995, the MIB Policy Locator Service may be able to find the missing policy for a fee. MIB is an association of more than five hundred United States and Canadian life insurance companies.

**POLICY LOCATOR WEB SITE:** www.policylocator.com  **MIB WEB SITE:** www.mib.com

### Treasury Direct

On the Treasury Direct Web site, click on "Treasury Hunt" to find out if your deceased parent owned security savings bonds, registered treasury notes, or securities. You will need your deceased's parent's Social Security number for the search.

**PHONE:** (800) 722-2678  **WEB SITE:** www.treasurydirect.gov/tdhome.htm

## OFFICE SUPPLY STORES

The following national office-supply stores offer shredders, electronic software, and paper products for sale online or in retail stores:

### Discounted Office Supplies

**PHONE:** (866) 302-5397  **WEB SITE:** discountofficeitems.com

### Office Max

**PHONE:** (800) 283-7674  **WEB SITE:** www.officemax.com

### Office Depot

PHONE: (800) 463-3768  WEB SITE: www.officedepot.com

### Staples

PHONE: (800) 378-2753  WEB SITE: www.staples.com

## ORGANIZATIONS FOR FINANCIAL ADVISORS AND PLANNERS

### American Institute for CPAs

Search here for a local financial advisor with a CPA/PFS designation in the "Personal Financial Planning" section of the AICPA Web site.

WEB SITE: pfp.aicpa.org

### Financial Planning Association

Search here for a Certified Financial Planner by location and specialty.

WEB SITE: www.plannersearch.org

### National Association of Personal Financial Advisors

This association's members are fee-only comprehensive financial planners.

WEB SITE: www.napfa.org

## ORGANIZATIONS FOR INDIVIDUAL INVESTORS

### American Association of Individual Investors (AAII)

AAII, a thirty-year-old independent nonprofit organization, supports the individual investor with investment education and resources. AAII's goal is to empower individuals to become effective and confident managers of their own financial assets through education. With an annual membership, you receive a monthly journal containing model portfolios, stock screens, portfolio management tips, and investor guides, plus access to local chapter meetings, an investment conference every other year, and the investment-advice-packed Web site.

PHONE: (800) 428-2244  WEB SITE: www.aaii.com

### Better Investing

This nonprofit organization—established over fifty years ago—offers individual investors financial education and investment clubs through local and national resources.

WEB SITE: www.betterinvesting.org

## ORGANIZATIONS FOR WOMEN INVESTORS

### Women's Institute for a Secure Retirement (WISER)

WISER is one of the only United States nonprofit organizations dedicated to educating women to make better financial choices and prepare for a more financially sound retirement through workshops, seminars, newsletters, reports, fact sheets, consumer guides, and a Web site. WISER has well-written and useful fact sheets on money and investment basics, IRAs, social security, health, widowhood, and pensions. An online budget worksheet coaches you through building a new budget. The quarterly financial newsletter, *WISERwoman*, is also available.

PHONE: (202) 393-5452  WEB SITE: www.wiser.heinz.org

### Women's Institute for Financial Education (WIFE)

Since 1988, WIFE, a nonprofit organization, led by financial advisor Ginita Wall and financial planner Candace Bahr, assists women on how to take financial control of their lives after major life transitions such as divorce or widowhood. WIFE's Money Clubs are located all around the United States for women to meet in small groups and grow in their knowledge of financial issues.

PHONE: (760) 736-1660  WEB SITE: www.wife.org

## PROFESSIONAL ORGANIZERS

### Local AARP Office   See page 165 for full description

### National Association for Professional Organizers   See page 164 for full description

## REGULATORY AGENCIES

### Financial Industry Regulatory Authority

This nongovernmental regulatory agency protects investors by regulating securities firms. The association also provides investor education through their Web site.

WEB SITE: www.finra.org

### Securities and Exchange Commission

This government agency protects investors by regulating the securities markets. The commission also provides investor education through their Web site.

WEB SITE: www.sec.gov

## SENIOR DISCOUNTS

**Heilman, Joan Rattner.** *Unbelievably Good Deals and Great Adventures That You Absolutely Can't Get Unless You're over Fifty.*
New York: McGraw-Hill, 2006.
Now in its seventeenth edition, this book can provide your over-age-fifty parent with great cost-cutting ideas and travel deals. This is a fantastic book for widowed parents to get ideas on organizations to get involved in.

### Senior Discounts
You can search discounts for people age fifty and older by state on the Web site for a small annual fee.
**PHONE:** (800) 372-7513   **WEB SITE:** www.seniordiscounts.com

## TAXES

### American Association of Retired Persons (AARP) Tax-Aide
AARP Tax-Aide, run by volunteers, offers free tax consulting, tax preparation, and online tax assistance. See page 165 for full description of AARP.
**PHONE:** (888) 687-2277   **WEB SITE:** www.aarp.org/money/taxaide

### Internal Revenue Service (IRS)   See page 222 for description

## TRADITIONAL PERSONAL ASSISTANTS

### Craigslist
The community Web site started in Northern California's Bay Area became the Bay Area's trusted resource to find jobs, stuff for sale, or anything anyone needed in their communities. Craigslist communities are now available in most major cities in the United States and around the world. Search the Web site for part-time local personal assistants.
**WEB SITE:** www.craigslist.com

### Domestic Placement Network
The company places personal assistants all over the world. You can also search their "do-it-yourself" Web site to recruit household help.
**PHONE:** (877) 206-5262   **WEB SITE:** www.dpnonline.com
**WEB SITE:** Do-It-Yourself Household Help: www.estatejobs.com

## Help Company

If you or your parent lives in New York City or Los Angeles, contact the Help Company to find personal assistants.

**PHONE:** (888) 435-7880 **WEB SITE:** www.thehelpcompany.com

## International Association of Administrative Professionals (IAAP)

IAAP is a nonprofit professional organization for administrative professionals. IAAP has approximately forty thousand members and six hundred chapters worldwide.

**PHONE:** (816) 891-6600 extension 2239 **WEB SITE:** www.iaap-hq.org

## Lindquist Group

If you need top-notch domestic support, contact the Lindquist Group. They have offices in Manhattan; Greenwich, Connecticut; Palm Beach, Florida; Atlanta, Georgia; and London, England.

**PHONE:** see Web site for specific office phone numbers

**WEB SITE:** www.thelindquistgroup.com

## VIRTUAL ASSISTANTS

**AssistU**  See page 215 for full description

## International Virtual Assistants Association

The International Virtual Assistants Association is a nonprofit trade organization for professional education and development of virtual assistants (VA) worldwide and educating the public on the role and function of the virtual assistant. A VA is an independent entrepreneur who provides administrative, financial, creative, and/or technical assistance for an hourly rate. Use this organization's public membership directory to find qualified virtual assistants to research pressing issues or track down paperwork.

**PHONE:** (888) 259-2487 **WEB SITE:** www.ivaa.org

# TECHNOLOGY TIME-SAVERS

## AUTOMATED MONTHLY SHIPMENTS

### Drugstore.com

At drugstore.com, you or your parent can enroll for auto delivery of regular shipments on certain items to arrive every 30, 45, 60, 90, or 180 days. The cost for shipping on repeat automated orders is $1.99. Click on "Help" then go to "What is the drugstore.com Auto Delivery program?" under questions for a full explanation of how it works.

**WEB SITE:** www.drugstore.com/templates/browse/default.asp?catid=94256&trx=GFI
-0-EVGR-MCN&trxp1=151&trxp2=94256&trxp3=2&trxp4=RD

### Netgrocer

Netgrocer sells groceries, health and beauty products, natural and organic products, kosher products, and toys and it delivers to all fifty states. At Netgrocer you can arrange to receive recurring grocery orders through its Web site. Netgrocer uses FedEx but does not require a signature for deliveries.

**PHONE:** (888) 638-4762  **WEB SITE:** www.netgrocer.com

## COMPUTER LEARNING CLASSES

### GCF Global Learning

GCF Global Learning offers free online classes accessible twenty-four hours a day, seven days a week regarding computers and software programs such as Windows XP,

Office, and money-management basics.
WEB SITE: www.gcflearnfree.org

## CONSUMER TECHNOLOGY RESEARCH

***Consumer Reports***  See page 224 for full description

## FAX BY E-MAIL SERVICES

### Efax.com

Efax offers a fee-based fax via e-mail service. You receive a toll-free fax number and all faxes are routed to your e-mail inbox.
PHONE: (800) 958-2983  WEB SITE: www.efax.com

### Godaddy.com

Go Daddy is a Web site hosting company that offers its Fax Thru E-mail service for a fee. You receive a toll-free fax number and all faxes are routed to your e-mail inbox.
PHONE: (480) 505-8877  WEB SITE: www.godaddy.com

## FINANCIAL ORGANIZERS

### National Association of Professional Organizers (NAPO)

See page 164 for full description

## HOME ACCOUNTING SOFTWARE

### Quicken  See page 219 for full description

## LOCAL TECH SUPPORT

### Geek Squad

Available in the United States and Canada, the national chain has more than seven hundred locations with both freestanding Geek Squad retail stores and locations affiliated with the Best Buy electronics chain store. Check its Web site for the most current pricing.
PHONE: (800) 433-5778  WEB SITE: www.geeksquad.com

### Geeks on Time

Geeks on Time provides real-time support through remote assistance. You can see a tech person moving around on your computer desktop when they work on your own computer in real time. Check the Web site for the most current pricing.

PHONE: (800) 433-5766  WEB SITE: www.geeksontime.com

## ONLINE TECH SUPPORT

### Ask Dr. Tech

Ask Dr. Tech uses remote assistance software to solve your PC problems for a fee. Check the Web site for the most current per-incident, monthly, or annual fee pricing.

PHONE: (914) 729-6620  WEB SITE: www.askdrtech.com

### PC Pitstop

Try the Web site if you or your parent is brave enough to face a PC problem alone. PC Pitstop offers free tech assistance by posting a link on its forums or live twenty-four-hour-a-day-seven-days-a-week assistance for a monthly fee. Check the Web site for the most current pricing.

WEB SITE: www.pcpitstop.com

### PC Pinpoint

PC Pinpoint uses a three-step process through diagnostic tests to determine your PC problem. You choose to solve the diagnosed problem yourself or choose to hire one of their computer technicians (from U.S.–based call centers) to work with you through remote-control software. PC Pinpoint charges per incident or an annual fee. Check the Web site for the most current pricing.

PHONE: (888) 897-7887  WEB SITE: www.pcpinpoint.com

### PlumChoice

PlumChoice makes technology work for consumers right over the Internet, offering setup, training and ongoing maintenance and repair on products ranging from PCs, networks and printers to MP3 players, PDAs, digital cameras and more. PlumChoice's service options are priced from $24.95 and include PC diagnostics, spyware and virus removal, wireless network setup, software installation, and support on more than 370 software products. Its flexible options allow customers to schedule support twenty-four hours a day, seven days a week around their busy timetable—a unique feature that, combined with the expertise of its top-ranked technicians, helped PlumChoice win both the *Laptop Magazine* and *PC Magazine* 2007 Editor's Choice awards for online technical support companies. PlumChoice was also included on the exclusive "O List" in *O, The Oprah Magazine,* December 2007, for outstanding holiday gift ideas. PlumChoice service is available direct to consumers and through partners such as Circuit City, firedog and EarthLink. Check its Web site for the most current pricing.

**PHONE:** (888) 758-6435  **WEB SITE:** www.plumchoice.com

## PASSWORD MANAGEMENT

### A1RoboForm

Save your multiple user names, passwords, and personal information for filling out forms on the Internet with this free product.

**WEB SITE:** www.pcworld.com/downloads/file_description/0%2Cfid%2C6380%2C00.asp

### Any Password

Store you or your parent's online passwords on a computer in an encrypted form with this free program for easy access. Only one password is required.

**WEB SITE:** www.romanlab.com/apw/index.html

### Splash Data

Palm users can store passwords encrypted on your Palm using this fee-based software.

**WEB SITE:** www.splashdata.com/splashid/index.asp

## REMOTE-ACCESS SOFTWARE

The following companies sell remote-access software that allows you remote access a parent's computer (if your parent will allow you access, of course). GoToMyPC seems to be the top-ranked product according to *PC World*. Check Web sites for current pricing and free trials.

### Avvenu's Access 'n Share

Access 'n Share is remote-access software that allows access to your (or a parent's) computer through a cell phone, personal digital assistant, or another computer. Basic service is free and an annual fee is charged for guaranteeing files can be shared or accessed when your computer is off or you aren't online.

**PHONE:** (877) 665-4266  **WEB SITE:** www.avvenu.com/products/access_share.php

## GoToMyPC

GoToMyPC offers remote access to clients' computers from any computer or wireless device for a monthly or annual fee.

**PHONE:** (888) 259-3826  **WEB SITE:** www.gotomypc.com

## Mionet

Mionet is remote-access software that allows file sharing among multiple computers in distant locations for a monthly or annual fee.

**PHONE:** (650) 496-1000  **WEB SITE:** www.mionet.com

## WIRELESS COMPUTER SOLUTIONS FOR PARENTS

## Dana by AlphaSmart

If your parent needs a lower-cost, lightweight laptop, consider a Dana. The AlphaSmart word processor Dana is one-third the cost of a laptop and can be equipped with wireless capabilities. The Dana is easy to carry and weighs two pounds.

**PHONE:** (866) 558-8452  **WEB SITE:** www.alphasmart.com/products/dana-w_In.html

# MOVING FORWARD

## BOOKS

**Levy, Naomi.** *To Begin Again: The Journey toward Comfort, Strength, and Faith in Difficult Times.*
New York: Ballantine Books, 1999.
The national best-selling book, written by a rabbi who lost her father, covers the topics of grief and loss, what brings comfort during grief, how to rebuild life again, transformation after grief, prayer, and ritual.

## CDS

*Your Present: A Half-Hour of Peace.* CD-ROM. Relax . . .
Intuit L.L.C, 2000.
This relaxing award-winning CD fosters deep relaxation and reduces stress.
**PHONE:** (888) 669-7352 **WEB SITE:** www.relaxintuit.com/main.asp

## CELEBRATE MILESTONES

### Blue Mountain Free E-Cards
Send yourself, a family member, or your parent an e-card celebrating small successes.
**WEB SITE:** www.bluemountain.com

**Bolton, Martha.** *Wow! Celebrations for the Successes of Life* (Exclamation Series). New York: Howard Books, 2005.
Written by a former Bob Hope staffer and author of more than fifty books, *Wow!* offers lists and enjoyable stories about celebrating the successes of life.

**Gordon, Lynn, and Karen Johnson.** *52 Ways to Celebrate Life* (Deck series.) San Francisco: Chronicle Books, 2005.
The pack of small, whimsically illustrated inspirational cards (about the size of a deck of playing cards) suggests fifty-two ways to celebrate life.

## Hallmark Cards
Send anyone an e-card celebrating small successes.
WEB SITE: www.hallmark.com

## CLASSES

## Learning Annex
The Learning Annex, a continuing-adult-education company, offers a variety of classes at the introductory level on such topics as spirituality, business and career, finance and investing, meeting people, health and healing, and being your own boss. Classes are available in Los Angeles, Minneapolis, New York, San Diego, San Francisco, and Canada.
PHONE: Phone numbers for each location are listed on the Web site.
WEB SITE: www.learningannex.com/default.taf?bizunit=annex

## Shaw Guides
See page 210 for full description

## GRIEF RECOVERY PROGRAMS

## Grief ❣ Recovery Institute
Local Grief ❣ Recovery Specialists teach the twelve-week Grief ❣ Recovery Outreach Program in various cities. The outreach program teaches participants ways to recover from unfinished emotional business and loss and move toward a healthier emotional life. Call the main office for local Grief ❣ Recovery Specialist contacts.
PHONE: (818) 907-9600  WEB SITE: www.grief.net

## MAGAZINES

*Living with Loss Magazine: Hope and Healing for the Body, Mind, and Spirit*
Inspirational stories and resources for the bereaved and by the bereaved. Featuring the most respected and experienced educators, presenters, speakers, facilitators, authors, and writers in the field. Offering compassion and hope with the most current resources, tools and perspectives to cope with the diverse issues and concerns that make each grief journey unique. Published quarterly by Bereavement Publications, Inc. $32 per year.
PHONE: (888)604-4673 **Website:** www.livingwithloss.com

## SHORT-TERM THINKING

**Cushnir, Raphael, and Pornchai Mittongtare.** *How Now: 100 Ways to Celebrate the Present Moment.*
San Francisco: Chronicle Books, 2005.
*How Now,* written by a former Hollywood screenwriter and director, offers simple ideas and exercises to bring your focus into the present moment.

**Duncan, Shannon.** *Present Moment Awareness: A Simple, Step-by-Step Guide to Living in the Now.*
Novato, CA: New World Library, 2003.
*Present Moment Awareness,* written by a self-made young millionaire, offers insights, exercises, and questions to ponder about present-moment awareness.

**Smollin, Anne Bryan.** *Live, Laugh, and Be Blessed: Finding Humor and Holiness in Everyday Moments.*
Notre Dame, IN: Sorin Books, 2006.
*Live, Laugh, and Be Blessed* offers advice about creating a positive, light, and grateful attitude toward life.

**Tolle, Eckhart.** *The Power of Now: A Guide to Spiritual Enlightenment.*
1st U.S. printing. Novato, CA: New World Library, 1999.
The powerful book discusses the benefits of present-moment thinking.

**Tolle, Eckhart.** *The New Earth: Awakening to Your Life's Purpose.*
New York: Dutton, 2005.
The role of ego and your "pain body" are discussed in the book and how they hold back

success. Tolle also discusses concepts revolving around inner consciousness.

## SPEAKERS

### Achievement Radio

An Internet fee-based radio station, Achievement Radio broadcasts motivational and inspiring addresses by speakers who focus on self-improvement topics to members. **PHONE:** (303) 330-9402  **WEB SITE:** www.achievementradio.com

### GetMotivation.com

To review many motivational speakers and their products in one place, go this Web site. **WEB SITE:** getmotivation.com/lists.html

# HOLIDAYS AND ANNIVERSARIES

## BOOKS

**Smith, Harold Ivan.** *A Decembered Grief: Living with Loss while Others Are Celebrating.* Kansas City, MO: Beacon Hill Press, 1999.
This book, written from the Christian perspective, offers practical and simple advice through short chapters on how to approach the holidays and deal with difficult holiday situations.

**Wolfelt, Alan D.** *Healing Your Holiday Grief: 100 Practical Ideas for Blending Mourning and Celebration during the Holiday Season.* Fort Collins, CO: Companion Press, 2005.
This book, written by the director of the Center for Loss and Life Transition, offers grievers advice on a hundred various difficult issues surrounding loss and the holidays in a simple one-idea-per-page format.

**Zonnebelt, Susan J. and Robert C. De Vries.** *The Empty Chair: Handling Grief on Holidays and Special Occasions.* Grand Rapids, MI: Baker Books, 2001.
*The Empty Chair* was written by a psychologist and a minister who both lost spouses. This book, written from the Christian perspective, blends the authors' personal experiences with loss and the holidays with spiritual and psychological guidance.

## HOLIDAY TRAVEL IDEAS

### Biking Trips

#### Abercrombie and Kent

Since 1962 the U.S.–based travel company Abercrombie and Kent (A&K) has provided upscale trips around the world traveling by bike, private jet, cruise ship, trains, horse, and more. A&K offers trips all over the world for small groups.
**PHONE:** (800) 462-7016 **WEB SITE:** www.abercrombieandkent.com

#### Backroads

Started in 1979, Backroads is a travel company offering biking, hiking, and multisport trips all over the world. Small groups of travelers staying in upscale inns or camping are led by one to two trained leaders well-versed in the location. Backroads offers trips for singles, couples, and families at varying prices and time frames.
**PHONE:** (800) 462-2848 **WEB SITE:** www.backroads.com

#### Mikebentley.com

A comprehensive list of biking tour company Web site links.
**WEB SITE:** www.mikebentley.com/bike/tourcomp.htm

### Caribbean Vacations

#### *Caribbean Travel and Life* Magazine

The official Web site of *Caribbean Travel and Life* magazine provides Caribbean destination information on hotels, activities, articles, and travel specials.
**PHONE:** (800) 588-1689 **WEB SITE:** www.caribbeantravelmag.com

#### Caribbean Tourism Organization

The Caribbean Tourism Organization Web site advertises and books Caribbean airline flights and hotels. The Web site also includes things to do while on vacation and festivals and events.
**PHONE:** (212) 635-9530 **WEB SITE:** www.caribbeantravel.com/

#### Turquoise Net

Turquoise Net advertises Caribbean and Central America travel suppliers.
**WEB SITE:** www.turq.com

## Club Med

### Club Med Resort

Club Med's worldwide resorts are destination vacations for couples, families, history and cultural buffs, sports-focused people, and travelers interested in relaxing and rejuvenating. A Club Med package covers lodging, food, open bar, snacks (at certain times), and all activities during your stay at the resort.

**PHONE:** (800) 258-2633  **WEB SITE:** www.clubmed.us

## Cruises

### Cruise411.com

The Web site sells cruises from many large cruise ships, offers current cruise deals, and makes destination and port activity suggestions.

**PHONE:** (800) 553-7090  **WEB SITE:** www.cruise411.com

### Cruisemates.com

Cruisemates is known for its unbiased information on the cruising industry. The Web site allows you to read reviews and articles from past guests of cruises of interest. Cruisemates does accept advertising but does not sell cruises.

**WEB SITE:** www.cruisemates.com

## Family Vacations

### Familytravelnetwork.com

Known for its unbiased approach, the Web site aids families in planning vacations. The Family Travel Network does not sell vacations through its Web site.

**PHONE:** (703) 905-9858  **WEB SITE:** www.familytravelnetwork.com

### FamilyTravelFiles.com

FamilyTravelFiles.com offers extensive information and ideas for planning various (beach, reunion, adventure, etc.) family trips.

**PHONE:** (813) 968-4799  **WEB SITE:** www.familytravelfiles.com

### Mousesavers.com

For discount information on everything related to Disney, check out the Web site.

**WEB SITE:** www.mousesavers.com

## Themeparkinsider.com

To review ratings, safety, hotels, and rides for theme parks, visit the Web site written by theme-park consumers.

**PHONE:** (626) 376-7787 **WEB SITE:** www.themeparkinsider.com

# General Adventure Travel/Outdoors

## Gorp.com   See page 213 for description

## iexplore.com

iexplore is an award-winning online discount seller of adventure travel trips including biking, hiking, and multisport tours as well as culinary and cultural trips.

**PHONE:** (800) 439-7567 **WEB SITE:** www.iexplore.com

## Lindblad Expeditions

Since 1979 Lindblad Expeditions has taken an intimate group of travelers on small ships to hard-to-access destinations all over the world, such as Egypt, the Galapagos, the South Pacific, and Antarctica. The company provides a trained leader and naturalist on trips.

**PHONE:** (800) 397-3348 **WEB SITE:** www.expeditions.com

## Natural Habitat Adventures

The company focuses on nature-based group trips providing naturalist guides. Choose trips in Africa, Latin America, the Galapagos, and many more countries.

**PHONE:** (800) 543-8917 **WEB SITE:** www.nathab.com

## Trails.com

Trails.com, offering fee-based access to its Web site, is all about trails and providing trail maps to hikers for trips in the United States and Canada.

**PHONE:** (206) 286-0888 **WEB SITE:** www.trails.com

## Wilderness Travel.com

Offering more than a hundred trips all over the world, this travel company (operating since 1978) focuses on small-group trips that combine cultural, wildlife, and hiking activities.

**PHONE:** (800) 368-2794 **WEB SITE:** www.wildernesstravel.com

## Golf

### Travel Golf

The Web site, created by Golf Publisher Syndications, is all about golf. Travel Golf offers information on courses, golf packages, golf blogs, current golf deals, and a reader's forum.
**WEB SITE:** www.travelgolf.com

## Home Exchange

### Homeexchange.com

The company provides a fee-based service assisting people in exchanging homes for varying periods of time worldwide.
**PHONE:** (800) 877-8723  **WEB SITE:** www.homeexchange.com

## Hotels and Bed-and-Breakfasts

### BedandBreakfast.com

You can search worldwide for bed-and-breakfasts, country inns, guesthouses, lodges, cabins, guest ranches, and other quaint lodging options on this Web site. In addition the site hosts reviews of lodgings, a newsletter, and current lodging deals.
**PHONE:** (800) 462-2632  **WEB SITE:** www.bedandbreakfast.com

### Placestostay.com

Based in Ireland, the Web site is a worldwide hotel-booking service.
**PHONE:** 011 353 66 9792779  **WEB SITE:** www.placestostay.com

### Tripadvisor.com

This travel-community Web site, written by other travelers, offers more than ten million reviews of more than 270,000 hotels, travel attractions, and restaurants all over the world.
**PHONE:** (781) 444-1113  **WEB SITE:** www.tripadvisor.com

## Ranches

### Duderanch.org

Search for specific types of ranch vacations on the Dude Ranchers' Association Web site that represents over one hundred dude ranches.
**PHONE:** (866) 399-2339  **WEB SITE:** www.duderanch.org

### Ranchweb.com

Ranchweb.com is a Web site dedicated to providing information to travelers about dude ranches, fly-fishing ranches, working cattle ranches, or ranch resorts. On the Web site you can book vacations, review information on selecting a ranch, search through available ranch activities, read the blog, and check past guest reviews.

**PHONE:** (707) 939-3801  **WEB SITE:** www.ranchweb.com

## Rent a Home or Villa Worldwide

### 1st Choice Vacation Rentals

Since 1994 the vacation rental Web site has offered travelers homes, villas, condos, ski locations, and time-share rentals worldwide.

**PHONE:** (800) 343-2891  **WEB SITE:** www.choice1.com

### Aqvaliving

The company rents unique Greek properties on the islands of Mykonos, Santorini, Rhodes, Hydra, and Crete.

**PHONE:** 44 207 0606 244  **WEB SITE:** www.livinginternational.net

### Barclayweb.com

Since 1963, Barclay has offered apartments, cottages, and villas for rent all over the world. Additional travel needs, such as rental cars, rail passes, and rental cellular telephones, are also available.

**PHONE:** (800) 845-6636  **WEB SITE:** www.barclayweb.com

### Chez Vous

Search the Web site to find a rental apartment in Paris, France.

**PHONE:** (415) 331-2535  **WEB SITE:** www.chezvous.com

### Homeaway.com

Homeaway.com lists rental condos and homes around the world advertised by the properties' owners. VRBO.com, also owned by Homeaway, lists over ninety thousand rental condos and homes around the world advertised by the properties' owners.

**PHONE:** (512) 493-0382  **WEB SITE:** www.homeaway.com  **WEB SITE:** www.vrbo.com

### Rentvillas.com

Since 1984 Rent Villas rents villas in Italy, Spain, France, Greece, Great Britain, Portugal, and Turkey to travelers.

**PHONE:** (800) 726-6702  **WEB SITE:** www.rentvillas.com

## RV Trips

### Byways.org

Part of the National Scenic Byways Program run by the United States Department of Transportation, the Web site highlights byways in all the fifty states and offers information to assist travelers in planning trips.

PHONE: (800) 429-9297 (option 3)  WEB SITE: www.byways.org

### Gorving.com

The Web site, created by RV manufacturers, related businesses, and campgrounds, provides information about RV traveling, buying or renting an RV, and things to do while on the road.

WEB SITE: www.gorving.com

### Roadsideamerica.com

Roadside America is a Web site dedicated to alerting travelers to quirky tourist attractions all over the United States.

WEB SITE: www.roadsideamerica.com

## Spas

### Destination Spa Group

The Web site offers information on spas in the United States, Canada, Mexico, and Thailand sorted by vacation type you desire or spa name, country or state.

PHONE: (888) 772-4363  WEB SITE: www.destinationspagroup.com

### SpaFinder   See full description on page 213

### Spa Magazine

*Spa Magazine* provides articles, reviews, and ideas on worldwide spas.

PHONE: (805) 690-9850  WEB SITE: www.spamagazine.com

## Tennis

### Tennis Resorts Online

Check out this Web site, written by a seventeen-year ex–*Tennis Magazine* writer veteran, to review tennis resorts, camps, and vacations.

WEB SITE: www.tennisresortsonline.com

## MEMORIAL IDEAS

### Fundraisers.com

The Web site offers you a way to search for worthy causes of importance to your loved one or family for grievers to donate to in lieu of flowers.

**PHONE:** (818) 482-9016  **WEB SITE:** www.fundraisers.com/causes/index.html

### Memory-Of   See description on page 168

### Personalized Memorial

You can post a memorial Web site, photos, and thoughts of a loved one through this Web site.

**WEB SITE:** www.personalizedmemorial.com

### *Scrapbooking* Magazine

The *Scrapbooking* magazine Web site offers many ideas for creating a scrapbook of memories, one type of memorial for a loved one.

**PHONE:** (760) 929-7090  **WEB SITE:** www.scrapbooking.com

### Team in Training

Train with Team in Training to run or walk a half marathon, marathon, or triathlons or bike the one-hundred-mile century bike ride to raise money for leukemia, lymphoma, and myeloma research.

**PHONE:** (800) 955-4572  **WEB SITE:** www.teamintraining.org

# MOVING MOM OR DAD

## BOOKS

**Miller, Judith. *Antiques Price Guide 2007.***
New York: DK Adult, 2006.
Updated annually, the book offers recent appraisal values and market trends for sellers of porcelain, glass, furniture, jewelry, textiles, and silverware, among other fine arts, all explained by a leading antiques expert.

**Morse, Sarah, and Donna Quinn Robbins. *Moving Mom and Dad: The Stress-Free Guide to Helping Seniors Move.***
Petaluma, CA: Lanier Press, 1998.
*Moving Mom & Dad*, written by the owner of Ultimate Moves (a senior transition specialist moving company based in Northern California), the book offers in-depth information to assist a parent with moving decisions including housing options, how to avoid problems in moving, and a cost worksheet.
**WEB SITE:** www.ultimatemoves.net

**Nagy, Mim. *The Complete Guidebook to the Business of Tag and Estate Sales.***
Spiral ed. North Ridgeville, OH: TLC Tag Sale Service & Pub. Co., 2002.
*The Complete Guidebook to the Business of Tag and Estate Sales,* covers every question you could imagine about with tag and estate sales and is written by a licensed antiques and collectibles appraiser.

**Perdigo, Cathy, and Sonia Weiss.** *The Pocket Idiot's Guide to Garage and Yard Sales.*
New York: Alpha, 2003.
*The Pocket Idiot's Guide to Garage and Yard Sales* spells out everything you need to know about hosting a garage or yard sale.

**Simmons, Sylvia.** *The Great Garage Sale Book: How to Run a Garage, Tag, Attic, Barn, or Yard Sale.*
New York: Backinprint, 2000.
*The Great Garage Sale Book,* written by a former advertising executive and experienced garage-sale holder, covers everything you need to know to have a successful garage sale.

**Walsh, Peter.** *How to Organize Just about Everything.*
See page 218 for full description

## DONATIONS

### Justgive.org

Justgive.org connects people with charitable organizations interested in donations of furniture and clothing, computers, cars, cell phones, pet supplies, or eyeglasses. The link offers a list of organizations and their particular donation needs.
**PHONE:** (866) 587-8448  **WEB SITE:** www.justgive.org

### Turbo Tax ItsDeductible

This free online program allows you to track individual donations—such as furniture, household goods, sporting goods, appliances, electronics, or clothing among others—to create the highest possible tax deduction. The program creates accurate values for donations based on current research from resale outlets and ebay.
**WEB SITE:** http://turbotax.intuit.com/tax-preparation/itsdeductible.jhtml

## ESTATE SALES/GARAGE SALES

### EBay

Ebay, an international online auction marketplace, provides an easy-to-understand e-commerce Web site where you can sell goods and services.
**WEB SITE:** www.ebay.com

### EHow: "How to Plan a Successful Estate Sale"

The step-by-step article on ehow.com explains how to do anything related to planning a successful estate sale.

**WEB SITE:** www.ehow.com/how_137449_successful-estate-sale.html

### Estate Sales

The companies listed on the Web site sell estate belongings for a fee.

**PHONE:** (888) 653-8468

**WEB SITE:** www.estatesales.net/estate-sale-companies/default.aspx

### PacKing.com

This company offers extensive packing supplies for all types of moves. You can fill out online forms to receive moving, packing, truck rental, or storage quotes from moving suppliers.

**PHONE:** (954) 742-4885    **WEB SITE:** www.pacKing.com

## HOME IMPROVEMENT

### Angie's List

The Web site offers referrals to home services, auto, pet, and entertainment companies that have competently served 600,000 homeowners in 124 major cities who are members of Angie's List. The Web site also posts reviews of vendors who have served Angie's List members. The Web site can be a great resource when moving Mom or Dad to a new retirement community where he or she doesn't have a list of local services.

**PHONE:** Check Web site for local Angie's list number    **WEB SITE:** www.angieslist.com

## MAGAZINES

### *AARP The Magazine*

*AARP The Magazine* is the official magazine of the American Association of Retired Persons (AARP). The magazine has articles that assist people with over-fifty lifestyle issues. Location Scout, available on the *AARP The Magazine* Web site, narrows your parent's retirement choices when he or she answers a questionnaire about retirement preferences. The magazine also is available in Spanish. See page 165 for full description of AARP.

**WEB SITE:** www.aarpmagazine.org    **WEB SITE:** http://web02.bestplaces.net/aarp/ls

### *Where to Retire* Magazine

*Where to Retire* highlights various retirement locations every month and gives information on cost of living, housing, and activities in each area.

**PHONE:** (713) 974-6903 **WEB SITE:** www.wheretoretire.com

## MOVING COMPANIES AND ESTATE ORGANIZERS

### Budget

Budget, a moving company, rents vans of various sizes, dollies, and packing supplies for local and cross-country moves to do-it-yourselfers.

**PHONE:** (800) 527-0700 **WEB SITE:** www.budget.com

### Door To Door

Door To Door brings self-storage containers to the client, the client fills them, and Door To Door transports them to the client's destination, where the client unpacks the container.

**PHONE:** (888) 505-3667 **WEB SITE:** www.doortodoor.com

### Exit Stage Right®

This estate-organizing company works closely as the agent of the estate administrator to organize the contents, information, and records of the home for the estate administrator to review. The owner of Exit Stage Right is a professional organizer with fifteen years of experience and has trained eighty other professional organizers around the country to work as professional estate organizers. Check under "Resources" on her Web site to locate a trained estate organizer in your area.

**PHONE:** (650) 493-3948 **WEB SITE:** www.exitstageright.com

### Moving Solutions

The national franchise company specializes in senior relocations. Moving Solutions is currently available in Connecticut, Delaware, Florida, New Jersey, New York, Pennsylvania, and South Carolina.

**PHONE:** (610) 853-4300 **WEB SITE:** www.movingsolutions.com

### National Association of Senior Move Managers

NASMM provides Senior Moving Managers all over the United States. Those managers assist older adults and their families with the emotional and physical aspects of relocation.

**PHONE:** (877) 606-2766 **WEB SITE:** www.nasmm.com

## PODS

PODS brings portable storage containers to clients' homes or offices to pack themselves. After a PODS container is packed, a PODS transport truck collects the container and delivers it to the destination of the client's request. The service is available in the United States, Canada, and Australia.

PHONE: (866) 229-4120  WEB SITE: www.pods.com

## U-Haul

U-Haul, a moving company, rents trailers and vans of various sizes, dollies, and packing supplies for local and cross-country moves to do-it-yourselfers.

PHONE: (800) 468-4285  WEB SITE: www.uhaul.com

## Ultimate Moves

The San Francisco company specializes in moving seniors and has facilitated more than 3,500 families relocations over the last sixteen years. The owner of Ultimate Moves, Donna Robbins, is the coauthor (with Sarah Morse) of the book *Moving Mom and Dad: The Stress-Free Guide to Helping Seniors Move.*

PHONE: (510) 703-7476  WEB SITE: www.ultimatemoves.net

## ORGANIZERS/STAGERS

### National Association of Professional Organizers (NAPO)

See page 164 for full description

### The International Association of Home Staging Professionals

You can search the Web site to find local home-staging professionals.

PHONE: (925) 686-2413  WEB SITE: www.iahsp.com/index.php

## PERSONAL-PROPERTY APPRAISERS

### Antiques Roadshow

The hit PBS television show Web site offers a searchable auction house and appraiser database.

WEB SITE: www.pbs.org/wgbh/pages/roadshow

### Appraisers Association of America

The Web site for the nonprofit association representing personal-property appraisers allows you to search online for a local appraiser member.

**PHONE:** (212) 889-5404 x 11  **WEB SITE:** www.appraisersassoc.org

## International Society of Appraisers

If you need to locate a certified and accredited personal-property appraiser, search on this Web site.

**PHONE:** (206) 241-0359  **WEB SITE:** www.isa-appraisers.org/ISA_form.html

## RECYCLING RESOURCES

## Earth 911

Search here to find a local recycling center that accepts specific recyclable supplies, such as automotive, household, lawn and garden, and electronics, if you are cleaning out a house.

**WEB SITE:** www.1800cleanup.org

## My Green Electronics

Search their database to find local electronic recycling drop-off programs for cell phones, computers, fax machines, printers, televisions, VCRs, and many other types of electronics.

**WEB SITE:** www.mygreenelectronics.org

## RETIREMENT COMMUNITIES

## Care Pathways

If your widowed parent is in need of assisted living, this Web site offers assistance in finding living arrangements for aging parents. The site was created by registered nurses.

**PHONE:** (877) 521-9987  **WEB SITE:** www.carepathways.com

## Retirement Living Information Center

The Web site is a general resource for finding information about senior retirement living. The Retirement Living Information Center includes information on taxes in each state, top places to retire, and new retirement communities. For a fee your parent can join and receive a personal online guide to guide him or her through retirement options based on interests, including two hundred locations in thirty-three states. The Web site also includes a list of many online senior publications.

**PHONE:** (203) 938-0417  **WEB SITE:** www.retirementliving.com

## SELLING THE HOME

**Carey, Bill, Chantal Howell Carey, and Suzanne Kiffmann.** *How to Sell Your Home without a Broker.*

Hoboken, NJ: John Wiley & Sons, Inc., 2004.

*How to Sell Your Home without a Broker* assists homeowners when they sell their homes without a real estate broker. Worksheets and contracts are provided.

### For Sale by Owner

The Web site assists property owners who sell their homes without a real estate broker.

**PHONE:** (888) 367-7253  **WEB SITE:** www.forsalebyowner.com

### Homes by Owner

The Web site provides information for sellers who sell their home without a real estate broker.

**WEB SITE:** www.homesbyowner.com

### National Association of Realtors

NAR is the national association of residential and commercial real estate agents given the designation Realtor. This designation requires adherence to a code of ethics and standard of practice and continuation of professional real estate classes for continuing development.

**PHONE:** (800) 874-6500  **WEB SITE:** www.realtor.org

**Nichole, Piper.** *The For Sale By Owner Handbook: FSBO FAQs: From Pricing Your Home Right and Increasing Its Curb Appeal to Negotiating the Contract and Hassle-Free Closing.*

Franklin Lakes, NJ: Career Press, 2005.

*The For Sale By Owner Handbook* describes how to tackle home-selling issues such as listing price, advertising, pictures, open houses, qualifying buyers, contracts, negotiating, and home inspections, among other home selling topics, without a real estate agent.

### Senior Residential Specialist Real Estate Agent

Realtors who are recognized as Senior Residential Specialists are trained specifically to serve seniors and their relocation needs.

**PHONE:** (800) 500-4564  **WEB SITE:** www.seniorsrealestate.com/sarec/index.jsp

# CHANGES IN FAMILY DYNAMICS

## COPING WITH CHANGE

**Adrienne, Carol.** *When Life Changes or You Wish It Would: A Guide to Finding Your Next Step Despite Fear, Obstacles, or Confusion.*
Reprint ed. New York: Harper Paperbacks, 2003.
*When Life Changes or You Wish It Would,* written by the coauthor of the *Celestine Prophecy,* discusses the cycles of change and how to trust those cycles. The book also discusses how to adapt a more adventurous and positive attitude.

**Deits, Bob.** *Life after Loss: A Personal Guide Dealing with Death, Divorce, Job Change and Relocation.*
3rd ed. Cambridge, MA: Fisher Books, 1999.
*Life after Loss,* written by pastor with twenty-five years of grief-support-group and counseling experience, assists readers with advice about intense feelings after loss, including a chapter on sudden loss versus prolonged loss.

**Perlitz, Cheryl.** *Soaring through Setbacks: Rise above Adversity . . . Reclaim Your Life.*
Hilton Head Island, SC: Cameo, 2004.
*Soaring through Setbacks* offers survival tactics to juggle change.
**WEB SITE:** soarwithme.com/products.html

**Yager, Jan.** *When Friendship Hurts: How to Deal with Friends Who Betray, Abandon, or Wound You.*
New York: Fireside, 2002.

Written by a sociologist expert on friendships, this book walks you through twenty-one types of negative friends and how to recognize them, why friendships go sour, and how to repair or end friendships.

## FAMILY DYNAMICS

**Becvar, Dorothy S.** *In the Presence of Grief: Helping Family Members Resolve Death, Dying, and Bereavement Issues.*
New York: Guilford Press, 2003.
*In the Presence of Grief* covers common problems, issues, and concerns of surviving family members.

**Converse, Linda J.** *She Loved Me, She Loved Me Not: Adult Parent Loss After a Conflicted Relationship.*
Bloomington, IN: 1st Books Library, 2001.
If you lost a parent with whom you had a difficult relationship, the book offers ideas and tools to resolve old feelings.

**Lerner, Harriet.** *The Dance of Connection: How to Talk to Someone When You're Mad, Hurt, Scared, Frustrated, Insulted, Betrayed, or Desperate.*
Reprint ed. New York: Quill, 2002.
Lerner explores the best ways to repair broken relationships and your own hurt, and includes personal stories.

**Levang, Elizabeth.** *When Men Grieve: Why Men Grieve Differently and How You Can Help.*
See page 171 for full description

**McGoldrick. Monica and Froma Walsh.** *Living Beyond Loss: Death in the Family.*
2nd ed. New York: W. W. Norton & Company, 2004.
A classic book on family dynamics examines the effect of death on families and offers therapeutic guidelines for improvement. The book discusses spirituality, traumatic deaths, and stigmatized losses, and well-known family therapists tell their own stories of loss and its effects.

### Sandwich Generation
The Web site offers information and seminars about elder parent issues.
**WEB SITE:** www.sandwichgeneration.com

## LIVING SPACES

**Ingham, Vicki, and HGTV.** *Six Steps to Design on a Dime.*
Knoxville, TN: HGTV, 2006.
The book explains six steps that create great designs on a $1,000 budget.

**Tincher-Durik, Amy, and HGTV.** *Design on a Dime: Achieve High Style on a $1,000 Budget.* Knoxville, TN: HGTV, 2003.
The book shows twenty-one transformations with budgets under $1000.

**Wong, Angi MA.** *Feng Shui Do's and Taboos: A Guide to What to Place Where.*
Palos Verdes Estates, CA: Pacific Heritage Books, 1999.
Angi MA Wong, a top feng-shui expert, gives advice about rearranging rooms in you or your parent's home to release blocked energy. Wong has been featured on *Oprah, CBS Morning News*, CNN, and in the *New York Times, Wall Street Journal*, and *USA Today*, among many other top media outlets.
**WEB SITE:** www.fengshuilady.com

## NATURAL HEALTH REMEDIES

**Balch, Phyllis A.** *Prescription for Nutritional Healing: A Practical A-to-Z Reference to Drug-Free Remedies Using Vitamins, Minerals, Herbs & Food Supplements .*
New York: Avery, 2006.
This natural-health bible offers in-depth descriptions of ailments and diseases as well as nutritional supplement suggestions on a wide variety of health topics.

**Chopra, Deepak.** *Perfect Health: The Complete Mind/Body Guide by Deepak Chopra,* M.D. New York: Harmony, 2001.
Deepak Chopra's book is worth reading if only to take the test to see what foods might better match your body type (and that of family members) according to Ayurveda (Indian traditional medical approaches). Chopra discusses Pranayama breathing to reduce stress and lower anxiety and the morning sun salute to flex the body, start the day, and remember yourself.

**Weil, Andrew.** *Natural Health, Natural Medicine: The Complete Guide to Wellness and Self-Care for Optimum Health.* Boston: Houghton Mifflin, 2004.
Dr. Weil's book on natural cures includes preventative home remedy treatments, resources, and tips for various ailments

# COMMUNITY

## EDUCATIONAL OPPORTUNITIES

### Adult Education/Continuing Education Centers

**Learning Annex**  See page 236 for full description

## COMMUNITY RETIREMENT CENTERS

### NC Center for Creative Retirement

Located in Asheville, North Carolina, the center opened in 1988 and offers a Paths to Creative Retirement workshop three times a year that costs $750. This life-transition program helps people evaluate the possibilities of the next step in creating a new life in retirement. The average age of attendees is fifty-seven years old. The NC Center also offers the Creative Retirement Exploration Weekend. This workshop discusses the pros and cons of relocating to a new host community.

**PHONE:** (828) 251-6140 (Asheville, NC)  **WEB SITE:** www.unca.edu/ncccr

## UNIVERSITIES OFFERING SENIOR DISCOUNTS

Encourage your parent to check his or her local universities for their senior discount offerings on classes. This list is just a few of the universities offering discounts:

### Boston University Evergreen Program

The Boston University Evergreen program allows community members over the age of fifty-eight to audit a class for fifty dollars a course and hear lectures and seminars by Boston University faculty for a small fee. When a community member registers to be an Evergreen sponsor and pays $300 a year, he or she can take classes and hear lectures and seminars for free.

**PHONE:** (617) 353-9852 (Boston, MA)  **WEB SITE:** www.bu.edu/evergreen

### Georgia Tech

If your parent is sixty-two years of age or older, he or she can apply to the university to sit in on classes, and pay only a nominal administrative charge (if space is available).

**PHONE:** (404) 894-4154 (Atlanta, GA)

**WEB SITE:** www.admiss.gatech.edu/62orolderprogram

### Princeton University

Princeton University offers the Princeton Community Auditing Program to community members. The program allows community members to sit in on regular undergraduate course lectures for a nominal semester fee. (The fee is waived in some alumni, docent, faculty, staff, and related-family cases).

**PHONE:** (609) 258-0202 (Princeton, NJ)

**WEB SITE:** http://web.princeton.edu/sites/pucsa/auditing.htm

### Rutgers

If your parent is sixty-two years of age or older, he or she can take classes at no cost, if space is available, on a noncredit basis.

**PHONE:** (732) 932-7823 (ext. 682) (New Brunswick, NJ)

**WEB SITE:** http://ur.rutgers.edu/community/senior.shtml

### University of Colorado at Boulder

If your parent is fifty-five years old or older, he or she can sit in on any daytime class at the university tuition-free. Attendees pay a nominal administrative charge.

**PHONE:** (800) 492-7743 (Boulder, CO)  **WEB SITE:** www.cualum.org/seniorauditor

### University of Denver

If your parent is sixty years of age or older, he or she can audit certain undergraduate classes for twenty-five dollars a course.

**PHONE:** (303) 871-2360 (Denver, CO)

**WEB SITE:** www.du.edu/specpro/additional-programs/senior-audit-program

## University of Minnesota Rochester

The University of Minnesota allows seniors sixty-two years of age and older to audit college credit classes for free if space is available. Seniors can also register for credit on the second day of registration. The cost is nine dollars a credit.

**PHONE:** (800) 947-0117 (Rochester, MN)

**WEB SITE:** www.r.umn.edu/07_student_services-senior_citizen.htm

## University of Nevada, Las Vegas

The University of Nevada allows seniors who are United States citizens, age sixty-two or over, and who have lived in Nevada for twelve consecutive months to take classes for free during fall and spring semesters if space is available. In the summers, seniors pay 50 percent of the tuition. Participants can audit the classes or take them for credit.

**PHONE:** (702) 895-2933 (Las Vegas, NV)

**WEB SITE:** http://seniorprograms.unlv.edu/academic_62plus.html

## University of Virginia

The University of Virginia waives fees and tuition for auditing classes if space is available for seniors over the age of sixty living in the Virginia community for twelve consecutive months. Seniors can enroll in three classes a semester.

**PHONE:** (434) 982-3200 (Charlottesville, VA)

**WEB SITE:** www.virginia.edu/registrar/records/98gradrec/chapter2/gchap2-1.15.html

# GROUP TRAVEL

## Biking/Hiking/Adventure Travel

### Abercrombie and Kent   See page 240 for description

### Backroads   See page 240 for description

### Specialty Travel Index

The Web site supplies you with links to four hundred adventure-tour operators who arrange special-interest trips from chocolate tours to llama packing trips. They also offer a biannual magazine for a small fee.

**PHONE:** (888) 624-4030   **WEB SITE:** www.specialtytravel.com

### 50-Plus Expeditions

50-Plus arranges adventure trips for people over the age of fifty who aren't into typical group tours. Trips go from Antarctica to the Amazon jungle.

**PHONE:** (866) 318-5050  **WEB SITE:** www.50plusexpeditions.com

## Book Your Own Group

### Groople.com

The Web site books cruises, air, train, and car trips for groups, especially weddings, family, alumni, sports, military, or religious groups.

**PHONE:** (888) 447-6675  **WEB SITE:** www.groople.com/hotels/Default.aspx

## Faith-Based Trips

### Adventures in Missions

The company offers coeducational and single-gender mission trips.

**PHONE:** (800) 881-2461  **WEB SITE:** www.adventures.org/a/adults/index.asp

### Globus Journeys/Religious Travel

"Travel the Lands of Faith Tours" are religious group trips offered by Globus Journeys. Twenty tours visit twenty different countries including the Lands of the Bible, Lands of Catholic Faith, Lands of Jewish Heritage, and Lands of Protestant Christianity.

**PHONE:** (800) 541-3788  **WEB SITE:** www.religioustravel.com

### World Mission Tours

World Mission Tours is a thirty-six-year-old travel company that specializes in Christian travel.

**PHONE:** (800) 225-7401  **WEB SITE:** www.womito.com

## Hobby Group Vacations

### Shaw Guides

The Web site lists both group and individual travel opportunities to take art classes, cooking schools, golf or tennis clinics, photography, or language classes in the United States and abroad.

**PHONE:** (212) 799-6464  **WEB SITE:** www.shawguides.com

### Learning Group Vacations

#### Elderhostel

Elderhostel offers affordable learning vacations for people fifty-five years of age or older from Key West to South Africa.

**PHONE:** (800) 454-5768  **WEB SITE:** www.elderhostel.org

### Men's Group Travel

#### Mancations

The Web site offers men's group travel vacation ideas such as golf packages, NASCAR trips, tailgating trips, houseboat trips, backpack trips, and fishing trips. Read the Mancations blog about men's group travel for more ideas.

**PHONE:** (916) 359-7700  **WEB SITE:** www.mancations.com

### RV Groups

#### RVUSA.com

A comprehensive guide to RV clubs and groups.

**PHONE:** (800) 709-3240  **WEB SITE:** www.rvusa.com/clubs.asp#national

### Spas

#### Canyon Ranch

Canyon Ranch, a high-end wellness center, offers healthy lifestyle living with education, workout classes, and fresh low-fat food in a group setting on vacation in Tucson, Arizona, and the Berkshire Mountains of Massachusetts. Vacationers are surrounded by others in workshops, exercise classes, and dining areas.

**PHONE:** (800) 742-9000  **WEB SITE:** www.canyonranch.com

#### SpaFinder

Destination spas offer a way for a newly widowed parent to travel alone but be surrounded by others at the same time.

See page 213 for full description

#### *Spa Magazine*

*Spa Magazine* provides spa articles, reviews, and ideas on spas around the world. Reviews can give your parent an idea if the spa caters to singles, couples, or groups.

**PHONE:** (805) 690-9850  **WEB SITE:** www.spamagazine.com

### Women's Group Travel

### Gordon's Guide

Gordon's Guide offers a list of various women's-trip tour operators.

WEB SITE: womens-travel.gordonsguide.com

### Gutsy Women Travel

If Mom is your widowed parent, the company offers female group trips all over the world that includes a tour manager or local escort. Trip types vary from adventure, fine homes, gourmet dining, mind-body-spirit, and music and the arts, among others.

PHONE: (866) 464-8879   WEB SITE: www.gutsywomentravel.com

### SWT Tours

The Web site lists trips for senior women (fifty or over) who want to travel, no matter if they are single, divorced, or married with a mate who doesn't enjoy travel.

PHONE: (917) 880-6732   WEB SITE: www.poshnosh.com/swt/index.htm

### Transitions Abroad

The Transitions Abroad Web site links to a list of extensive women's group travel companies.

WEB SITE: www.transitionsabroad.com/listings/travel/women/websiteswomenclubs.shtml

## JOBS IN RETIREMENT

## AARP Best Employers for Workers Over 50 List

The AARP Best Employers for Workers Over 50 list shows whom AARP supports as the best companies to work if you are a mature worker over the age of fifty. See page 165 for full description of AARP.

WEB SITE: www.aarp.org/money/careers/employerresourcecenter/bestemployers

## Experience Works

Experience Works helps low-income seniors gain job skills needed to receive a job offer.

PHONE: (866) 397-9757   WEB SITE: www.experienceworks.org

**Heilman, Joan Rattner. *Unbelievably Good Deals and Great Adventures That You Absolutely Can't Get Unless You're over Fifty. McGraw-Hill, 2006.***

See page 228 for full description

## Retired Brains

Use the Web site to connect a retired widowed parent to part-time, full-time, and volunteer opportunities. Retired Brains also provides information for seniors.

WEB SITE: www.retiredbrains.com

## Retirement Jobs

The Web site connects hiring companies with job-seeking older workers. The service is free to job seekers. The Web site offers assistance with resumés, relevant articles, stories of other retirements, and dream jobs.

PHONE: (781) 235-1329 (option 2)  WEB SITE: www.retirementjobs.com

## Senior Community Service Employment Program

The AARP-sponsored program offers job assistance, training, and support to low-income workers fifty-five years of age and over. The program has seventy-eight offices in twenty-two states.

PHONE: see web site for specific local phone numbers

WEB SITE: www.aarp.org/money/careers/findingajob/jobseekers

## Senior Service America

Your parent can use the Web site to find a job or volunteer opportunities if he or she is fifty-five years old or older.

PHONE: (301) 578-8900  WEB SITE: www.seniorserviceamerica.org

## Seniors for Hire

Connect widowed parents ages fifty and over to available jobs through the Web site.

PHONE: (714) 848-0996  WEB SITE: www.seniors4hire.org

## Silver Staffing

An Atlanta-based company, Silver Staffing places workers more than fifty years of age in temporary and permanent jobs.

PHONE: (404) 252-4088  WEB SITE: www.silverstaffing.com

**Stone, Marika and Howard.** *Too Young to Retire: 101 Ways to Start the Rest of Your Life.*
1st ed. Waterville, ME: Thorndike Press, 2004.

*Too Young to Retire,* written by a couple who chose a nontraditional retirement, offers insight and ideas into a variety of retirement options.

WEB SITE: www.2young2retire.com

## Vocation Vacations

Before your parent goes back to school or work, encourage him or her to try out a dream job first. Your parent can choose from jobs such as private investigator to dog trainer to pastry chef and many more.

**PHONE:** (866) 888-6329   **WEB SITE:** www.vocationvacations.com

## Workforce 50

If your parent is over the age of fifty, have your parent check out Workforce 50 for part-time, full-time, temporary work, or volunteer opportunities in his or her community. There is also an area to post a resumé.

**WEB SITE:** www.workforce50.com

## ONLINE COMMUNITIES FOR OLDER SINGLES/DATING

**Culbreth, Judsen.** *The Boomers Guide to Online Dating.*
Emmaus, PA: Rodale Books, 2005.
Judsen Culbreth, the editor-in-chief of *Working Mother* and executive editor of Redbook, updates the thirty-five-plus-aged woman about the best ways to find dates online.

## Eharmony.com

Eharmony, created by a clinical psychologist, uses a scientific approach to match individuals with its Compatibility Matching System to connect potential mates.

**WEB SITE:** www.eharmony.com

**Helgoe, Laurie A.** *Boomer's Guide to Dating (Again).*
Reissue ed. New York: Alpha Books, 2004.
Laurie A. Helgoe, a clinical psychologist, offers advice for baby boomers about how to reenter the dating arena in midlife.

## Match.com

Match.com is an online dating Web site. When you join, you fill out a profile and have the option to post a picture. After you register, you receive e-mails from interested potential dates and contact those who interest you. A monthly fee is charged for the service.

**WEB SITE:** www.match.com

## Meetup.com

An online social networking Web site, Meetup.com connects people with specific inter-

ests with each other to meet up as a group in their local community. Some of the current interests that have created local groups include books, politics, specific dog breeds, knitting, poker, travel, faith, and newcomers who have recently moved to a community.
**WEB SITE:** www.meetup.com

## VOLUNTEERING

### Senior Corps

The Senior Corps, part of Corporation for National and Community Service and a federal agency, unites people over the age of fifty-five with volunteer opportunities using their skills. The Foster Grandparent Program joins seniors over the age of sixty with children with varying needs. The Senior Companion Program offers people age sixty or older to assist the elderly with daily tasks. RSVP is a program to connect volunteers past the age of fifty-five with tasks in the community matching their skills and interests.
**PHONE:** (202) 606-5000  **WEB SITE:** www.seniorcorps.gov

### VolunteerMatch

The organization, supported by various foundations, connects volunteers with service opportunities in local communities.
**PHONE:** (415) 241-6872  **WEB SITE:** www.volunteermatch.org

# LEGAL CONCERNS AND DIRECTIVES

## HEALTHCARE DIRECTIVES AND PROXIES

**Carlson, Lisa.** *Caring for the Dead: Your Final Act of Love.*
Hinesburg, VT: Upper Access Books, 1998.
*Caring for the Dead,* written by the executive director of the Funeral and Memorial Societies of America, provides an overview of death and funeral issues along with specific state requirements and laws that surround death and funeral practices.

**Irving, Shae, ed.** *Nolo's Encyclopedia of Everyday Law: Answers to Your Most Frequently Asked Legal Questions.*
6th ed. Berkeley, CA: Nolo Publishing, 2005.
Nolo publishes legal guides on various legal topics and revises those guides with new law changes. The particular legal reference book covers many issues with regard to wills and estate planning—including wills, probate, executors, living trusts, estate and gift taxes, funeral planning, and body and organ donations. The book also provides information on healthcare directives, including durable power of attorney and conservatorships.

### National Hospice and Palliative Care Organization's Caring Connections
The Web site allows free access to view and download all fifty U.S. states' advance healthcare directives and instructions for each state.
**WEB SITE:** www.caringinfo.org

## Quicken WillMaker Plus 2008 by Nolo

If you or your parent need to create legal documents, the software program allows you to create a will, living trust, healthcare directive with healthcare power of attorney, financial powers of attorney, and executor documents, among others. The software costs between thirty-nine and forty-nine dollars depending on if you require the CDs or are able to download the product.

**WEB SITE:** www.nolo.com/product.cfm/objectID/6E9ED903-C9B4-42E0-9C2E2 35DD87A0A8A/309/

## United States Living Will Registry

The Web site stores an electronic version of a person's living will or healthcare proxy or both and makes all documents available to healthcare providers or family members when requested. The service can be valuable when you or your parent has to travel to out-of-state hospitals for emergency treatment or gets sick when you or your parent travels internationally.

**WEB SITE:** www.uslivingwillregistry.com/faq.shtm

## WILLS

## AARP's "Worksheet for Your Will"

"Worksheet for Your Will" is a simple worksheet to guide you when you assemble all of your important assets and wishes on paper before you craft a formal will. See page 165 for full description of AARP.

**WEB SITE:** www.aarp.org/families/end_life/a2003-12-04-endoflife-will.html

**Irving, Shae, ed.** *Nolo's Encyclopedia of Everyday Law: Answers to Your Most Frequently Asked Legal Questions.*

6th ed. Berkeley, CA: Nolo Publishing, 2005.

See description on page 266

**Palermo, Michael T.** *AARP Crash Course in Estate Planning: The Essential Guide to Wills, Trusts, and Your Personal Legacy.*

New York: AARP Books and Sterling Publishing, 2005.

*AARP Crash Course in Estate Planning,* written by an AARP's legal specialist and certified financial planner, covers many topics and questions about estate planning, including trusts and wills.

**Quicken WillMaker Plus 2008.** CD-ROM.
Berkeley, CA: Nolo Publishing, 2007.
See description on page 267

**Randolph, Mary. "Make a Will"**
The online article on Nolo Publishing's Web site, written by an attorney, provides a step-by-step process of considerations to make prior to writing a will.
**WEB SITE:** www.nolo.com/article.cfm/objectID/C7217F40-D912-490A-920D6C7C 3B29FDDC/catId/FD1795A9-8049-422C-9087838F86A2BC2B/309/CHK

## PRENUPTIAL AGREEMENTS FOR REMARRIAGE

**Choudhri, Nihara K.** *What to Do Before the I Do: The Modern Couple's Guide to Marriage, Money, and Prenups.*
Naperville, IL: Sphinx Publishing, 2004.
Written by a graduate of Columbia Law School and the author of *The Complete Guide to Divorce Law*, the book reviews marital and financial questions your widowed parent should ask before he or she walks down the aisle again.

**Dublin, Arlene.** *Prenups for Lovers: A Romantic Guide to Prenuptial Agreements.*
New York: Villard, 2001
*Prenups for Lovers*, written by a family law attorney, covers the reasons to have a prenuptial agreement, how to create a prenuptial agreement, and unique situations, such as same-gender relationships, lovers in business together, marriages created later in life, and cohabitation relationships.

**Stoner, Katherine E., Irving and Shae Irving,** *Prenuptial Agreements: How to Write a Fair and Lasting Contract.*
2nd ed. Berkeley, CA: Nolo Publishing, 2005.
*Prenuptial Agreements*, written by attorneys, offers legal information about prenuptial agreements. The book helps your parent decide if a prenuptial agreement is needed for a serious relationship and what additional financial information to include in a prenuptial agreement draft. Additionally *Prenuptial Agreements* provides sample worksheets and sample prenuptial agreements to review.

# EPILOGUE

As you assist a newly widowed parent, you will test your patience, stamina, boundaries, and faith while you juggle your own life. New roles, responsibilities, or hard choices surface daily, which disrupt your comfortable habits and schedules. As you join new support groups or try new holiday routines, you may feel jolted by all the changes. If you sign a caregiver contract, you test family relationships and trust. You may lose income or job security if you reduce your work schedule. If your parent must sell your childhood home, strong emotions may brew. Changes occurring after the loss of a parent create stress and can affect your health if you don't take care of yourself. If you will reach out for help from others, you will preserve your own well-being.

As you move forward during the transition after loss, new choices and hard decisions present themselves. You can choose to see them as difficulties, problems, opportunities for growth and positive change, or ways to connect with others. The trick to survival is reaching out to others for help. When you ask for assistance, many people receive great joy when they lend a hand. As you encounter new choices or tasks, use the more than five hundred resources in this book to assist you. When you use the many resources available to you, God can work through others to provide you with solutions. You are not alone.

As you work through issues with your newly widowed parent, preserve your boundaries. You can easily forget about yourself when you have many tasks to complete. No matter if you take a walk, sip a cup of coffee, or a talk with a friend, when you preserve your own time and honor your own needs, you keep your own life intact for when you return to it after your family duties lessen. Celebrate your small successes and milestones day by day.

One day the extra duties will end. Over time you and your widowed parent will look back and see the many benefits of your journey where you worked together and with others to provide life-changing solutions. I wish for you great blessings, comfort, and many extended hands reaching out to you and your widowed parent as you both step out on your own unique journeys after loss.

# A WORD TO READERS

## FROM CAROLINE HAVERKAMPF
(Jamieson's widowed mother)

*The Effects of My Husband's Death*

I never would have imagined that my world—my existence as I knew it—would be shattered and torn apart in one horrifying instant when a doctor said, "Your husband has non-Hodgkin's lymphoma." For a minute I could not breathe and the ground seemed to give way underneath me. I thought, *Is this really happening to us?*

Eleven months later, my daughters' and my lives had changed in one instant with my husband's death in hospice. The day he died, my world as I knew it left with him. I was not part of a couple anymore. I was the first widow in my group of friends. I was fifty-six years old—the average age for widows today.

Suddenly alone, I was living an extrovert's nightmare intensified by the previous year of isolation imposed by my husband's illness. I was now known and referred to as a *widow*. My social life shifted as the former couples we socialized with stopped calling and offering invitations. My reality turned into unchartered territory. I couldn't find another widow in my age range who had also lost her husband and survived the transition who could shepherd me through the journey. I reached out to newly divorced friends but quickly realized we struggled with very different loss issues. Each day I felt as if I was walking through my life in a surreal fog—my former expectations of retirement with my husband surrounded by my children and grandchildren were shattered.

The first few years after his death, I found it difficult to stay in the present as my mind floated back to a past I could not fix or change. I had been a daily caregiver to my husband during his cancer, and after his death I found it difficult to focus on my own self-care and health. Without my two daughters' support and guidance, I would not have known where to begin. As I grieved my husband's death, I realized a large part of me died with him.

Many changes happened during the months and years following his death. I changed my holiday traditions so that I wasn't constantly reminded of my loss.

Nine months after my husband's death, I moved to a larger city with more social, educational, and cultural activities for single women. The most difficult part of my new life was only having one person to do the work two people used to do. I was unfamiliar with many of the financial tasks my husband did for many years. It has taken me years to feel comfortable with many of these financial responsibilities. Somehow my husband's death left all of us without our previous support network, and we would have to build a new network over time. In hindsight I wish all of us—Jamieson, Ivy, and myself—had been given resources to find good grief counseling and support groups before, during and after my husband's death.

After the funeral, my daughters helped me pour through my husband's financial records and assisted me with organizing the next steps. I was glad not to have to organize everything myself or meet alone with our estate attorney. In a sense, my daughters put their lives on hold to help their father and mother. I am very grateful for their previous and continued support.

## My Life Now

A lot of people ask me if I regret the way we handled things after my husband died. I don't. I only regret not having more access to available resources to assist with the many crucial tasks and decisions. I believe we did the best we could with what we knew at the time.

I force myself every day to focus on how my gifts and experience can help others. In 2005 I walked a half marathon to raise money in my husband's name for the Leukemia & Lymphoma Society and cancer research. I prayed I could finish the race and marveled at the generosity of my contributors. In addition I now use my gifts and experiences to help others through various volunteering organizations in Atlanta.

Since my husband's death, I have grown and pushed myself through involvement in many different activities and groups. I renovated rental properties with my daughters and took classes in investments, real estate, Spanish, and Chinese at a local university's adult-continuing-education program. I developed an interest in spirituality, joined a local women's Bible study group, and now regularly attend church services. I went on a yoga retreat and learned about meditation. I explored retirement communities. My most recent endeavor is my pursuit of a master's degree and then a PhD in holistic nutrition. My most important activity every day is to get out of the house.

The holidays are always challenging. My children and I always try to do something different since the holidays never felt the same after my husband's death. We have found volunteering and mixing with other families during the holidays diverts the focus off ourselves and our loss and invites in new friends and memories.

As I continue to talk to more married women my age about widowhood, I rarely meet women who have created a "plan B" for their life in case they are widowed. More often I speak with married women my age who have no idea what they would do if their husband dies before they do.

I look back at the beginnings of my widowhood and know that my daughters' encouragement and resourcefulness enabled me to make great personal progress as a newly single woman in the world. Although the transition through widowhood hasn't been easy, I can see a new foundation firming underneath me—filled with new friends, spirituality, and interests. I know my husband would have been so proud to know our suffering resulted in a resource book to help other families in a similar situation.

If you are a new widow or widower, I can't imagine how the loss of your spouse has affected your life. You may hear different widow or widower "rules" of what you should and should not do and when is the appropriate time for different things. Do what feels right to you. The right decision is different for everyone. My best advice is to find a supportive community, ask for help, eat nutritious foods, get lots of rest, and rent before you decide to move. I wish you wise guidance for healing your grief; an expansive circle of comforting friends, family and resources; and a future filled with hopeful new memories.


Caroline Haverkampf

# APPENDIX A

# SAMPLE OBITUARIES

If you are faced with writing an obituary for your deceased parent, or helping your surviving parent with this daunting task, the following samples may help you prepare this significant tribute to your parent.

## OBITUARY SAMPLE #1: FEMALE ACADEMIC

Dr. Chelsea King, a cognitive-development psychology professor at the University of California (UC) Berkeley for 20 years, died suddenly Tuesday in a car accident. She was 59.

Dr. King thrived on Berkeley's campus with her students. A successfully published author of many books in the field of cognitive development, Dr. King juggled teaching, writing and speaking in the local Northern California community. An avid hiker and self-taught watercolor artist, Dr. King valued curiosity, environmental protection and time with her family.

Dr. King enjoyed volunteering at the University of California San Francisco (UCSF) Children's Hospital and various environmental organizations. Born and raised in London, England, she earned a bachelor's degree from Oxford University and her master's degree and Ph.D. in cognitive development from UC Berkeley.

Dr. King received worldwide respect for her work, including the American Psychological Association's Distinguished Scientific Contribution Award and a

Guggenheim Fellowship. She also served as president of the Association for Psychological Science and as an advisory board member of the University of California San Francisco Children's Hospital and was a large contributor to the Northern California Environmental Grassroots Fund.

In lieu of flowers, the family requests that donations be made to the Center for a Livable Future (www.jhsph.edu/clf) or UCSF Children's Hospital (www.ucsfhealth.org/childrens/index.html).

Dr. King is survived by her husband of fifteen years, Simon, and their adopted daughter, Ju Ling. She is also survived by her parents, Eleanor and Clive Ward of Portland, Oregon, and her sister, Louisa Taylor, of New York, New York. Dr. King's memorial service will be held this week in Berkeley followed by a private funeral in Portland. For more information contact the Berkeley Student Affairs or the Central London Funeral Home located at 25-27 Beetle Street, London, AP8 1RJ, United Kingdom. Phone: 44 10 3429 9845.

## OBITUARY SAMPLE #2: SUCCESSFUL LAWYER

Davidson Higgs IV, a partner of the Boston law firm Higgs Patterson and Wagner, passed away Saturday from liver cancer. He was 65.

During the last 25 years of his life, Mr. Higgs built his successful law firm, which specialized in intellectual property in the Boston area. He believed in boldness, determination and risk. Mr. Higgs enjoyed mentoring his firm's young rising stars, contributing to the Boys and Girls Club of Boston, and volunteering legal aid to various Boston community organizations.

Born and raised in Dallas, Texas, Mr. Higgs earned a bachelor's degree from Southern Methodist University and his law degree at Yale University. Mr. Higgs graduated summa cum laude from Yale Law School and was highly involved with the Jerome N. Frank Legal Services Organization at Yale.

Mr. Higgs received frequent requests to be a keynote speaker at various local universities and intellectual-property law seminars because he served as past president of the Boston Bar Association and became an active member of the Massachusetts Bar Association. The American Intellectual Property Law Association elected him vice president of its organization in 1994.

In lieu of flowers, the family requests that donations be made to the American Cancer Society by mail. Checks can be sent to the American Cancer Society, P.O. Box 22718, Oklahoma City, Oklahoma, 73123-1718 or see www.cancer.org for further donation options. The Higgs family chose the American Cancer Society to fund research on liver cancer.

Mr. Higgs is survived by his wife of 35 years, Connie, and their three sons, Jack, Davidson and Taylor. He is also survived by his parents, Betty and Davidson Higgs III. Davidson's memorial service will be held this week in Dallas. For more information contact the Legacy Funeral Home in Dallas, Texas.

## OBITUARY SAMPLE #3: A FULL, GOOD, ORDINARY LIFE

Donatella H. Fiorelli passed away peacefully in her sleep on January 2, 2000, after an energetic, passionate and rich 95 years of life. "Dona" and her predeceased husband Vincent Fiorelli shared a cherished lifetime of loving memories.

With a love of music and community service, Dona also gave back to her Brooklyn community. She was a piano teacher and singer as a young adult and taught piano throughout her marriage. A keyboard enthusiast and songstress, she loved teaching children, sharing her passion for instruments and songs.

She is survived by her two daughters, Marguerite Ottavio and Nicoletta Gambino of New York, New York. Mrs. Fiorelli is also survived by four grandchildren, Vinni Ottavio, Isabella Ottavio, Marcella Gambino and Alfonso Gambino, and two great-grandchildren, Raffaella and Sofia, who brought her much joy. Mrs. Fiorelli had a full life with many supportive friends and a large extended family.

A funeral mass is scheduled for 12:00 p.m. Monday, January 7, 2000, at St. Andrew the Apostle Roman Catholic Church in Brooklyn. Immediately following the funeral mass, burial ceremonies will occur at Hillside Memorial Park in Brooklyn. A reception at Mrs. Fiorelli's home will follow, hosted by family and friends. Please call the Valentina Funeral Home in Brooklyn for viewing times and additional details.

# LEGAL CONCERNS AND DIRECTIVES

Preparing in advance for the legalities related to healthcare and the end of life will make decisions for your loved ones much simpler when the time comes. In addition, some legal concerns may become paramount following death or when a surviving parent may decide to remarry. All of these concerns can be proactively considered by following these suggestions.

## HEALTHCARE DIRECTIVES AND PROXIES

Emergencies, diseases, or unexpected events happen. Such events can catch you and your family off guard and have horrific consequences. You need to be prepared ahead of time to avoid additional difficulty when an unexpected death or accident happens and a loved one becomes incapacitated or incompetent. Two documents will provide you and your family some security and comfort for those times, a healthcare proxy also called a healthcare directive, and a living will.

### Healthcare Proxy: Healthcare Directive or Advance Healthcare Directive

A healthcare proxy is a written document, also called a medical power of attorney, that allows an appointed person to have the legal authority to make decisions about your medical care when you become unable to make your own decisions. A healthcare proxy is usually included with a living will. When you have a written healthcare proxy, your appointed proxy can stop a court or hospital from making decisions on your behalf.

## Living Will

When written before sickness occurs, a living will allows you to decide your preference of treatments to be conducted or not administered if and when you become ill or experience an accident. A living will describes a person's considerations and wishes if he or she becomes incapacitated in various ways, including situations such as dementia, a vegetative state, terminal condition, or coma. A living will spells out if you want to be on artificial life support, artificially receive food and water, and receive care for pain management. A healthcare proxy, also called a healthcare directive, can be included in a living will as well. When you draft two separate legal documents, you can change one or the other when needed, and this strategy reduces legal costs.

Different states limit medical care and choices. United States government Web sites outline different state's rules and provide electronic documents to review. Also check the **Caring Connection** Web site (p. 266) from the National Hospice and Palliative Care Organization to find out more about each state's specific laws with regard to living wills and healthcare proxy. Encourage your parent to register his or her will or healthcare proxy with the **U.S. Living Will Registry** (p. 267) to create easy access in emergencies.

After you create these documents, make photocopies and give them to close friends and family members who might be involved in your healthcare. Keep the originals in a safe, accessible place. If you place them in a safe deposit box, make sure your designated proxy has access.

## Resources and Options

For more information on living wills, healthcare directives, and wills, consult *Nolo's Encyclopedia of Everyday Law* (p. 266) and **Quicken WillMaker Plus** software (p. 267). For additional healthcare directive and proxy resources, see Part III: Resources. Create a living will and healthcare proxy in case of an emergency. When the documents are needed, patients and their loved ones both benefit.

## THE IMPORTANCE OF WILLS

Wills provide two major benefits: (1) they make death easier on your family members by avoiding probate, and (2) they give direction for estate distributions as you wished. Without a will, the laws of the state you live in determine how your estate is distributed. You must create a will and keep the information within the will current—such as beneficiaries on insurance policies and investment portfolios. When you create a will and keep the document safely stored, you invite peace of mind.

## The Benefits of a Will

A will is a written document that expresses your unique wishes on how various aspects of your estate will be distributed to beneficiaries upon your death. When you write a will, ponder and address the following important issues:

* Delineate your valuable assets.
* Set your beneficiary or beneficiaries.
* Exclude any particular family members you want to exclude.
* Specify the desired division of possessions, cash, stocks, bonds, real estate, or other assets to a beneficiary or beneficiaries.
* Assign guardians for young children.
* Assign an executor of your estate.
* Donate assets or cash to charities.
* Specify the desired division of fine art, furniture, jewelry, or collectibles to a beneficiary or beneficiaries.
* Clarify instructions on how to handle your business if you are self-employed.
* Handle other specific details.

## If You Die without a Will

If you die without a will, or "intestate," difficulties arise and your estate holdings may not be distributed as you wish. During probate—the legal proceedings to settle an estate of a deceased person—state law determines the way an estate is distributed. If you die without a will, the state courts determine a beneficiary or beneficiaries according to the laws where you lived.

## Keep Your Will Current

You must update your will whenever a family change occurs, including divorce, death, new sons-in-law or daughters-in-law, adoption, a change in a child's marriage status, births, or when you move to a different state. Make sure you update your will's beneficiary or beneficiaries—as well as their contact information—on life insurance policies and investment portfolios regularly.

After you take the time to create a will, make photocopies and keep the original in a safe and accessible place. If you place them in a safe deposit box, make sure your executor has access and a key. One choice for safekeeping your will is to keep the original on file with your attorney.

 ## Resources and Options

No matter what assets are owned, both you and your parent should create a will. If you have accumulated no property or substantial items yet, any monies in banks will be needed for a surviving spouse. Without a will on file, bank accounts may be frozen and the courts will determine who gets what. Encourage your parent to work through the **AARP "Worksheet for Your Will"** (p. 267) if he or she has not created a will. Read the online article **"Make a Will"** (p. 268) on the Nolo Publishing Web site or read the book *AARP Crash Course in Estate Planning: The Essential Guide to Wills, Trusts, and Your Personal Legacy* (p. 267). For additional will resources, see Part III: Resources.

If you change your will every few years or when a family change occurs, you will keep your will current with your latest intentions and create easy access to accounts when needed. When you write a will and put the document in a safe place, you experience peace of mind, and you give that piece of mind to your spouse and family at the time of your death as well.

## PRENUPTIAL AGREEMENT FOR REMARRIAGE

Falling in love is easy but staying in love proves harder. Unfortunately not all relationships last. Because of this fact, prior to remarrying, many widows or widowers create prenuptial agreements, or "prenups," to protect assets and financial interests built prior to the pending marriage in case the new marriage fails. Without a prenuptial agreement, state laws determine the fate of assets in the event of a divorce or death of a spouse.

## What Is a Prenuptial Agreement?

A prenuptial agreement is a written agreement between two people prior to marriage. A typical prenuptial agreement lists the assets and liabilities of each person and defines what his or her property rights will be if the marriage dissolves or one of the couple dies.

When someone dies who has a will and a prenuptial agreement, a current will trumps a prenuptial agreement, although a will could refer to the prenuptial agreement for details. If a will is older and a newer prenuptial agreement exists, the prenuptial agreement may be used successfully in probate court to declare the will invalid. Attorneys who specialize in those matters have good legal knowledge about such matters and can make legal recommendations about specific issues related to prenuptial agreements and wills and occurrences when they coexist.

## Who Needs a Prenuptial Agreement?

In the past, Hollywood celebrities and the rich and famous seemed to be the only people who needed prenuptial agreements because of their obvious wealth and assets. Nowadays everyday people prepare prenuptial agreements, especially for second or third marriages, when people want to protect assets for children from previous marriages. Prenuptial agreements are also useful for future spouses to define the financial responsibilities of each person during as well as after the marriage. If either person has debts to repay, a prenuptial agreement can define the terms of repayment and who is responsible.

## What if I Decide Not to Have a Prenuptial Agreement?

If a person decides not to have a prenuptial agreement when he or she remarries, state laws may decide who owns the assets accumulated during a marriage. Upon a person's death or divorce, if a prenuptial agreement was not created, state laws will decide the fate of the assets. Additionally, without a prenuptial agreement, state law can determine what happens to property accumulated prior to a second or third marriage.

## Resources and Options

If you or your parent write your own prenuptial agreement, use two attorneys from separate firms—one for the bride and one for the groom—to review the document and make sure it meets state laws where the couple plans to live. A good book to review and discuss with your widowed parent and potential mate is ***Prenuptial Agreements: How to Write a Fair and Lasting Contract*** (p. 268) produced by the legal publisher, Nolo Publishing. Additional books about prenuptial agreements are listed in Part III: Resources. When you or your parent write a prenuptial agreement, think about the following questions:

- Do I have valuable property acquired prior to my current relationship, including real estate, jewelry, antiques, stocks, a business, partnerships, etc.?
- Do I anticipate earning future royalties or income from work accomplished prior to the marriage?
- If my marriage fails, will I offer to pay alimony? How much alimony will I offer to pay and for how long?
- Do I own property I wish to leave to my children upon my death?
- Do I want alimony if the marriage fails?
- Does my future husband or wife have any debts?
- What other financial assets do I want to protect for myself or my children from previous relationships?

Suggest a prenuptial agreement to your widowed parent before he or she walks down the aisle again. Prenuptial agreements prevent financial tugs-of-war because they protect assets, establish financial boundaries, and avoid expensive disagreements if the relationship fails. Many books and resources are available to assist you or your parent when you write your own prenup. If you or your parent chooses to write a prenuptial agreement, hire an attorney to review the final draft to ensure protection and meet local state requirements.

If your parent owns assets, the decision to protect them with a prenuptial agreement is smart. This document protects a parent's assets, if only, perhaps, for his or her children's best interests. Without a prenuptial agreement, the state laws where your parent lives will determine who acquires what property, and the state's decision may not be what your parent wished. Review the resources provided and have your widowed parent talk to his or her future spouse to see what works best. We can all hope the relationship flourishes and the document will not be needed, but better to have one than to be sorry later.

# WORKSHEETS

## GENERAL PAPERWORK TO GATHER WORKSHEET

In the days, weeks, and months following your parent's death, many decisions will need to be made about funeral arrangements, finances, and other paperwork. You will help your widowed parent deal with these issues more easily by gathering the following list of documents.

- ☐ 10–15 certified copies of death certificates
- ☐ Any stocks or bond certificates of the deceased
- ☐ Bank statements of the deceased
- ☐ Car registration(s) and title(s) owned by the deceased
- ☐ Credit cards of the deceased
- ☐ Current bills of the deceased
- ☐ Deeds and titles to property of deceased
- ☐ Health insurance of the deceased
- ☐ If military, discharge papers or VA claim number of the deceased
- ☐ Life insurance policy number(s) and policy or policies of deceased
- ☐ Marriage and birth certificate of deceased
- ☐ Mortgage papers of the deceased
- ☐ Passwords to online accounts of the deceased
- ☐ Recent income tax forms and W2 forms of the deceased
- ☐ Social Security card of deceased
- ☐ Social Security records of deceased
- ☐ Wills or trusts of the deceased

## SAMPLE FILING CATEGORIES WORKSHEET

If you or your widowed parent needs to reorganize household and personal paper-work, the following list of sample filing categories may be useful:

**Automobile**
- Car loan
- Gas
- Maintenance

**Bank Charges**

**Childcare**

**Clothing**
- Dry cleaning
- Purchases
- Repairs

**Donations and Charities**

**Education**
- Books
- Student loan
- Tuition

**Food**
- Dining out
- Groceries

**Gifts**
- To others
- To yourself

**Healthcare**
- Dentist
- Hospital
- Optometrist
- Physician
- Prescriptions

**Household**
- Cable
- Electricity
- Garbage and recycling
- Homeowner association dues
- Home phone
- Cell phone
- Housecleaning service
- Mortgage
- Natural gas/oil
- Office supplies
- Internet service
- Repairs
- Supplies
- Water and sewer
- Yard service

**Income**
- Employee
- Other
- Self-employed

**Insurance**
- Car insurance
- Disability insurance
- Homeowner's or renter's insurance
- Health insurance
- Life insurance
- Long-term healthcare
- Liability umbrella policy

**Leisure**
- Books
- CDs and DVDs
- Cultural events
- Entertaining
- Movie rentals
- Sporting events
- Sporting goods
- Toys/games
- Vacations

**Memberships**
- Clubs
- Groups/associations
- Health club

**Miscellaneous Bills**
- Postage and shipping

**Pets**
- Food
- Health insurance
- Toys and treats
- Veterinarian

**Professional Services**
- Attorney
- CPA

**Subscriptions**
- Magazines
- Newsletters
- Newspapers

**Taxes**
- Current year
- Last six years' returns

## 12 STEPS TO A MOVE WORKSHEET

Making a move in the months, even years, following the death of a spouse is a huge decision, often filled with many emotional challenges. Once your parent has made the decision to move, help them undertake this major task by following these twelve steps:

☐ Decide if your parent will hire a real estate agent or sell the home "by owner."

☐ Decide if your parent wants to hire organizational help through a senior move manager or estate organizer.

☐ Plan an appropriate and realistic moving schedule.

☐ Identify what items will move with your parent.

☐ Identify what items will be given to family members.

☐ Decide what to do with remaining items.
- Sell at garage/estate sale.
- Donate.
  + Call nonprofits to arrange pickup or drop-off of donated items.
  + Track donations.
- Hire personal-property appraiser to assess items value.
- Hire liquidator to sell price and sell items.

☐ Decide if parent will hire movers to pack and move the contents of the home.
- Decide how car(s) will be transported to the new home.
- Gather packing supplies and arrange for portable storage containers (if needed) if your parent wants to pack themselves.
  + Hand pack delicate or valuable items yourself.
  + Arrange for cases of water for moving day to be available.

☐ Create workable schedule to clean out the home.
- Coordinate with professionals, friends, or family members.
- Start with easier rooms first.
- Reward yourself for progress with breaks, walks, food, or phone calls to friends.

☐ Research local approved recycling facilities to discard toxic products.
- Recycle old paint cans.
- Recycle metal items.
- Recycle computer equipment.

☐ Merge, purge, and automate paper files and bills with parent.
- Create new mobile file system for move.

☐ Make arrangements for moving day.
- Arrange daycare for pets on moving day.
- Print out driving directions to new home.

☐ Arrange for assistance at new home location.
- Make sure assistance is available at the new home if no moving company is hired.
- Arrange for water and food to be available at the new home.

## NEW FAMILY JOBS WORKSHEET

The list below shows six roles or jobs typically needed to support a newly widowed parent, all of which can be divided among friends and family. Use the list as a starting point to share support roles in the family.

### 1. Finances
- ☐ Bills and accounting _____
- ☐ Budgets_____
- ☐ Investments _____
- ☐ Tax prep coaching _____

### 2. Legal
- ☐ Estate planning_____
- ☐ Settling the estate _____

### 3. Local Issues (person lives near parent)

### 4. Moving/Real Estate Coordinator
- ☐ Donations_____
- ☐ Mortgage _____
- ☐ Packing and coordinating cleaning out the home

_____

### 5. Organizing and Paperwork
- ☐ Files _____
- ☐ Finding outside assistance _____
- ☐ Systems_____

### 6. Technology Support
- ☐ Purchases _____
- ☐ Ongoing maintenance and issues_____

## COMMUNITY EXTRA-HANDS WORKSHEET

When your widowed parent moves to a new area, the following worksheet will be helpful in developing a list of needs for him or her in order to begin building a community of "extra hands" for various tasks.

### Community
- ☐ Local Chamber of Commerce (business referrals) _____
- ☐ Local travel groups _____
- ☐ Senior work opportunities _____
- ☐ Senior volunteering opportunities _____
- ☐ Singles groups for people fifty years old or older _____
- ☐ Travel agent_____

### Finances
- ☐ CPA_____
- ☐ Financial planner (specialist in widows and widower issues) _____
- ☐ Money manager _____
- ☐ Trust company _____

### Funeral and Memorial Service
- ☐ Chef or caterer _____
- ☐ Event planner _____
- ☐ Florist _____
- ☐ Funeral director _____

### Household
- ☐ Appliance repair _____
- ☐ Air-conditioning or heater maintenance _____
- ☐ Automotive mechanic_____
- ☐ Charitable donations pickup service _____
- ☐ Computer recycling service _____
- ☐ Dentist _____
- ☐ Doctors _____
- ☐ Electrician _____
- ☐ Errand runner_____

- ☐ Handyman _____
- ☐ Gardener and landscaping company _____
- ☐ Grocery and takeout food delivery _____
- ☐ Housekeeper/cleaning service _____
- ☐ Locksmith _____
- ☐ Movie delivery service _____
- ☐ Personal shopper _____
- ☐ Pet daycare _____
- ☐ Pet sitter and pet walker _____
- ☐ Pizza delivery _____
- ☐ Plumber _____
- ☐ Toxic materials pickup service _____

## Moving

- ☐ Moving company _____
- ☐ Realtor _____
- ☐ Senior moving specialist and organizer _____

## Paperwork

- ☐ Bookkeeper _____
- ☐ Estate attorney _____
- ☐ Personal assistant and virtual assistant _____
- ☐ Professional organizer _____

## Support

- ☐ AARP local office _____
- ☐ Therapist or grief counselor _____
- ☐ Local spousal loss support groups _____
- ☐ Psychologist _____
- ☐ Spiritual advisors (rabbi, priest, minister) _____
- ☐ Spiritual communities (synagogues, churches, temples, mosques) _____
- ☐ Dial 2-1-1 _____
- ☐ Widow and or parental-loss support group _____

## Technology

- ☐ Local tech support _____
- ☐ Online tech support _____

# PAYMENT OPTIONS
# FOR FUNERAL HOMES

Paying for a funeral can be costly, especially if not planned for in advance, and the decisions related to funeral planning are filled with emotion and difficulty for those who have to make arrangements. Use the following information to help your parent make the financial decisions related to the funeral or memorial service.

## TERMS OF PAYMENT

Most funeral homes set terms of payment for within thirty to forty-five days. Most funeral homes accept personal checks, credit cards, and life insurance checks.

If you are comfortable with the funeral home staff, you can assign the life insurance policy to the funeral home, and the funeral home will handle the filing for you. If the amount of life insurance exceeds the amount of the bill, once the funds are received by the funeral home, you receive the refund. In general, but particularly with a large life insurance policy, have an attorney review everything; this strategy ensures proper payout by the insurance company and prevents legal problems. If the amount is less than the bill, you pay the balance.

Dr. R. E. Markin, author of *The Affordable Funeral: Going in Style, Not in Debt* (p. 167), suggests it is wise to only assign an amount of the policy to cover the funeral home's "fair estimate" of total costs. If you assign the entire amount, the funeral home can hold it in their own account gaining interest for ninety days or more after they are paid. Markin says that some funeral homes offer monthly installment plans to cover costs, but he cautions to be aware that this is a "repackaged" product—another loan company actually does the loan—and the funeral home collects additional interest from you. If you use a bank or a loan company instead, you can reduce your costs. Also, if the funeral home holds the notes themselves, Markin says the interest rate is typically 18 to 25 percent.

## IF YOU HAVE LIMITED FUNDS AVAILABLE FOR PAYMENT

As with any business, the funeral home is a for-profit business. Reputable funeral directors try to guide families to affordable funerals. A large range of merchandise in varying price ranges is available, including the type of casket and vault. Some funeral homes allow you to create a payment plan for a funeral, while others will not. Some funeral conglomerates even have finance divisions that accommodate varying payment terms. Ask and understand the funeral home's payment policies before you hire the company.

You may chose within a price range for a casket or vault or even choose cremation, a less-expensive option. Some families prefer to buy their own loved one's casket at a casket store or online rather than purchase from funeral homes as a way to reduce cost (for low-cost funeral vendors, see **Funeral Planning Web Sites and Services** on (p. 165). Funeral homes are owned by a wide variety of owners, from private families to corporate firms, therefore no general policy exists regarding prices or arrangements.

## EXPECTED COSTS

Funeral can cost more or less, depending on what type the family wants and the budget. The cost of the cemetery plot is another issue to factor into funeral expenses. A person pays for the space, the opening of the grave, and the marker or tombstone (typically a plaque made in bronze or stone).

According to the *Funeral Monitor,* the typical funeral with ground burial currently costs $10,650—roughly $6,650 is spent at the funeral home with the rest at the cemetery. Markin says this amount does not include a marker or monument—the average cost in 2005 of a marker was $1,400. Markin suggests you plan a funeral for a weekday instead of a weekend to save on costs—up to a thousand dollars—because most cemeteries have a "sliding scale" for opening and closing fees, with the weekends and holidays being the most expensive. Keep in mind that different traditions and their related costs vary from region to region and from religion to religion.

## CURRENT UNITED STATES FUNERAL HOME LAWS

The **Funeral Rule** (p. 166), designed by the Federal Trade Commission (FTC), requires funeral homes to give every consumer an itemized general price list upon the consumer's first visit to the funeral home to make funeral arrangements. If caskets and outer burial containers are not included on the general price list, they are required to show you a copy of this price list. Markin says that few funeral homes will give you a copy to take to compare prices at other places, but if they offer you the list, the funeral home may be more trustworthy and reasonably priced. The **FTC** (see Part III: Resources) has two brochures: "Paying Final Respects: Your Rights when Buying Funeral Goods and Services" and a more-detailed guide, "Funerals: A Consumer Guide" for more information on funeral home costs and practices.

# ELDERCARE RESOURCES

## COMMUNICATION

**Lebow, Grace, Barbara Kane, and Irwin Lebow.** *Coping with Your Difficult Parent.*

New York: Harper Collins, 1999.

If you are struggling with communicating with a troublesome parent, this book can help you find the right dialogue and way to approach your parent with success. Topics covered in the book include dependency, black-and-white thinking, negative behavior, self-centered behavior, control issues, self-abuse and depression, fearfulness, and grief and loss.

**Solie, David.** *How to Say It to Seniors: Closing the Communication Gap with Our Elders.*

Upper Saddle River, NJ: Prentice Hall Press, 2004.

This book aids in understanding the unique perspective of senior parents and creating more successful communication.

### General Handbooks

**Abramson, Alexis.** *The Caregiver's Survival Handbook.*

New York: Perigree Trade, 2004.

This book for caregivers, written by an expert on aging issues, offers advice on typical problems—juggling many responsibilities, guilt, getting other family members to help, conflict with your parent, and your parent's independence. Resources are also included.

**Morris, Virginia. *How to Care for Aging Parents.***
Rev. and exp. ed. New York: Workman Publishing Company, 2004.
This large resource book covers virtually every aspect of caregiving and elderly parents, including financial, legal, health, daily living and body issues; where to find help; family and doctor issues; mental issues; hospitals; insurance; moving and nursing homes; and grief after loss.

## Personal Information Organizers

*Exit Strategies: A Plan and a Place for Your Estate Information (CD)*
This interactive software program assists you in building an electronic file to store vital personal information such as financial, insurance, home, health, vehicle, property, and advisor records for an elderly parent, your spouse, or yourself. The CD costs $49.95.
**WEB SITE:** www.exitstageright.com/store/default.htm

# ABOUT THE AUTHOR

Ms. Jamieson Haverkampf gleaned intimate knowledge of balancing her own life with a newly widowed parent when she aided her fifty-six-year-old widowed mother in Virginia, while still running her real estate business in California, after the early unpredicted loss of her father to cancer.

Haverkampf, a certified Grief ❧ Recovery Specialist, lives in Atlanta, Georgia, with her dog, Fritz. For more information on the author and Blooming Women Press L.L.C, please visit www.theparentlossbook.com.

# INDEX

To order additional copies of
*Mom Minus Dad: The Essential Guide for Busy Adults with Newly Widowed Parents*
as a gift for friends or family members struggling with parent loss,
please go to www.amazon.com.

Printed in the United States
104928LV00005B/93-500/P

9 781934 953198